WITHDRAWN

D1127204

APPALACHIAN
WOMEN

APPALACHIAN WOMEN

WOMEN

An Annotated Bibliography

———————

SIDNEY SAYLOR FARR

THE UNIVERSITY PRESS OF KENTUCKY

Library of Congress Cataloging in Publication Data

Farr, Sidney Saylor, 1932–
  Appalachian women.

  Includes index.
  1. Women—Appalachian region—Bibliography.
I. Title.
Z7964.A127F37 [HQ1438.A127] 016.3054'0974 80-5174
ISBN 0-8131-1431-4   AACR2

Copyright © 1981 by the University Press of Kentucky

Scholarly publisher for the Commonwealth,
serving Berea College, Centre College of Kentucky,
Eastern Kentucky University, The Filson Club,
Georgetown College, Kentucky Historical Society,
Kentucky State University, Morehead State University,
Murray State University, Northern Kentucky University,
Transylvania University, University of Kentucky,
University of Louisville, and Western Kentucky University.

Editorial and Sales Offices: Lexington, Kentucky 40506

Z
7964
.A127F37

This book is dedicated to
ALFRED H. PERRIN
Invaluable friend and adviser

WILLIAM F. MAAG LIBRARY,
YOUNGSTOWN STATE UNIVERSITY

Contents

Foreword

In a special way this annotated list of over a thousand books, short stories, magazine articles, and oral history tapes concerning Appalachian women is a personal, pioneer effort. The compiler was born and raised on Stoney Fork near Pineville in Eastern Kentucky. She lived as a girl in an isolated mountain hollow, later in small towns and in a large city outside of Kentucky. She has by years of effort and desire read herself into an education. She was married at age fifteen. For some time now, she, her second husband, and her son have been involved in the academic life of a Kentucky college community. "This bibliography," she writes, "is something I have long wanted to do and I have tried to bring to it as objective a viewpoint as possible while still being true to myself as a mountain wife, mother, and worker-student."

The bibliography is indebted to the few bibliographies and lists which are already available, but in large part comes from examination of the books and magazines themselves. Her work she considers as a "step-ahead" towards what is bound to come later, a full-scale bibliography of Appalachian women.

As a writer, Sidney Farr has great admiration and respect for other Appalachian women writers, such as Harriette Arnow, Wilma Dykeman, and Elizabeth Madox Roberts, to name just a few, as well as for the real-life mountain heroines such as Mother Jones of union organizing fame, Mary Breckinridge of the Frontier Nursing Service, the dedicated women who founded the settlement schools, and for Juanita Kreps, former Secretary of Commerce, and all the women miners, women editors, women on the picket lines, in classrooms, and in soup kitchens. She has been fortunate in having the outstanding Weatherford-Hammond Appalachian Collection resources of Berea College readily available for her research.

Both regional and national publications were consulted. The listings extend back in time to include pertinent early material. Daniel Boone's patient wife and their daughter, who was kidnapped by Indians and rescued by her father, are included. Works before 1850 specifically dealing with mountain women are comparatively few in number. The earliest entry used is a book published in 1825, but most nineteenth-century books are dated after 1850. The listings then stretch through 1979.

It was probably inevitable that out of the material read for annotations the compiler reports that she emerged with a deep respect for some of the writers who have faithfully portrayed the people of the Appalachian area, but with contempt for those works, obviously hastily written "pot-boilers," which purport to reveal, through careless generalities and cruel caricatures, the supposed degraded traits of the mountain people and their way of life.

I am sure there was a temptation for her to censor material and limit listings and annotations only to those works which she felt gave a true portrayal of the mountain woman. She rejected this and chose instead to list as many items as could be found which presented some aspect of the mountain woman—whether the writing perpetuated certain stereotypes, was melodramatic or even patently false, or was factual, perceptive, and realistic.

While the man of the mountain family has often been treated as a hillbilly caricature in fiction, on television, and in the comics, his women, with some notable exceptions, have remained in the shadows, housebound and worn out by bringing up a new baby each year while making do in the kitchen. But the war on poverty of the 1960s and the woman's liberation movement of the 1970s, the coal strikes and the picket lines have caused the Appalachian woman to reexamine and reevaluate her role in the family and the community.

There is but little question that mountain women have a voice today. How long have they had that voice and how did they get it? Writers, even newspaper reporters, are now doing research to find out what the Appalachian woman is really like and how important she was and is in regional affairs and history. Books and articles have proliferated. The 1980s will see more. At the same time, many regional colleges and universities recently have been busy setting up Appalachian Studies centers, with new courses and new fields of regional research. Women's studies programs are also springing up throughout the country. Students in these classes are asking questions, seeking source material, tracing roots. This list was compiled to help meet the needs of these researchers, and to consolidate and extend background information on Appalachian women and their families, their growing relationships with other women, even with their husbands' labor unions, and the problems of their neighborhoods and communities.

What significance does such a listing, by one woman of words written about a relatively small segment of mountain women, have today, considering the large number of Appalachian women who have lived and died in the last 135 years? I am reminded of Rupert Brooke's lines:

Preface

For a hundred years and more the Appalachian woman has been exhibited in many different settings, illuminated with different shadings of light, and extolled or criticized. She has been depicted as beautiful and ugly, weak and strong, young and old, a follower, a leader, a housewife, an activist—depending upon which particular voice one hears and which picture one sees. But the same thing can be said about women the world over—Jewish, Irish, Puerto Rican, Greek. It depends on one's perspective.

Appalachian women have been set apart by some writers, who have portrayed them as poorly dressed, snuff-dipping or pipe-smoking, strange-speaking creatures. It is true that poverty and geography have in some ways dictated the lives of women in the mountains. It is true that mountain women are warped or shaped by their environment, the mores of their culture, the restrictions of their religious beliefs, and the traditions handed down from mothers and grandmothers. Many of them still speak a language that sometimes sounds like Elizabethan English. Some still rely on folk remedies, knowledge that is orally transmitted, the signs of the zodiac for planting crops, supernatural powers and their Calvinistic belief in predestined events.

Appalachian women are very insular; time, circumstances, and location have forced this on them. They have let the man assume any prominent family role in community and political affairs; they imply that he is head of the household and his word is law to his family—and in truth this is often the way it is. For generations. as women in other parts of the country were beginning to realize various degrees of personal freedom, the mountain woman was thought of or accepted, not as an individual, but as a mere extension of the man in her life. So quite often the mountain woman has to work behind the scenes to have her way. She resorts to cunning and craft, using devious methods to achieve her goals. But ironically enough the blood kinship so vital in Appalachian relationships gives her strange sources of power. The woman is the giver of life.

In the list of works which I have compiled here, it will be seen that mountain women do seem to have some special powers and special hardships. Because of the roles they have been forced to play, because of geographic and social restrictions, because they are the mainstay of most mountain families, they have retained longer than most women in our country the self-reliant strength and responsibility commonly associated with frontier women in pioneer days.

As a mountain woman, born and raised in Eastern Kentucky, my personal perspective has been congenial to the task of compiling a bibliography on Appalachian women. For a number of years I have lived in an urban setting and, as a student and free-lance writer, I have tried to keep up with all the rapid changes which this decade has brought to women, both regionally and nationally. I have also kept close ties with the women in the mountain community where I grew up and where my mother and sister still live. I have vivid memories of my mother, my grandmother, and other women of the community. I want to see them interpreted as they really were and are, not as stereotyped classifications. Because of my own background, therefore, it has been hard to refrain from eliminating some material I discovered in my research which I felt did not give a true picture of the mountain woman. I have not done this, however, but have included good, bad, and indifferent accounts. If a work made an attempt to portray the characteristics of mountain women, it was included in this bibliography.

For the most part, these works deal with the area generally identified as the Southern Appalachians. There are a few exceptions, however. I found a few articles and stories specifically about southern women but displaying characteristics which I know from personal experience to be true also of Appalachian women. One article, for example, entitled "Magnolias Grow in Dirt," is about the ribald jokes and stories southern women have heard and related down through the years. Some mountain women I know also enjoy risque stories.

In compiling this bibliography, I have used everything I could find that is about mountain women: books, chapters from books, magazine articles, short stories, manuscripts, theses and dissertations, oral history tapes, and various other studies. For the most part the research was done in Special Collections at Hutchins Library, Berea College. I have relied on some bibliographies, notably Charlotte Ross's *Bibliography of Southern Appalachia; The Southern Mountaineer in Literature,* by Lorise C. Boger; *The Kentucky Novel,* by Lawrence S. and Algernon D. Thompson; *The Southern Appalachians: A Bibliography and Guide to Studies,* by Robert F. Munn; *North Carolina Fiction, 1734–1957,* edited by William Stevens Powell; and *Appalachian Outlook,* by the West Virginia University Library at Morgantown. I also found Cratis Williams's doctoral dissertation, *The Southern Mountaineer in Fact and Fiction,* published by University Microfilms at Ann Arbor, Michigan, an invaluable resource. A few items listed here are not annotated; these, without exception, I picked up from one of these bibliographies.

Some children's books are included here where the story is about a mountain girl and shows her growth and relationship with her family and acquaintances. I have not systematically searched for children's books, however. Those I listed are ones I happened to know about.

Neither have I been able to include all the oral history material done by colleges and schools in the Appalachian area. Hutchins Library has a Union Catalog listing oral history tapes and transcripts done at Alice Lloyd College, Lee's Junior College, Emory and Henry College, and Appalachian State University. Entries from that catalog dealing with mountain women are included here in the Oral History section. I have not had the time or resources to make a thorough search for all the oral history tapes and transcripts available on this subject.

Articles from a large number of regional and national periodicals are included in the listings. Those for which relatively complete coverage is represented (through 1979) are: *Appalachia*; *Appalachian Heritage*; *Appalachian Journal*; *Appalachian South*; *Appalachian Women*; *Berea Quarterly*; *Foxfire*; *MAW*; *Mountain Call*; *Mountain Life & Work*; *Mountain Living*; *Mountain Memories*; *Mountain Review*; *Mountain Trace*; *The Plow*; *Sing Out!*; *Southern Exposure*; *Tennessee Folklore Society Bulletin*; and *World Evangel*.

The material is arranged here under several general subject headings to facilitate use by researchers. For more specific topics, the reader should consult the index, which also lists authors, and the titles of most works. Subjects dealt with in the Fiction and Drama section, the Poetry section, and the Oral History section are not indexed. Within each section, works are arranged alphabetically by author, or by title if the work was published anonymously. Where multiple works by a single author are listed, they are in chronological order.

I am sure that in my search many books have been overlooked. No single bibliographer can be sure of finding every item on a subject. Nevertheless, it seemed to me important to get this listing into print so that students and other researchers will have at least this much information available to them on this important subject.

In compiling a book of this sort there are always many people who help make it a reality. A special note of thanks goes to Loyal Jones, director of Berea College's Appalachian Center, who first suggested to me the idea of compiling a bibliography of Appalachian women. The late Arthur Flandreau, director of Hutchins Library from 1974 to 1979, was strongly supportive of the project from its inception. Mr. Alfred H. Perrin gave encouragement and support in many tangible and intangible ways and has been invaluable as friend and adviser. Dr. Gerald Roberts, director of Archives and Special Collections at Berea College, was generous in his moral support and technical advice, which are deeply appreciated. My very special thanks go to Charlotte Cline, and

Lois Tompkins, who did a fine job in typing the manuscript, and to students and friends on the Berea College campus who brought to my attention many specific works which have been included in this bibliography. And last but certainly not least, deep appreciation that words cannot adequately express to my husband, Grover, and my son, Bruce, for their help in the research and preparation of the bibliography, as well as their moral support and encouragement during those periods when I was overwhelmed by the amount of time required for this undertaking.

Autobiography & Biography

1. Adams, Robert G. *Nancy Ward, Beautiful Woman of Two Worlds.* Chattanooga, Tenn.: Hampton House, 1979.

   A biography of Nancy Ward, a Cherokee princess born and raised in what is now known as East Tennessee. Nancy played a significant role in the history and development of Tennessee.

2. Agee, James. "Emma's Story: Two Versions." *Sou. Expos.* 7 (Spring 1979): 8–17.

   Agee writes of Emma, 18 years old, married for two years to a man old enough to be her father. A tender, poignant description of a young Alabama girl and the two men (a writer and a photographer) who entered her life for a short time.

3. Ambrose, Luther. "A Mountain Mother." *Mt. Life & Work* 4 (Apr. 1928): 21–28.

   A true story about Ambrose's mother, a remarkable mountain woman. She raised a large family, all of whom were educated. To help earn desperately needed money, she began experimenting in weaving. Later she instructed workers at Berea College in the art of weaving, and Fireside Industries was born.

4. ———. "To Read, To Learn." *Mt. Life & Work* 45 (Sept. 1969): 13–17.

   A tribute to the author's mother and her zeal for learning—a zeal triumphant over circumstances that are now part of legend.

5. Anderson, Elsie. "Our Life with Grandmother, Rebecca Caudill Tackett." *Appal. Heritage* 6 (Summer 1978): 11–12.

   A woman remembers when her grandmother was ill and the family moved in to help take care of her. A good glimpse of an old woman, a young wife and mother, and a young girl.

6. Anderson, Rufus. *Memoir of Catherine Brown, A Christian Indian of the Cherokee Nation.* Boston: Armstrong & Crocker & Brewster; New York: Haven, 1825.

   Catherine's memoir deals primarily with her life and work at Brainerd Mission School for the Cherokee. She was born in present-day Wills Valley; both Wills Valley and Brainerd are now suburbs of Chattanooga, Tennessee.

7. Angel, Samuel P., and Scott, Samuel W. *History of the Thirteenth Regiment, Tennessee Volunteer Calvary, U.S.A., Including a Narrative of the Bridge Burning, the Carter County Rebellion, and the Suffering of the Union Men and Women of Carter and Johnson Counties, Tennessee, During the Civil War.* Knoxville, Tenn.: The authors, 1903.

The title describes the work. A number of women are portrayed.

8. Angier, Suzanne. "Florence and Lawton." *Foxfire* 7 (Fall 1973): 192–208, 225–27.

A mountain couple remember their youth, adventures, and way of life.

9. "Annie Perry." *Foxfire* 9 (Summer/Fall 1975): 143–62.

Through interviews conducted over a four-year period, the personality of an 83-year-old mountain woman shines.

10. Appleton, Elizabeth P. "A Half-life and Half a Life." *Atlantic Monthly* 13 (Feb. 1864): 157–82.

An extremely articulate Kentucky girl from a coal-mining district relates achievements and failures in her attempts to improve her life.

11. Arnow, Harriette. "Recollections and Literary History." *Appal. Heritage* 1 (Fall 1973): 11–15.

A brief autobiography covering Arnow's career as a published author.

12. "Aunt Addie Norton." *Foxfire* 10 (Fall 1976): 192–210.

Born in 1890 in Rabun County, Georgia, Aunt Addie talks of her life and beliefs.

13. Axelrod, Jim, ed. *Thoughts of Mother Jones Compiled from Her Writings and Speeches.* Huntington: Appalachian Movement Press, 1971.

Beginning her career as a union organizer in midlife, Mother Jones became a legendary figure in the labor movement.

14. _____. "Growin' Up Country: Logan County, West Virginia." Clintwood, Va.: Resource and Information Center, Council of the Southern Mountains, 1973.

Susan recalls the struggles and hardships of growing up.

15. _____. "A Letter from Perry County, Kentucky. Peg." *Growin' Up Country.* Clintwood, Va.: Resource and Information Center, Council of the Southern Mountains, 1973.

Peg, a young mountain woman, learns who she is.

16. Baer, Barbara L. "Harriette Arnow's Chronicle of Destruction." *Nation* 22 (Jan. 31, 1976): 117–20.

A survey of Arnow's life and novels. All of her books have realistic characterizations of Appalachian women.

17. Baker, Edna Ritchie. "Memories of Musical Moments." *Appal. Heritage* 5 (Summer 1977): 59–64.

The importance of music for the Ritchie family is discussed. Lyrics from several songs are included.

18. Baker, Madge. "I Know It's Me They're Calling when I Hear 'Ms. Tumbleweed.'" *Appal. Women* 1 (Fall 1979):15, 28.

Baker, a native of Tennessee, is known to her fellow truck drivers as "Tumbleweed." She writes about her experiences driving a tractor-trailer.

19. Ball, Bonnie Sage. *Red Trials and White.* New York: Exposition, 1955.

A biography of Caty Sage and her abduction by Indians. The story of her life was reconstructed from family letters and legends.

20. Beard, Ida M. *My Own Life.* Winston-Salem: Winston Printing Co., 1900.

An autobiography of a deserted wife, left with two sons and no money to support them in the days when work opportunities for women were very scarce.

21. Behymer, F. A. "The Queen of the Barge Still Reigns along Troublesome Creek." St. Louis *Post-Dispatch* Sunday magazine, Oct. 23, 1932, pp. 1–4. (Excerpts from this article also appear as "The Queen of Troublesome Creek, Kentucky" in *Literary Digest* 114 [Nov. 19, 1932]: 26, 28.)

When all the men in her family were killed in a feud, Stella Combs came into power. She announced that she hoped for peace but would not hesitate to extend her realm if the opportunity came.

22. Berman, Connie. "Dolly Parton Scrapbook." *Good Housekeeping* 188 (Feb. 1979): 140–43, 203–09.

Dolly Parton tells of her childhood in the Smoky Mountains of Tennessee, and how she was able to realize her dreams of being a superstar and having a great deal of money.

23. Breckinridge, Mary. *Wide Neighborhoods.* New York: Harper, 1952.

The autobiography of the remarkable woman who founded the Frontier Nursing Service in Leslie County, Kentucky, and the story of the nurse-midwives who ride over the hills and up the hollows delivering babies and caring for mothers. Beginning in Chapter 17 are varied accounts of mountain life and mountain people, especially women.

24. Brown, Rick, and Thrasher, Sue. "Loretta Lynn." *Sou. Expos.* 2 (Spring/Summer 1974): 20, 22.

An interview with the singer, daughter of an Eastern Kentucky coal miner. She talks about her life as a mountain girl and young woman, and her music and career. Her music is interwoven so closely into her life that when she speaks of one she is also telling of the other.

25. Buck, Pearl. *Once Upon a Christmas.* New York: Day, 1972.

Recollections of this famous writer's West Virginia childhood.

26. Burke, Pauline Wilcox. *Emily Donelson of Tennessee*. Richmond: Garrett & Massie, 1941.

The stirring events of history as they took place around Emily Donelson. When her aunt, Rachel Jackson, died, Andrew Jackson asked Emily to be hostess at the White House.

27. Byers, Tracy. *Martha Berry: The Sunday Lady of Possum Trot*. New York: Putnam, 1932.

An account of how this southern woman established the Berry School in Georgia. A few good characterizations of mountain girls.

28. Caldwell, Kate Livingston. *Diary of Kate Livingston, 1859–1868*. Nashville: WPA, 1938.

A biography of Kate Livingston and much county history of Hamblen County, Tennessee.

29. Carnahan, Opal. "A Mountain Girl on Education." *Mt. Life & Work* 18 (Fall 1942): 8.

A girl from Harlan County, Kentucky, speaks at her commencement service at Dorland-Bell School about the few educational opportunities for her peers in the mountains, and urges them to take advantage of what is there.

30. Carpenter, Brenda. "Making a Cucumber Doll." *Foxfire* 9 (Winter 1975): 376–78.

An interview with Florence Brooks in which she shows how she has made dolls from childhood to the present.

31. "Carrie Stewart." *Foxfire 5*. Eliot Wigginton, ed. Garden City, N.Y.: Anchor Press/Doubleday, 1979.

Carrie Stewart, over 100 years old, lives in Franklin, North Carolina. She tells about her father, who was a slave, and her active life of rearing ten children and being a midwife.

32. Carver, Kaye. "Annie Perry." *Foxfire 4*. Eliot Wigginton, ed. Garden City, N.Y.: Anchor Press/Doubleday, 1977.

An interview with an 83-year-old woman who talks about her childhood in a pre-Civil War house, her young adulthood, and her life now in the Georgia hills.

33. Caudill, Harry M. *Dark Hills to Westward*. Boston: Little, Brown, 1969.

This book is based on legendary accounts of Jenny Wiley, a white woman and Kentucky pioneer who was captured by Indians.

34. Caudill, Rebecca. *My Appalachia*. New York: Holt, Rinehart & Winston, 1966.

A native of Appalachia, Caudill gives us a moving, personal narrative of how life was when "the snow was still clean before the mines came."

35. _____. *A World of Books*. Chicago: Children's Press, 1970.

The author, a Kentucky woman, speaks of her long struggle to become a writer and teacher.
36. Chaffin, Lillie D. *8th Day 13th Moon.* Pikeville, Ky.: Pikeville College Press, 1975.
A book of poetry in which Chaffin tells of the world for Appalachian women as she sees it.
37. _____. "Regionalism." *Appal. Heritage* 7 (Fall 1979): 47–51.
The author, a mountain woman, talks about her writing, how she views the region and her place in it, education, and other topics.
38. Clark, Septima Poinsette. *Echo in My Soul.* New York: Dutton, 1962.
A black school teacher and native of South Carolina relates her experiences in working for the advancement of her people, including her arrest at the Highlander Folk School in Tennessee and the closing of the school.
39. Click, Ellen M. "Mulberry Gap." *Mt. Life & Work* 4 (Apr. 1928): 11–15.
The author writes of her grandmother, her mother, and herself, all mountain women, and their love of beauty and education. Click's mother owned an unabridged dictionary and refused to sell it for $10.00 at a time when money was desperately needed for her six daughters.
40. Cole, Effie. "Granny's Diary." *Mt. Rev.* 5 (1975): 19–20.
Excerpts from a diary kept by a literate woman in Civil War days, a woman recently settled in the mountains. Characteristic of the hardihood of pioneer women and some of their superstitions.
41. Conti, Susan. "Mary S. Ferguson: Weirton's 'Historian Laureate' Is Also Talented Artist." *Goldenseal* 2 (Jan./Mar. 1976): 14.
The 77-year-old native of Hancock County, West Virginia, is introduced. Pages 15–18 present her "Christmas Memories."
42. Cooper, Wilma Lee. "You Can't Talk about Women in Country Music. . . ." An interview by Alice Gerrard. *Sing Out!* 26, no. 2 (1977): 2–7.
Cooper says of her background: "Grandmother married a Ware and had four children, and the littlest one was six months old . . . when Grandfather died. . . . My grandmother worked like a man." Cooper reveals her own character and those of her grandmother and mother.
43. "Cora Whitaker of Whitaker's Music Store: Roots." *Mt. Life & Work* 51 (May 1975): 26–27.
Cora has operated a music store since 1948 in Jenkins, Kentucky.
44. Cory, Richard. *Mary N. Murfree.* United States Author Series, no. 121. New York: Twayne, 1967.
A critical look at the life and works of the woman who first focused

the nation's literary attention towards Appalachia.

45. Counts, Cat. "Coal Mining and Women." *Mt. Life & Work* 54 (July 1978): 9.

> Counts, the mother of five, is a coal miner. "I can't stay home and draw welfare," she says. "I'm not old enough for Social Security. So I have to work somewhere."

46. Crittenden, Edward B. *The Entwined Lives of Miss Gabrielle Austin, Daughter of the Late Rev. Ellis C. Austin and of Redmond, the Outlaw Leader of the North Carolina Moonshiners.* Philadelphia: Barclay, 1880.

> The story of Gabrielle Austin who, at 16, taught school for a time in "a back county of Virginia." In distressing circumstances, she went to Asheville, North Carolina, to stay with a cousin. Captured by the outlaw Redmond, she was later set free and married the man she loved. The latter third of the book is about Redmond.

47. Darcy, Jean. "Paradox of Patricia Rodionoff-Peck." *MAW* 1 (Sept./Oct. 1977): 5–10.

> An interview with a sculptor who returned to her small hometown after years in a large city because "things become real here."

48. Darden, Norma Jean, and Darden, Carole. *Spoonbread and Strawberry Wine.* Garden City, N.Y.: Anchor Press/Doubleday, 1978.

> The authors researched their family backgrounds and wrote this collection of traditional recipes, photographs, health and beauty secrets, and stories about celebrations and rituals. Along with this are ten short biographies of women in the Appalachian region and the surrounding area.

49. David, Cheryl. "To Be Happy." *Mt. Life & Work*, Special Issue (June 1974), pp. 9–10.

> The story of a black woman who has lived all her life in the coal-mining area of Fayette County, West Virginia. After two attempts at suicide, she is trying to find the support she needs from a community health center.

50. Davidson, Josephine Martin. *Josie M. Davidson: Her Life and Work, by Herself.* Prestonsburg, Ky.: Mrs. A. J. Davidson, 1922.

> The autobiography of a Kentucky mountain woman who grew up during the Civil War and Reconstruction.

51. Davis, Dera. "Green Fields Far Away." *Such As Us: Southern Voices of the Thirties.* Chapel Hill: Univ. of North Carolina Press, 1978.

> A long, articulate account by an Alabama woman who married a coal miner. She talks of their success before the 1929 crash and the desperate years afterwards.

52. Davis, Julia. *Legacy of Love.* New York: Harcourt, Brace, 1961.

Two sets of grandparents—the intellectual Davises of Clarksburg, West Virginia, and the lively McDonalds of the Shenandoah Valley of Virginia—make the years of childhood a time of division.

53. DeGering, Etta. *Wilderness Wife: The Story of Rebecca Bryan Boone.* New York: McKay, 1966.
   A biography of the woman who married adventure and followed it westward all her life. Rebecca is admired and respected by mountain women.

54. Depree, Gladis Lenore. *The Self-Anointed.* New York: Harper & Row, 1978.
   Depree is the daughter of John Vogel, founder and director of a home for orphaned children in Corbin, Kentucky. She talks freely of her life there and the other girls in the establishment, and of her escape from physical bondage and from the bondage of an unhealthy love shown her and the other girls by her father.

55. Dewey, Maybelle Jones. *Push the Button: The Chronicle of a Professor's Wife.* Atlanta: Tupper & Love, 1951.
   A biography of a Cartersville, Georgia, woman and her life as wife of the director of the Emory Glee Club.

56. Dickens, Hazel. "As Country As I Could Sing." *Growin' Up Country,* Jim Axelrod, ed. Clintwood, Va.: Resource and Information Center, Council of the Southern Mountains, 1973.
   Dickens talks with Alice Gerrard about life, being a woman, and singing country music.

57. Dillard, Annie. *Pilgrim at Tinker Creek.* New York: Harper's Magazine Press, 1974.
   A woman's sojourn in the Blue Ridge Mountains, near Roanoke, Virginia.

58. Dillard, Colonel John H. "The Story of Rowena Roberts." *Mt. Life & Work* 4 (Apr. 1928): 19–20, 31.
   A true story of a North Carolina mountain girl who makes good. Against many odds the lovely Rowena gets an education because, through long years of hardship, she never gives up her dream. After her schooling is completed she leaves her native hills, gets work in a big city, and is very successful.

59. Dunn, Durwood. "Mary Noailles Murfree: A Reappraisal." *Appal. Journal* 6 (Spring 1979): 196–204.
   Murfree (*pseud.* Charles Egbert Craddock) wrote almost exclusively about mountaineers in the Cumberland and Great Smoky mountains. For decades, her works remained the principal text for anyone outside the region desiring to know anything about mountain people. Many of her books have women as central characters. After a brief biographical statement, the author does a

WILLIAM F. MAAG LIBRARY
YOUNGSTOWN STATE UNIVERSITY

critical analysis of both her writings and what critics have said about her since the 1880s.

60. Dykeman, Wilma. *Look to This Day*. New York: Holt, Rinehart, & Winston, 1968.

Dykeman, who has lived for many years in the Appalachian area, writes of one woman's thoughts and feelings. Her viewpoint is universal as she relates a sunrise from her kitchen window, gives tribute to an elderly Negro teacher in Tennessee, and talks about a trip to Italy.

61. _____. "Diminished by His Going, Better for His Presence." *Appal. Heritage* 7 (Winter 1979): 4–6.

Dykeman, author of several books with mountain women as main characters, women who loved, suffered, and lost, writes about her own loss in a disciplined but direct cry from the heart.

62. Eckley, Wilton. *Harriette Arnow*. New York: Twayne, 1974.

A critical study of Arnow, an Appalachian woman and novelist. Included are a short biography and a bibliography.

63. "Ethel Corn." *Foxfire* 7 (Winter 1973): 260–67.

A woman speaks of her life, her faith, her views of contemporary life, and the war in Vietnam.

64. Fanning, John. "Mountaineer of the Month: Shirley Bradley." *Mt. Call* 30 (May 1977): 10, 17–18.

The author's childhood memories of Shirley Bradley and her husband, and a recent visit with Shirley. "Shirley's refusal to 'move in' with her son's family is characteristic of Appalachian mountain women. There must be dozens of old widowed women living alone in little houses here in our watershed."

65. Farr, Sidney. "Dark Hollow and Other Memories." *Appal. Journal* 4 (Winter 1977): 164–68.

Conversations with the author's relatives concerning mountain life. Good characterization of the great-grandmother, a remarkable pioneer woman during the frontier days in Eastern Kentucky.

66. Fetherling, Dale. *Mother Jones, the Miners' Angel: A Portrait*. Carbondale: Southern Illinois Univ. Press, 1974.

An interesting biography of this remarkable woman who did so much for coal miners and their families.

67. Fowler, William W. *Women on the American Frontier*. Hartford, Conn.: Scranton, 1876.

Historical accounts of the strong, brave women, as well as the weaker ones, who helped to settle America. Chapter 10 specifically deals with the women of Appalachia.

68. Gaines, Judith. "Women of Appalachia." *Appalachia* 11 (Apr/May 1978): 14–25.

Biographies of three women: a teacher, a member of the Council on Women, and a student at Berea College.

69. Gillespie, Paul. "Granny Reed: A Testimony." *Sou. Expos.* 4, no. 3 (1976): 33–37.

"A proud member of the Church of God in Western North Carolina," a 90-year-old woman describes her life in the mountains and her religious experiences.

70. Gordon, Norma Baker. "The Discovery of the World." *Mt. Life & Work* 35 (Winter 1959): 39–41.

Gordon, raised in Cutshin, Kentucky, tells of how her discovery of the world of books led her to the discovery of the world. At the time of writing, she was a senior at Berea College.

71. ———. "Spring Is a Feeling." *Mt. Life & Work* 36 (Spring 1960): 22–26.

A reminiscence by a young mountain woman about her life at home on a mountain farm: "a riot of sensory pleasures for a child whose world is a mountain hollow."

72. Gore, James H. *My Mother's Story.* Philadelphia: Judson, 1923.

The author's mother, Sidney Sophia Gore, was born in 1828 in Virginia. We see her as a young girl, wife, and mother, strong, dedicated, and true to her ideals all through the devastating Civil War.

73. Govan, Christine Noble. *Rachel Jackson: Tennessee Girl.* Indianapolis: Bobbs-Merrill, 1955.

A biography of the wife of Andrew Jackson. Rachel's family moved to Tennessee and she finished her growing up years in what is now Nashville. Written for the teenage reader.

74. Gray, Edna. *One Woman's Life: The Steppings of Faith.* Atlanta: Harrison, 1898.

Most of the story takes place in Western North Carolina. Gray married a man who soon reverted to brutal habits. Her life was one of extreme mental anguish for a number of years, but her faith in God carried her through.

75. Green, Archie, ed. "Aunt Molly Jackson Memorial Issue." *Ky. Folklore Rec.* 7 (Oct./Dec. 1961): 129–75.

A discographic compilation of works about this remarkable singer and songwriter from the mountains. Alan Lomax, Zonweise Stein, John Greenway, and D.K. Wilgus pay warm tribute to her. "I have brought to light the first in print vignette . . . by the late Ben Robertson . . . the folklorist who knew her best. [Mary Elizabeth Barnicle] has much to offer about her friend."

76. Green, Lewis. "Mary." *Mt. Rev.* 1 (Spring 1975): 37–38.

A description of a 74-year-old mountain woman and of her courage and fortitude.

77. Hall, Nora K. "What's Wrong with Our Schools?" *Mt. Rev.* 1 (Sept. 1974): 29.

   The author, who taught in Eastern Kentucky schools for 40 years, says political control and poorly trained teachers are the main reasons schools in Appalachia are deficient. A look at the problem from a mountain teacher's viewpoint.

78. Ham, Tom. "Close-up of a Hillbilly Family." *Amer. Mercury* 52 (1941): 659–65.

   An account of the way of life of the Long family in the North Georgia hills.

79. Hannum, Alberta Pierson. *Look Back with Love: A Recollection of the Blue Ridge.* New York: Vanguard, 1969.

   "This is a personal remembrance of a time that was, and perhaps will never be again: of mountain friends . . . a different look at the Appalachian people. . . ."

80. Hardin, Gail. *The Road from West Virginia.* Chicago: Children's Press, 1970.

   The story of a school dropout, a coal miner's daughter, who tells about factory jobs she has held which make her value a high school diploma.

81. Harrington, Etta. "Witch Stories." *Foxfire* 9 (Winter 1975): 364–72.

   Excerpted from a book manuscript are "stories told at night by father and grandparents" of the narrator. We gain insight into the narrator's life style as she relates the stories.

82. Harris, Corra May White. *A Circuit Rider's Wife.* Philadelphia: Altemus, 1910.

   A semi-autobiographical book about the trials and tribulations of a minister's wife. A gleam of humor and evidence of a strong, independent woman run through the book.

83. _____. *Eve's Second Husband.* Philadelphia: Altemus, 1911.

   Autobiographical fiction from the North Georgia hills.

84. _____. *A Circuit Rider's Widow.* New York: Doubleday, Page, 1916.

   A semi-autobiographical novel about the author's life in North Georgia as the widow of a Methodist minister.

85. _____. *My Book and Heart.* Boston: Houghton Mifflin, 1924.

   The autobiographical memoir of a feminist, minister's wife, and novelist.

86. Healy, Dora, and Franklin, Annie. "A Day on the Farm." *Such As Us: Southern Voices of the Thirties.* Chapel Hill: Univ. of North Carolina Press, 1978.

   Healy (68 years old) and Franklin (70) have made a success of their farm without the help of a man.

87. Hitchcock, Carolina [Hanks]. *Nancy Hanks: The Story of Abe Lincoln's Mother.* New York: n.p., 1899.

   This author, presumably a descendant of the family, says that Nancy Hanks was an indentured servant in Swain County, North Carolina.

88. Hoffius, Steve. "I Expect I'll Get A Plaque." *Sou. Expos.* 7 (Summer 1979): 74–76.

   Septima Poinsette Clark has acquired a mythic reputation. A black woman, she taught school in South Carolina and worked for a period at the Highlander Folk School in Monteagle, Tennessee.

89. Hudson, Elsie. "Their First Home, the Haunted House." *Appal. Heritage* 6 (Summer 1978): 14–16.

   Hudson writes about her mother, Annie Anderson, age 82. Both women are revealed—the old woman and the younger one, who has migrated to Michigan.

90. Huff, Jane. *Whom the Lord Loveth: The Story of James A. Huff.* New York: McGraw-Hill, 1961.

   A wife's account of her brief and happy marriage to a young, seriously ill minister from East Tennessee.

91. Hughes, Emily M.A. *Dissipations at Uffington House.* Memphis: Memphis State Univ. Press, 1975.

   From 1881 to 1887 Hughes wrote to a friend in England describing everyday life in Rugby, Tennessee, established by her father and uncle in 1880. The settlement was to be for younger sons of English families, victims of the law of primogeniture. (There are now plans to restore the settlement.)

92. "Ida Belle Marcum: Little Laurel Lady." *Mt. Call* 1 (Mar. 1974):4–6, 18.

   An 89-year-old woman is interviewed and describes many aspects of her life.

93. Ingles, Andrew Lewis, ed., and Steel, Roberta Ingles. *Escape From Indian Captivity: The Story of Mary Draper Ingles and Son Thomas Ingles.* Radford, Va.: Commonwealth Press, n.d.

   Not available for annotation.

94. Ivey, Saundra K. "Aunt Mahala Mullins in Folklore, Fakelore and Literature." *Tenn. Folklore Soc. Bull.* 41 (Mar. 1975): 1–8.

   The "printed and orally transmitted references to . . . a colorful Tennessee folk character."

95. Jackson, Annis Ward. "The Graves." *Mt. Living* 9 (Summer 1978): 24–25.

   Jackson relates an anecdote her grandmother told about two graves in a clearing on the mountain which had been there "nigh

onto a hundred years." In the telling, the mountain grandmother
is revealed to the reader.

96. _____. "The Pokeberry Sow." *Mt. Living* 9 (Aut. 1979): 39–41.
A short story about the author's childhood and her grandmother,
Annie. She relates an incident that happened when Annie was a
young girl.

97. James, Betty Payne. "The Road Back." *Mt. Rev.* 3 (May 1972):
10–13.
A native mountain woman who left the area for a while after she
finished college now tries to find her way back. The main theme
is displaced Appalachians who find their way home again.

98. James, Oleona. *My Colorful Days*. Boston: Christopher, 1940.
The author spent years as a social worker and teacher among
women and their families in the mountains.

99. Jemison, Stokes Marie. "Ladies Become Voters." *Sou. Expos.* 7
(Spring 1979): 48–59.
The author has worked for civil rights for blacks and the Equal
Rights Amendment, and did research about the fight by southern
women for suffrage before 1920. Here she writes about Pattie
Ruffner Jacobs, born in West Virginia in 1885, and her great work
with women for the cause. "She was a woman . . . far in advance
of her time."

100. Jenkins, Anita; Carver, Bit; and Queen, Myra. "Aunt Lola Cannon." *Foxfire* 4. Eliot Wigginton, ed. Garden City, N.Y.: Anchor
Press/Doubleday, 1977.
An 83-year-old woman talks of her childhood, school days, and
young wifehood, when women first got the vote.

101. "Joe and Mandy Hannah: A Thanksgiving Memorial." *Mt. Call* 1
(Nov. 1973): 4–6.
The story of a mountain couple who endured loss and great hardships and came through with dignity, their lives rich and mean-
ingful.

102. Johnson, Geremiah, and Johnson, Phyllis. "Mama Remembers."
Mt. Memories, no. 10 (Fall/Winter 1978): 32–34. Pippa Passes, Ky.:
Students of the Appalachian Oral History Project, Alice Lloyd Coll.
"For generations the women in our family have stood in the
shadows while their men received all the recognition. One such
woman is Hazel Mae Johnson."

103. Jones, Mary Harris. *The Autobiography of Mother Jones*. Mary
Field Parton, ed. New York: Arno Publishers and *New York Times*,
1969; Charles H. Kerr, 1974.
Mother Jones tells of her long fight for unionization of the mines.
Four photographs.

104. Justice, Mari R. "Daughter of Pioneers." *Appal. Heritage* 2 (Summer 1974): 45–48.

An account of the author's grandmother, who kept alive the traditions of her pioneer ancestors.

105. Kary, Lee. "She Started Something." *Mt. Life & Work* 40 (Winter 1965): 8–11.

The story of Catherine Whitener, who reintroduced the old art of tufting textiles in Dalton, Georgia. The production of bedspreads and other tufted items has raised the economic level of women in Whitfield County.

106. Kinder, Alice J. "Brave Candle in the Dark." *Mt. Life & Work* 37 (Winter 1961): 53–56.

Kinder tells about her aunt, a native of the Kentucky mountains, "who had acquired only a sprinkling of education in a country school, but in the school of experience she . . . mastered a course not offered in a college curriculum."

107. _____. "We'll Shave the Razorbacks Today." *Mt. Life & Work* 40 (Fall 1965): 36–37.

The narrator tells of her grandmother, Big Mama, and how she secured her winter meat around the middle of December each year.

108. _____. *Mama's Kitchen Window*. Kansas City, Mo.: Beacon Hill, 1977.

Vignettes from life in the Kentucky hills. Chapters include "Mama's Rose China Platter," "Mama's Sunday Bonnet," "Mama's Wedding ring," "Mama and the Missionary Barrel," etc.

109. King, E. Sterling. *The Wild Rose of the Cherokee*. Nashville, Tenn.: University Press, 1895.

A semi-biographical book about Nancy Ward, the girl born to an English woman and a Cherokee Indian. Nancy was instrumental in promoting peace and good will between the Cherokee and white races. She has been called the "Pocahontas of the West."

110. Kiser, Mabel. "Mountain Childhood." *Mt. Rev.* 1 (Summer 1975): 12–13.

What it was like when the author was a child growing up in the mountains.

111. Lauritzen, Mrs. J. R. *Some Sketches from My Life, Written for My 80th Birthday, May 1, 1910*. Knoxville: n.p., 1910.

Not available for annotation.

112. Lawson, Sidney. "Rosa Brooks Beason, Artist." *Mt. Life & Work* 42 (Spring 1966): 24–26.

An interview with Beason at her home in Middlesboro, Kentucky. She is a self-taught artist who waited until her family was grown before she had time and space to paint. "In my day girls were taught that a wife's first responsibility was to her husband, a mother's first duty was to her children."

113. Lenski, Lois. *Coal Camp Girl*. New York: Lippincott, 1959.

An autobiographical story of a young mountain girl growing up in a West Virginia coal camp.

114. "Letcher County Woman Tells Her Story." *Mt. Life & Work* 52 (Feb. 1976): 5.

A Linefork, Kentucky, woman describes her life of hardships: sick husband, hungry children, and nineteen dollars a month income for all of them.

115. "Letters from Annie: Part I & II." *Foxfire* 8 (Spring and Summer 1974): 25–40, 135–46.

A collection of letters revealing the life of a young mountain girl.

116. Little, Joan. "I Am Joan." Rebecca Ranson, ed. *Sou. Expos.* 6, no. 1 (1978):42–47.

Ranson taped, organized, and edited this autobiographical material: Little's account of her jail experience, trial for murder, acquittal, and escape from jail.

117. Long, Priscilla. *Mother Jones, Woman Organizer, and Her Relations with Miners' Wives, Working Women, and the Suffrage Movement*. Cambridge, Mass.: Red Sun, 1976.

"Her unique position as a woman in the male labor movement, combined with her symbolic importance as a champion of workers, causes her life and attitudes to illustrate interesting aspects of the tension between class and sex."

118. "Lordy, What a Woman." *Appal. Heritage* 1 (Winter 1973): 62–64.

Relates a visit with Aunt Josie Tackett on Beefhide Creek in Pike County, Kentucky.

119. "Lottie Thompson." *Mt. Trace* 1 (Spring 1975): 76–79.

A 92-year-old woman describes her life on a farm.

120. Lunsford, Kern. "Diary of Jennie Louise Lunsford." Typescript prepared at Jonas Ridge, N. C., July 1973. Buncombe County, N. C., Archives.

Jennie Lunsford lived on Hanlon Mountain in Buncombe County, North Carolina. Her diary records some of the happenings of the Lunsford family from 1903 to 1907.

121. Lynn, Loretta, with Vecsey, George. *Loretta Lynn: Coal Miner's Daughter*. Chicago: Regnery, 1976.

The singer's life from its beginning in Eastern Kentucky to stardom in Nashville. The book was made into a motion picture, which was released in 1980.

122. McBain, Anna D. "What It Means to Be a Teacher." *Berea Quarterly*, May 1901, pp. 19–21.

The author of this short essay, a black girl who attended the Normal School division of Berea College, writes about her experiences teaching in Garrard County, Kentucky.

123. McBroyer, Emma Lee Van Arsdell. *Grandmother Bond.* Lawrenceburg, Ky.: Lawrenceburg Printing Co., 1976.

A short biography of the author's grandmother, who was born and raised in Barbourville, Kentucky, and later moved to Anderson County with her bridegroom, a minister.

124. McCloud, Emma. "So I Sung to Myself." *Sou. Expos.* 7 (Spring 1979): 18–26.

Emma's story in her own words 40 years after James Agee wrote about her and her family. (See #2, above.) She talks about her life as a tenant farmer, nurse's aide, housewife, and mother of five.

125. McKinney, Aunt Tobe. "Talking Is My Life." *Such As Us: Southern Voices of the Thirties.* Chapel Hill: Univ. of North Carolina Press, 1978.

Aunt Tobe is a Tennessee woman. "Now, I know some folks back through here in Big Ivy will say Aunt Tobe McKinney is a gossip. Law ha' mercy, a gossip is a sharp-tongued woman and I'm not that."

126. McVey, Frances Jewell. "The Blossom Woman." *Mt. Life & Work* 10 (Apr. 1934): 1–5.

Weavers, basket makers, and former Pine Mountain and Hindman Settlement pupils gather at a mountain home and tell stories of Katherine Pettit and May Stone, who worked hard to establish the schools. We get insights into some of the women as they talk.

127. Maggard, Sally. "Eastern Kentucky Women—International Woman's Day." *Mt. Life & Work* 51 (Apr. 1975): 19–23.

A report of a meeting at Wheelwright in Floyd County, Kentucky, on International Woman's Day. Women born and raised in Appalachia speak about themselves.

128. _____, and McSurely, Al. "Granny Hager: In Memory and Honor." *Mt. Life & Work* 51 (Apr. 1975): 15–18.

Granny Hager, sometimes compared with Mother Jones, worked hard helping the miners get organized. She believed a union was the only way the miners could win the right to a safe place to work.

129. Marler, Martha Griffis. *Kentucky Jane.* San Antonio: Naylor, 1962.

The life of a young mountain girl: autobiographical sketches.
130. Marsh, Ruby Kenan. *Keeper of Memories*. Asheboro, N.C.: n.p.,
1965.
> Biographical sketches of Confederate widows living in North
> Carolina (several of them in the western part of the state) from
> 1861 to 1961.
131. Marshall, Catherine Wood. *Christy*. New York: McGraw-Hill,
1967.
> Partly a biography of the author's mother, a North Carolina na-
> tive, presented as fiction. A young girl accepts a teaching post in
> East Tennessee, where she finds love and a vocation, and where
> she relates on a deep level with the mountain women.
132. Matthews, Aaron, and Matthews, Mary. "He said nobody should
keep no dam' books on his place. . . ." *Such As Us: Southern Voices of
the Thirties*. Chapel Hill: Univ. of North Carolina Press, 1978.
> Both husband and wife talk about sharecropping in the early
> 1920s and the desperate poverty of their lives.
133. Matthias, Virginia. "Alice Slone: Mountain School Builder." *Mt.
Life & Work* 33 (Winter 1957): 5–10.
> How a teacher helped a community build its own school.
134. Mayhall, Kane. "Miz. Bennett." *Appal. Heritage* 3 (Summer
1975): 21–24.
> A story of the author's grandmother, a mountain woman.
135. Merzer, Meridee. "Kathy Kahn: Voice of Poor White Women."
Viva 1 (Apr. 1974): 74–78.
> The story of Kathy Kahn (author of *Hillbilly Women*), who came
> to Appalachia ten years ago and has been active as spokeswoman
> and organizer of women's groups.
136. Moore, Martha Kiser. "The Appalachians of Wilma Dykeman's
Fiction." Master's thesis, East Tennessee State Univ., 1975.
> A close look at the way Dykeman portrays Appalachian people.
> Since Dykeman is noted for her characterizations of mountain
> women, this affords another viewpoint on them.
137. Morgan, Lucy. *Gift from the Hills*. Chapel Hill: Univ. of North
Carolina Press, 1971.
> The story of the Penland School of Handicrafts in North
> Carolina.
138. Myers, Elizabeth P. *Angel of Appalachia: Martha Berry*. New
York: Messner, 1968.
> What can one woman do in Appalachia to make life better for
> many people? Martha Berry, a southern belle, established a
> school and gave new opportunities to those she called "my
> thousands of children."

139. Noble, Cora M. *Memories*. Boston: Christopher, 1964.
    The author was court clerk in Breathitt County, Kentucky, for many years. She recounts her memories of childhood there.
140. Noble, Hollister. *Woman with a Sword: The Biographical Novel of Anna Ella Carroll of Maryland*. New York: Doubleday, 1948.
    A novel about women and the Civil War in the mountains.
141. Norwood, Hayden. *The Marble Man's Wife: Thomas Wolfe's Mother*. New York: Scribner, 1947.
    Wolfe's mother grew up in the mountains of Western North Carolina and ran a boardinghouse in Asheville to help support her family.
142. Pamplin, Lily May. *The Scamps at Bucksnort*. New York: Exposition, 1962.
    Memories of life in the foothills of Tennessee.
143. Parks, Edd Winfield. *Charles Egbert Craddock*. Chapel Hill: Univ. of North Carolina Press, 1941.
    A good study of Mary Noailles Murfree under her pseudonym. She wrote many books about mountain women.
144. Perry, Beulah. "My Grandfather Came Here from Africa as a Slave." *Foxfire* 8 (Summer 1974): 150–67.
    Perry, 80 years old, tells her life story.
145. Phelan, Mary Kay. *Martha Berry*. New York: Crowell, 1972.
    Martha Berry founded a school for mountain children which in later decades became Berry College.
146. Plantz, Steve. "Women in the Mines: One Woman's Story." *Mt. Call* 2 (Aug. 1975): 4, 17.
    The story of a woman miner, Ruth Ann Parker.
147. Pollack, Barbara. *The Collectors: Dr. Claribel and Miss Etta Cone*. Indianapolis: Bobbs-Merrill, 1962.
    Claribel and Etta Cone were sisters of industrialist Moses Cone. They helped establish the Cone Craft Center on the Blue Ridge Parkway.
148. Prichard, Arthur C. "Phoebia G. Moore, M.D.: The First Woman to Study Medicine at West Virginia University." *Goldenseal* 5 (Oct./Dec. 1979): 36–41.
    The story of how Phoebia Moore broke down the wall of sex prejudice thrown around the medical courses at West Virginia University and received her M. D. in 1903.
149. Purkey, Lena P. *Home in Madison County*. Johnson City: East Tennessee State Univ., Research Advisory Council, 1975.
    A personal account of the years 1904–1926, when the author was growing up in Madison County, North Carolina.
150. Raper, J. R. *Without Shelter: The Early Career of Ellen Glasgow*.

Southern Literary Studies. Baton Rouge: Louisiana State Univ. Press, 1971.

> Glasgow's writings are tangentially Appalachian. This is about her early years.

151. Reece, Florence. "Which Side Are You On?" *Sou. Expos.* 4, no. 1 & 2 (1976): 90.

> A brief account of the author's background as daughter and wife of miners, and of how her famous song of that title came to be written.

152. Reed, Ida Lillard. *My Life Story.* N.p.: The author, 1912.

> An autobiography of a West Virginia churchwoman. It includes anecdotes of her childhood in the hills.

153. Reston, James, Jr. "The Innocence of Joan Little." *Sou. Expos.* 6 (Winter 1978): 30–38.

> Excerpts from a forthcoming book. Joan Little's case has been taken up by national groups. A black woman, she says she'll be murdered if taken back to a South Carolina jail to finish serving her sentence.

154. Rhodes, Mary. "Ada Kelly." *Foxfire* 6 (Summer/Fall 1972): 80–87.

> An interview with an active, courageous, outspoken 83-year-old woman who lives at Kelly's Creek in North Carolina.

155. Riddle, Almeda. *A Singer and Her Song.* Baton Rouge: Louisiana State Univ. Press, 1970.

> The author is a noted singer of traditional ballads. A good glimpse into her background and life.

156. Ridgway, Florence Holmes. "Women's Industrial: A Story of Sharing." *Mt. Life & Work* 32 (Autumn 1956): 30–35.

> How the Berea Women's Christian Temperance Union formed an association concerned with the welfare of those in need in 1890.

157. Ritchie, Edna. "The Singing Ritchies." *Mt. Life & Work* 29 (Summer 1953): 6, 8–10.

> The Ritchies are among the most famous singing families of the Southern Highlands. Edna, one of the daughters, tells what it was like growing up as one of the Ritchies.

158. Ritchie, Jean. *Singing Family of the Cumberlands.* New York: Oxford Univ. Press, 1955; Oak Publications, 1963.

> A charming, tender, delightfully humorous account of the well-known folksinger's growing-up years in Appalachia, her family, her friends, and people in the community.

159. Rogers, Lucille. *Light from Many Candles.* Nashville: McQuiddy, 1960.

> A history of pioneer women in education in Tennessee.

160. Ross-Robertson, Lola. "Ida L. Reed: 1864–1951; Barbour County Hymn Writer, Poet." *Goldenseal* 2 (Oct./Dec. 1976): 25–32.

A brief biography of this remarkable woman and some selections from her writings.

161. Russell, Elizabeth, and Campbell, Henry. *Paths of Glory.* Richmond, Va.: Whittet and Shepperson, 1961.

"A simple tale of a faring bride, Elizabeth, sister of Patrick Henry and wife to William Campbell and William Russell, who were prominent in activities on the Virginia frontier."

162. Sexton, Daveena. "Mattie Profitt: An Interview." *Mt. Rev.* 1 (Sept. 1974): 27–28.

An Eastern Kentucky Schoolteacher describes her experiences, the political control of the schools, and her present life.

163. Shackelford, Laurel. "Home." *Mt. Rev.* 1 (Sept. 1974): 5–6.

A Louisville woman compares city life to her prior life style in Floyd County, Kentucky.

164. Sharp, Molly. "There's Always a Judas." *Such As Us: Southern Voices of the Thirties.* Chapel Hill: Univ. of North Carolina Press, 1978.

Sharp, living with her daughter and son-in-law (a Baptist preacher) in North Carolina, talks about her life, her daughter's work in the cotton mills, and the preacher's work in the mill villages.

165. Simmons, Lola. "From the Mountains Faring." *Such As Us: Southern Voices of the Thirties.* Chapel Hill: Univ. of North Carolina Press, 1978.

Lola says she and her common-law husband came "faring down from the mountains to Knoxville, and ain't never going back again. I miss them mountains sometimes. Yes, I miss that steep old land."

166. Slone, Verna Mae. *What My Heart Wants to Tell.* Washington, D.C.: New Republic Books, 1979.

Primarily a biography of a mountain man, written by his daughter, whose voice is authentic as she relates anecdotes about her father, mother, and various other mountain people.

167. Smith, Barbara. "Pilgrimage for Jenny." *Appal. Heritage* 7 (Summer 1979): 52–57.

A modern-day woman writes about Jenny Wiley, the Kentucky mountain woman who was captured by Indians and taken away after her children were killed. The author relates the events surrounding Jenny's escape and return home, and talks about Jenny Wiley Park and her grave.

168. Smith, Lilly. *Call of the Big Eastatoe.* Columbia, S.C.: State Printing Co., 1970.

An autobiographical novel of rural and family life in the South Carolina mountains.

169. Stanley, Len. "Custom Made Woman Blues." *Sou. Expos.* 4 (Winter 1977): 92–93.

Interviews with Hazel and Alice, a folksinging duo especially liked by women. Hazel was born and raised in West Virginia and worked in a textile mill before she got into folksinging. Her partner is a college-educated folksinger from Los Angeles.

170. Stevens, Bernice A. *A Weaving Woman.* Gatlinburg, Tenn.: Buckhorn Press, 1971.

One woman's obsession with weaving. The book includes illustrations and instructions.

171. Stevenson, Gloria. "That's No Lady, That's Mother Jones." *Worklife* 1 (July 1976): 24–28.

Summarizes the life of Mother Jones and her aid to striking coal miners in West Virginia and elsewhere.

172. Stivers, Louise. "Buildin' and Destroyin'." *Mt. Rev.* 2 (Mar. 1976): 6–7, 10.

A transcription of an oral history interview with a woman whose family has lived in Clay County, Kentucky, for six generations.

173. Stuart, Jesse. "A Woman of Stature." *Appalachia* 7 (Oct./Nov. 1973): 35–40.

An account of a student in Jesse Stuart's school when he was a young teacher. Anne worked hard to secure an education and walked 104 miles in two days to take state examinations.

174. Sudano, Betty. "In the Mines." *Mt. Life & Work* 51 (Feb. 1975): 35–36.

Sudano talks about being a mountain woman and deciding to become a miner. "I worked there about 1947 or 1948. . . . I worked ten or eleven years for Jewell Ridge in Tazewell County, Virginia."

175. Sullivan, Ken. "Out in the Weeds and Briers: The Recollection of Rosie Lee Shanklin." *Goldenseal* 4 (Apr./Sept. 1978): 26–30.

The author talks with a 91-year-old woman, a native of Summers County, West Virginia, who speaks of her early (arranged) marriage, changes in the community, differences in people.

176. Sutton, Margaret. *Jemima, Daughter of Daniel Boone.* New York: Scribner, 1942.

The story of Jemima Boone from six to sixteen. Most of the text is the well-known Boone story as seen through the eyes of a young girl. Though not Appalachian *per se*, this book is about a young pioneer girl in the frontier days of Kentucky, and some of the pioneer girls and women of that era settled in the hills.

177. Talford, Theresa. "Coal Mining and Women." *Mt. Life & Work* 54 (July 1978): 8–9.
    Talford, a bridge operator at Clinchfield's Pilgrim Mine, talks about her experience in the mines.

178. Talmadge, John Erwin. *Rebecca Latimer Felton: Nine Stormy Decades.* Athens: Univ. of Georgia Press, 1960.
    Becky Felton, early feminist and labeled a character, was the first woman to serve in the United States Congress. She was a controversial figure in Bartow County, Georgia, for most of her 90-odd years.

179. Taney, Mary Florence. *Kentucky Pioneer Women.* Cincinnati: Robert Clarke, 1893.
    Rebecca Byran Boone and Susanna Hart Shelby, natives of North Carolina, Keturah Leitch Taylor and Mary Hopkins Cable Breckenridge from Virginia, and Henriette Hunt Morgan and Susan Lucy Barry Taylor of Kentucky are the pioneer women depicted. They lived during a period when those who survived possessed courage and great strength.

180. Terry, Peggy. "Our America: A Self-Portrait at 200: The Hillbilly." *Newsweek* 88 (July 4, 1976): 54, 61.
    An interview with a woman originally from Kentucky and Oklahoma facing poverty and prejudice in Chicago.

181. Thomas, Jean. *The Traipsin' Woman.* New York: Dutton, 1933.
    An account of Thomas's experiences as a traveling court stenographer in Eastern Kentucky. she has good insights into the mountain culture.

182. ———. *The Sun Shines Bright.* New York: Prentice-Hall, 1940.
    The autobiography of Jean Thomas, the "Traipsin' Woman," who collected mountain ballads and songs.

183. Thrasher, Sue. "The Woman behind Minnie Pearl." *Sou. Expos.* 2 (Winter 1975): 32–40.
    A tape-recorded interview with entertainer Minnie Pearl, who talks about her public and private lives.

184. Trivette, Janese. "Sing Me Home before I Die." *Plow,* Aug. 1976, pp. 5–6, 14.
    An interview with Ruth and Lehman Stamper at their home in Poor Valley, Virginia. They talk about their hillside farm, the handcrafted items they make to sell, and their music.

185. Tucker, Emma Curtis. "The Little Lady of the Transformation." *South Atlantic Quarterly* 21 (Oct. 1922): 327–34.
    An article about Alice Lloyd and her work at Caney Creek, Kentucky.

186. Turner, Debbie. "That's One Night I'll Never Forget." *Mt. Life & Work* 52 (June 1976): 22–26.

A young mountain girl tells about losing her husband during the explosion at the Scotia Mines in March 1976 and what it is like to be a young widow with a child in Eastern Kentucky.

187. Tyler-McGraw, Marie. "But After All Was She Not a Master-piece as a Mother and a Gentlewoman. . . ." *Goldenseal* 3 (Oct./Nov./Dec. 1977): 28–34.

Anna Maria Reeves Jarvis, a nineteenth-century West Virginia woman who worked for health and peace, was the inspiration for Mother's Day.

189. Warren, Harold F. "Aggie Lowrance, a Late-blooming Wild Flower." *A Right Good People*. Boone, N.C.: Appalachian Consortium Press, 1974.

At 71 years of age, Aggie Lowrance has blossomed into an "un-usually creative designer, teacher and craftswoman."

190. Werstein, Irving. *Labor's Defiant Lady*. New York: Crowell, 1969.

Mother Jones was a remarkable woman deserving of all the books and articles written about her. This is another look at the woman as well as her deeds.

191. West, Hedy. "No Fiddle in My Home." *Sing Out!* 26, no. 5 (1978): 2–6.

This internationally known performer of songs from her native folk and other traditions writes about her grandmother, Lillie West, a folksinger from a singing family.

192. Wharton, May Cravath. *Doctor Woman of the Cumberlands: The Autobiography of May Cravath Wharton, M.D.* Pleasant Hill, Tenn.: Uplands, 1953.

A deeply moving account of a woman doctor's life and practice in the Cumberland mountains.

193. Wheeler, Arville. *White Squaw: The True Story of Jennie Wiley*. Boston: Heath, 1968.

A biography of Kentucky pioneer Jennie Wiley, her life, and her captivity by Indians.

194. "Which Side Are You On?" *Mt. Life & Work* 48 (Mar. 1972): 22–24.

An interview with Florence Reece, who tells about her early years and the coal mining conditions behind her labor song "Which Side Are You On?" which tells of the conflict between union men and company thugs.

195. White, Alma. *The Story of My Life*. New Jersey: Pillar of Fire, 1919.

White, one of seven sisters, was born in 1862 at Kinnikinneck in Lewis County, Kentucky. Her mother and sisters were typical mountain women. She yearned for an education, was later converted, became a minister, and founded the Pillar of Fire Church.

196. White, Helen. *From the Mountain*. Memphis: Memphis State Univ. Press, 1972.

An account of the lives and literary endeavors (including the *North Georgia Review*) of Paula Snelling and Lillian Smith.

197. White, Timothy. "Portrait of a Hill Person: Nancy Kincaid." *Mt. Call*, July 1976, p. 6.

Kincaid, a native of West Virginia, tells how two of her homes have been marred or ruined by dynamite, floods, and mud, all a result of stripmining activities.

198. Williams, Clara. "No Union for Me." *Such As Us: Southern Voices of the Thirties*. Chapel Hill: Univ. of North Carolina Press, 1978.

A short narrative setting forth Williams's strong feelings about the unions in Virginia and North Carolina.

199. Williams, Cratis. "Hedy West: Songbird of the Appalachians." *Appal. South* 1 (Summer 1965): 8–11.

Williams, a folksinger in his own right, writes with perception and clarity about folksinger Hedy West and her people, mountaineers since the American Revolution.

200. Wilson, Beryl. "My Grandmother." *Mt. Life & Work* 17 (Summer 1941): 25, 27.

A Berea student tells about her mountain grandmother, who "loved all life and especially baby life, human and animal. . . . flowers were her hobby."

201. Winter, Oakley. "Vesta, A 'Modern' Woman." *Mt. Life & Work* 40 (Winter 1965): 31–32.

Winter writes of her Tennessee grandmother, a strong woman who raised a large family. She had a keen mind and made it her business to keep track of the yield of the land as well as every detail of her household.

202. Withington, Alfreda Bosworth. *Mine Eyes Have Seen: A Woman Doctor's Saga*. New York: Dutton, 1941.

The author returned to the Kentucky mountains to practice medicine. An account of her experiences.

203. Wolfe, Thomas. *Look Homeward, Angel*. New York: Grosset & Dunlap, 1929.

The story is primarily about Eugene Gant, Wolfe's father, and his brothers, but Wolfe's mother, iron-willed Eliza Gant, is also portrayed throughout this very powerful, semi-autobiographical novel.

204. _____. *The Short Novels of Thomas Wolfe.* C. Hugh Holman, ed. New York: Scribner, 1961.
Of the five novels in this collection, the most interesting is "Web of Earth." It is primarily about Eliza Gant, modeled along the lines of Wolfe's mother.

205. "Women's Voices: Thoughts on Women's Music in America." *Sing Out!* 25, no. 2 (1976): 3–6.
A good article profiling some noted women, especially Lily May Ledford, one of the original Coon Creek Girls at Renfro Valley, Kentucky.

206. Wood, Violet. *So Sure of Life.* New York: Friendship Press, 1950.
The story of doctor Robert F. Thomas and his wife Eva. She is a teacher and he is the only doctor in the area. The author tells of their life in the Smoky Mountains and of the people they meet there.

207. Wright, Muriel Hazel. *Springplace: Moravian Mission and the Ward Family of the Cherokee Nation.* From the genealogical notes of Miss Clara Alice Ward and other sources. Guthrie, Okla.: Co-operative Publishing Co., 1940.
Not available for annotation.

208. Wyker, Mossie Allman. "Yes! There Is Hope for Rural Appalachia." *World Call* 49 (Nov. 1967): 21–22.
Anna Hobbs, wife and mother of four children, is the motivating force in developing her community, Kerby Knob, Kentucky.

Coal Mining

209. Addington, Luther F. "Flowers." *Mt. Life & Work* 36 (Summer 1960): 36–38.
About an Appalachian black woman whose husband was a miner. He was shot and killed in the fall; she died during the winter. A neighbor, a white man, kept working in her flowers the next

spring and summer: "She was a lover of flowers... so... I've come to hoe her flowers."

210. Ansley, Fran, and Thrasher, Sue. "The Ballad of Barney Graham." *Sou. Expos.* 4, no. 1 & 2 (1976): 137–42.

An interview with the woman who wrote the ballad about her father gives us an insight into her own character. She talks about the United Mine Workers, her father's death at the hands of company thugs, the hardships she and her family endured, and their migration to Ohio.

211. Aumiller, Grace. "In the Mines." *Mt. Life & Work* 51 (Feb. 1975): 36–37.

"My name is Grace Aumiller and I live in Baltimore, Maryland. I worked [in the mines] 11 years. I started around 1938 or 1939 at Laurel Creek in Sears, West Virginia... for Jewell Ridge Coal Company."

212. Axelrod, Jennifer. "Appalachia, Women and Work." MAW 3 (Jan./Feb. 1978): 7–11.

A historical overview encompassing Appalachia women in unions, the labor force, coal mining, textile manufacturing, and hospital work.

213. Axelrod, Jim, ed. *Thoughts of Mother Jones: Compiled from Her Writings and Speeches.* Huntington: Appalachian Movement Press, 1971.

Beginning her career as a union organizer in midlife, Mother Jones became a legendary figure in the labor movement.

214. Bernard, Jacqueline. "Dark as a Dungeon Way Down in the Mines." *Ms.* 3 (Apr. 1975): 21.

Claims for black-lung benefits have been filed by two women in Tazewell County, Virginia.

215. _____. "Pikeville's Methodist Hospital: One More Rejection." *Sou. Expos.* 3 (Winter 1976): 27–28.

Nurses, aides, and other workers at the Appalachian Regional Hospital strike for better pay, better treatment. The three-year-long strike has been strangled by red tape and lack of support from the United Mine Workers and the Methodist Church.

216. Bethel, Thomas. "1974: Contract at Brookside." *Sou. Expos.* 4, no. 1 & 2 (1976): 114–24.

In this long strike, the women joined the men on the picket lines. As one miner describes it: "The women was a real important factor. Women can get away with more than men—as far as the law is concerned. Course they got manhandled a little bit, they come out real well... they was brave women."

217. Bishop, Bill. "1931: The Battle of Evarts." *Sou. Expos.* 4, no. 1 & 2 (1976): 92–113.

> Deals with the strike at the Evarts Mine in 1931, and shows through prose and photographs the effects of the strike on people generally and on the women specifically. "Miners' wives bore the strike's greatest hardships, but had the least control over the union movement . . . women saw the organizing drive through the eyes of their hungry children."

218. Bowman, Lois. "Coal Mining and Women." *Mt. Life & Work* 54 (July 1978): 10.

> Bowman works at Pittston Company's Clinchfield Mine at Splashdam near Haysi, Virginia.

219. Brittain, Carol. "First Women Delegates." *Mt. Life & Work* 52 (Oct. 1976): 36–37.

> "Women in the mines are working out well. You could do it. My mother could do it. Your mother could do it . . . now that I've gotten into it and into the Union. I wouldn't trade it for nothing."

220. Brooks, Gwen. "I Am a Union Woman." *Growin' Up Country.* Jim Axelrod, ed. Clintwood, Va.: Resource and Information Center, Council of the Southern Mountains, 1973.

> Brooks talks about three women—Granny Hager, Aunt Molly Jackson, and Florence Reece—who were very active and vocal in the union at the mines and the strikes.

221. Brooks, Nell. "Little Children of a Coal Miner." *Mt. Rev.* 3 (Oct. 1976): 29–31; 3 (Winter 1977): 1–5.

> Growing up in a miner's family in Benham, Harlan County, Kentucky.

222. Brown, Ruby. "Coal Mining and Women." *Mt. Life & Work* 54 (July 1978): 7–8.

> Brown tells about the mine where she works and what it is like to be a miner.

223. Burns, Barbara. "Why I Decided to 'Go Underground.'" *McCall's* 104 (Sept. 1977): 69, 73, 82.

> The author, who lives in Craigsville, West Virginia, became the first woman coal miner in her area. She writes about some of the pressures she encountered.

224. Cain, James Mallahan. *The Butterfly.* New York: Knopf, 1947.

> A young woman comes back to the West Virginia-Kentucky border mine camp where she was born. The story deals with moonshining practices and coal-camp life styles.

225. Church, Ruth, and Stanley, Cathy. "Women Miners—In the 40s; Today." *Mt. Life & Work* 50 (Nov. 1974): 14–15.

> Two women working in the Virginia mines describe their work;

and two women who worked in the mines in the 1940s talk about filing for black-lung benefits.

226. "Coal Companies Keep Women from Work in the Mines." *Mt. Life & Work* 50 (Oct. 1977): 10–11.

"West Virginia coal companies don't advertise job openings in ways that reach potential women applicants."

227. Combs, Ruby. "Coal Mining and Women." *Mt. Life & Work* 54 (July 1978): 8.

Combs works in Pocahontas No. 4 Mine in Virginia, where she was injured in May 1978. She relates a few of her experiences.

228. Counts, Cat. "Coal Mining and Women." *Mt. Life & Work* 54 (July 1978): 9.

Counts, the mother of five, is a coal miner. "I can't stay home and draw welfare," she says. "I'm not old enough for Social Security. So I have to work somewhere."

229. Davis, Dera. "Green Fields Far Away." *Such As Us: Southern Voices of the Thirties.* Chapel Hill: Univ. of North Carolina Press, 1978.

A long, articulate account by an Alabama woman who married a coal miner. She talks of their success before the 1929 crash, and the desperate years afterwards.

230. Dos Passos, John. *Adventures of a Young Man.* New York: Harcourt, Brace, 1938.

This novel is set in Slade, Harlan County, Kentucky, where Glenn Spotswood spends some time assisting the striking miners of the Muddy Fork Local. Children and women are portrayed. Wheattey Napier is especially well characterized.

231. Edwards, Debbie; Tiller, John; and Johnson, Linda. "Brookside, Kentucky." *Mt. Life & Work* 49 (Oct. 1973): 2–5.

Miners (aided by women) strike for recognition at Eastover Mining Company's Brookside Mine in Harlan County. This was a tense struggle, reminding one of former days in Eastern Kentucky.

232. Evans, Helen. "Coal Mining and Women." *Mt. Life & Work* 54 (July 1978): 9.

"I used to work in a factory. I could not make enough money, so I went to work where the money could be made . . . in the coal mines."

233. Ewald, Wendy, ed., *Appalachia: A Self-Portrait.* Foreword by Robert Coles, text by Loyal Jones. Frankfort, Ky.: Gnomon Press for Appalshop, 1979.

Photographs of people and places, a number of them of mountain women and girls. There is an especially good photograph of three women miners.

234. Fetherling, Dale. *Mother Jones, the Miners' Angel: A Portrait.* Carbondale: Southern Illinois Univ. Press, 1974.

An interesting biography of this remarkable woman, who did so much for coal miners and their families.

235. Fugate, Deloras. "Coal Mining and Women." *Mt. Life & Work* 54 (July 1978): 9.

"I went to work in the mines because that is the only place I could earn enough money to support my little girl."

236. Gibbs, Libby. "That's An Awful Word—Widow." *Mt. Life & Work* 52 (June 1976): 11–21.

A young mountain girl, widowed when her husband was killed in the Scotia Mines, talks about him, their life together, the mine officials, and what it has been like for her and her two boys in the months since the tragedy.

237. Green, Archie, ed. "Aunt Molly Jackson Memorial Issue." *Ky. Folklore Rec.* 7 (Oct./Dec. 1961): 129–75.

A discographic compilation of works about this remarkable singer and songwriter from the mountains. Alan Lomax, Zonweise Stein, John Greenway, and D.K. Wilgus pay warm tribute to her. "I have brought to light the first in print vignette . . . by the late Ben Robertson . . . the folklorist who knew her best. [Mary Elizabeth Barnicle] has much to offer about her friend."

238. Gunning, Sarah. "My Name is Sarah Ogan Gunning. . . ." *Sing Out!* 25, no. 2 (1976): 15–16.

A songwriter and singer of traditional songs writes about her life in the coal mining counties of southeastern Kentucky.

239. Hunter, Sally. "A Widow Speaks." *Mt. Life & Work* 50 (Dec. 1974): 18.

Hunter interviews the widow of a miner who was trapped inside Consolidation Coal Corporation's mine near Mannington, West Virginia. The company has not recovered the bodies of twenty-three of the men, even after six years. The widows have formed a group to fight for passage of the federal Health and Safety Act.

240. "In the Mines . . . Two Women Remember." *Mt. Life & Work* 51 (Feb. 1975): 35.

Two of the first women miners on record are interviewed. They describe many aspects of their lives: duties, safety, and health.

241. "Lady Miner Digs Her Job: A Young Mother of Eight Strikes Coal." *Ebony* 29 (Oct. 1974): 116–18, 120, 122.

A widowed black woman works in the Nanty 610 mine near Johnstown, Pennsylvania.

242. Lawrence, Randy. "Make a Way Out of Nothing: One Black Woman's Trip from North Carolina to the McDowell County Coalfields." *Goldenseal* 5 (Oct./Dec. 1979): 27–30.

> An interview with a black woman who had worked in a tobacco factory in North Carolina before her family migrated to the coal fields of West Virginia. She worked in various jobs, sang in church choirs, and had a firm belief that God takes care of His children.

243. Lawson, Sidney. "Appalachia, 1965." *Mt. Life & Work* 40 (Winter 1965): cover.

> A poem telling how one mountain woman views her native hills and her people since stripmine operations began in Appalachia.

244. Lenski, Lois. *Coal Camp Girl.* New York: Lippincott, 1959.

> An autobiographical story of a young girl growing up in a West Virginia coal camp.

245. Long, Priscilla. *Mother Jones, Woman Organizer, and Her Relations with Miners' Wives, Working Women, and the Suffrage Movement*, Cambridge: Red Sun Press, 1976.

> "Her unique position as a woman in the male labor movement, combined with her symbolic importance as a champion of workers, causes her life and attitudes to illustrate interesting aspects of the tension between class and sex."

246. Maggard, Sally and McSurely, Al. "Granny Hager: In Memory and Honor." *Mt. Life & Work* 51 (Apr. 1975): 15–18.

> Granny Hager, sometimes compared to Mother Jones, worked hard helping the miners get organized. She believed a union was the only way the miners could win the right to a safe place to work.

247. Nelson, Linda. "Women." *Mt. Life & Work* 48 (Nov. 1972): 8.

> "A Weekend for Women" brought together a variety of women in West Virginia. Among them were daughters, wives, and sisters of coal miners, who discussed what it means to be related to a miner.

248. Plantz, Steve. "Women in the Mines: One Woman's Story." *Mt. Call* 2 (Aug. 1975): 4, 17.

> The story of a woman miner, Ruth Ann Parker.

249. Rasnick, Elmer. "Women File for Black Lung—Expecting Trouble." *Mt. Life & Work* 50 (Sept. 1974): 11.

> Five women worked in the Laurel Creek Mines in Tazewell County, Virginia, from 1940 to 1952. Two plan to file for black-lung benefits but fear they will not be believed.

250. Reece, Florence. "Which Side Are You On?" *Sou. Expos.* 4, no 1 & 2 (1976): 90.

> A brief account of the author's background as daughter and wife of

miners, and of how her famous song of that title came to be written.

251. Ritchie, Jean. "Black Waters." *Appal. Heritage* 1 (Summer 1973): 53–54.

Ritchie, noted folksinger and author, shares her feelings about the stripmining in Perry County, Kentucky,—her homeplace—in the words and music of this protest song.

252. Sammons, Donna. "Woman Coal Miner." *MAW* 1 (Nov./Dec. 1977): 17–18.

An Eastern Kentucky woman expresses her reasons for becoming a miner and discusses attitudes toward women miners.

253. Stanley, Cathy, and Church, Ruth. "Olga Coal Company Causes Misery and Suffering." *Mt. Life & Work* 59 (Nov. 1974): 16–19.

An interview with Madeline James, who lives in McDowell County, West Virginia. She and her neighbors believe their community is threatened by two coal-waste dams; they are fighting for strict measures to make the dams safer.

254. Stevenson, Gloria. "That's No Lady, That's Mother Jones." *Worklife* 1 (July 1976): 24–28.

Summarizes the life of Mother Jones and her aid to striking coal miners in West Virginia and elsewhere.

255. Still, James. *On Troublesome Creek.* New York: Viking, 1941.

A novelette composed of nine episodes, each one basically a short story, which tell of the life and times of a miner's family living on Troublesome Creek, Kentucky. Women of all ages and young girls are strongly characterized.

256. Sudano, Betty. "In the Mines." *Mt. Life & Work* 51 (Feb. 1975): 35–36.

Sudano talks about being a mountain woman and deciding to become a miner. "I worked there about 1947 or 1948. . . . I worked ten or eleven years for Jewell Ridge in Tazewell County, Virginia."

257. Talford, Theresa. "Coal Mining and Women." *Mt. Life & Work* 54 (July 1978): 8–9.

Talford, a bridge operator at Clinchfield's Pilgrim Mine in Virginia talks about her experiences in the mines.

258. Thornton, Marcellus Eugene. *My "Budie" and I.* New York: Neely, 1899.

A mountain girl, Louise Stewart, meets the owner-manager of a coal mine at Pigeon Roost, North Carolina. The two, from widely differing backgrounds, fall in love and the story ends happily. Much of the book deals with coal mining during the decade 1880–1890.

259. Turner, Debbie. "That's One Night I'll Never Forget." *Mt. Life &
Work* 52 (June 1976): 22–26.

A young mountain girl tells about losing her husband during the
explosion at the Scotia Mines in March 1976 and what it is like to
be a young widow with a child in Eastern Kentucky.

260. "UMWA Women from Mother Jones to Brookside." *UMW Journal* 87 (Mar. 1976): 10–27.

Discusses Mother Jones, women working in the mines, women in
labor activities and community development, and widows' problems.

261. Ward, Charlie. *Silk Stocking Row.* Parsons, W. V.: McClain,
1975.

Men and women living in a West Virginia coal camp are the
characters in this novel. Several mountain women play major
roles.

262. Werstein, Irving. *Labor's Defiant Lady.* New York: Crowell,
1969.

Mother Jones was a remarkable woman, deserving of all the books
and articles written about her. This is another look at the woman
and her deeds.

263. Whalen, Eileen. "Women Save the Strike: Harlan Miners Fight
for Union." *Sou. Patriot* 31 (Nov. 1973): 1, 4.

Describes the women's role in the Brookside, Kentucky, strike.

264. "Which Side Are You On?" *Mt. Life & Work* 48 (Mar. 1972):
22–24.

An interview with Florence Reece, who tells about her early years
and the coal mining conditions behind her labor song "Which
Side Are You On?" which tells of the conflict between union men
and company thugs.

265. White, Timothy. "Portrait of a Hill Person: Nancy Kincaid." *Mt.
Call,* July 1976, p. 6.

Kincaid, a native of West Virginia, tells how two of her homes
have been marred or ruined by dynamite, floods, and mud, all a
result of stripmining activities.

266. Williams, Clara. "No Union for Me." *Such As Us: Southern
Voices of the Thirties.* Chapel Hill: Univ. of North Carolina Press,
1978.

A short narrative setting forth Williams's strong feelings about the
unions in Virginia and North Carolina.

267. Witt, Matt. *In Our Blood.* New Market, Tenn.: Highlander Research Center, 1979.

This book of photographs and text depicts four coal-mining

families. In each case, the woman's point of view is given along with that of her husband.

268. "Women: Miners' Wives and Widows." *Mt. Life & Work* 51 (Dec. 1975): 34–35.

A short article about the widows of 78 miners killed in the Mannington Number Nine disaster. The women remember the fight for safety, the fight to get the men out of the mine. They talk about plans for a statewide widows' organization.

269. "Women and the Union." *Mt. Life & Work* 52 (Oct. 1976): 33–35.

The editors interviewed several women who speak out for the union and the strike at the Brookside Mine in Eastern Kentucky.

270. "Women Coal Miners." *Mt. Life & Work* 55 (Jul./Aug. 1979): 3–28.

A special section of this issue is devoted to articles and photographs about women miners.

271. "Women Miners Organize to Fight Sex Bias." *Mt. Life & Work* 54 (Oct. 1978): 13–15.

A group of women miners met in Norton, Virginia, in September 1978 to form a local organization to protect women miners from sex discrimination in promotion and job hiring in the coal industry.

272. Women of Eastern Kentucky. "We Will Stop the Bulldozers: A Statement, January 20, 1972." Berea, Ky.: Council of the Southern Mountains, 1972.

Mountain women band together, vowing not to let the hills be ripped apart by stripmining or corporations from outside the area.

273. "Women Organize at Stearns." *Mt. Life & Work* 53 (May 1977): 3–5.

"200 miners on strike at the Justus Mine in Stearns, Kentucky, have been strengthened in their fight for UMWA representation by their women."

274. "Women Push Coal Employment." *Mt. Life & Work* 54 (Aug. 1978): 22–23.

The story of women miners who rallied in front of the Capitol in Washington, D.C., for the Equal Rights Amendment in June 1978. Six coal companies are vulnerable to legal action unless they hire more women miners.

275. "Women Seek Jobs in Kentucky Coal Mines." *Mt. Life & Work* 51 (May 1975): 18.

Two women residents of Cumberland, Kentucky, have applied for mining jobs but cannot even get interviews with personnel managers.

276. "Women Stop School Busses." *Mt. Life & Work* 54 (Oct. 1978): 9–10.

> An account of the women in Harlan County, Kentucky, who blocked school bus routes in an effort to stop Jericol Mines' armored trucks from traveling the roads after a school bus was caught in the line of fire. This action shows the women changing to a more aggressive, militant stance instead of staying home and letting the men do most of the fighting.

277. "Women Sue 153 Coal Companies." *Mt. Life & Work* 54 (June 1978): 3–6.

> Women have asked the federal government to review "the blatant pattern of sex discrimination" in the coal industry.

278. Woolley, Bryan, and Reid, Ford. *We Be Here When the Morning Comes.* Foreword by Robert Coles. Lexington: Univ. Press of Kentucky, 1974.

> The authors lived with the family of a miner during the last few weeks of the bitter 13-month strike at Brookside mine in Harlan County, Kentucky. They recorded the feelings of the striking miners and their wives about their jobs, their struggle to unionize, their communities, and their lives. The role of the women, who were arrested for picketing, is especially well presented. Several good photographs of the women.

Education

279. Ambrose, Luther. "A Mountain Mother." *Mt. Life & Work* 4 (Apr. 1928): 21–28.

> A true story about Ambrose's mother, a remarkable mountain woman. She raised a large family, all of whom were educated. To help earn desperately needed money, she began experimenting in weaving. Later she instructed workers at Berea College in the art of weaving, and Fireside Industries was born.

280. _____. "To Read, To Learn." *Mt. Life & Work* 45 (Sept. 1969): 13–17.

> A tribute to the author's mother and her zeal for learning—a zeal triumphant over circumstances that are now part of legend.

281. Anderson, Rufus. *Memoir of Catherine Brown, A Christian In-*

dian of the Cherokee Nation. Boston: Armstrong & Crocker & Brewster;
New York: Haven, 1825.

Catherine's memoir deals primarily with her life and work at
Brainerd Mission School for the Cherokee. She was born in
present-day Wills Valley; both Wills Valley and Brainerd are now
suburbs of Chattanooga, Tennessee.

282. "Appalachian Women?" *Mt. Life & Work* 52 (Aug. 1976): 22–23.

In addition to problems of housing, employment, and education,
mountain women in the city must deal with stereotypes about
Appalachian people, which are often reinforced by the media.

283. Badyer, Earladeen D. "A Mother's Training Program—A
Sequel." *Children Today* 1 (May/June 1972): 7–11, 36.

In Chattooga County, Georgia, low-income mothers are instructed in how to teach one- and two-year-old children at home.

284. Ballangee, Judith. "Lend-a-Hand Lives Up to Its Name." *Appalachia* 4 (Aug./Sept. 1971): 15–19.

The Lend-a-Hand health center, established in 1958 by a nurse
and a schoolteacher in Knox County, Kentucky, is described and
reviewed. Young girls and women have been served since its
inception.

285. Bland, Marion F. "Superstitions about Food and Health among
Negro Girls in Elementary and Secondary Schools in Marion County,
West Virginia." Master's thesis, West Virginia Univ., 1950.

Not available for annotation.

286. Bradley, Frances Sage. "The Redemption of Appalachia." *Hygeia*
9 (Jan. 1931): 26–30.

Lack of health education in the mountains is illustrated by the
woman who sent for her children and would not let them go back
to the boarding school because there was an outbreak of measles.

287. Brandstetter, Anne. "Mountain Teens Learn at East End School."
Youth Mag. 27 (Sept. 1976): 44–47.

Sue Schaeffer's parents were born and raised in Appalachia; the
family now lives in Cincinnati's East End. The article is about her
and others like her—migrants from the hills—attending the East
End Alternative School.

288. Byers, Tracy. *Martha Berry: The Sunday Lady of Possum Trot.*
New York: Putnam, 1932.

An account of how this southern woman established the Berry
school in Georgia. A few good characterizations of mountain
girls.

289. Campbell, Marie. *Tales from the Cloud-Walking Country.*
Bloomington: Indiana Univ. Press, 1958.

When the author taught at the mountain settlement school on

Caney Creek in Knott County, Kentucky, she met many mountain women who told her folktales. Seventy-eight of those tales are recorded here, old European folktales told in the mountain dialect.

290. Carnahan, Opal. "A Mountain Girl on Education." *Mt. Life & Work* 18 (Fall 1942): 8.

A girl from Harlan County, Kentucky, speaks at her commencement service at Dorland-Bell School about the few educational opportunities for her peers in the mountains, and urges them to take advantage of what is there.

291. Caudill, Rebecca. *Schoolhouse in the Woods.* New York: Holt, Rinehart & Winston, 1949.

The main character of this book for young readers is a mountain girl named Bonnie. The book describes her experiences in her first year of school.

292. ———. A *World of Books*. Chicago: Children's Press, 1970.

The author, a Kentucky woman, speaks of her long struggle to become a writer and teacher.

293. Chaffin, Lillie D. "Regionalism." *Appal. Heritage* 7 (Fall 1979): 47–51.

The author, a mountain woman, talks about her writings, how she views the region and her place in it, education, etc.

294. Clark, Septima Poinsette. *Echo in My Soul.* New York: Dutton, 1962.

A black schoolteacher and native of South Carolina relates her experiences in working for the advancement of her people, including her arrest at the Highlander Folk School in Tennessee and the closing of the school.

295. Click, Ellen M. "Mulberry Gap." *Mt. Life & Work* 4 (Apr. 1928): 11–15.

The author writes of her grandmother, her mother, and herself, all mountain women, and their love of beauty and education. Click's mother owned an unabridged dictionary and refused to sell it for $10.00 at a time when money was desperately needed for her six daughters.

296. Coogan, Mercy Hardie. "Infants and Mothers 3, Mortality 0." *Appalachia* 12 (July/Aug. 1979): 1–13.

This article talks about mothers and infants in Appalachia and programs to reduce the mortality rate. Good photographs of women of various ages.

297. Davis, Mary. "Women and Vocational Education." *Mt. Rev.* 1 (Summer 1975): 20.

Contains suggestions for more effective career education planning for women in Appalachia.

298. Dillard, Colonel John H. "The Story of Rowena Roberts." *Mt. Life & Work* 4 (Apr. 1928): 19–20, 31.

A true story of a North Carolina mountain girl who makes good. Against many odds the lovely Rowena gets an education because, through long years of hardship, she never gives up her dream. After her schooling is completed she leaves her native hills, gets work in a big city, and is very successful.

299. Dingman, Helen H. "The Spinning Wheel." *Mt. Life & Work* 3 (Jan. 1928): 7–8, 20.

Dingman visited Berea College and the Log House, where young mountain girls were spinning and weaving. She feels they have many advantages in their educational experience there.

300. Dutton, William Sherman. *Stay on Stranger: An Extraordinary Story of the Kentucky Mountains.* New York: Farrar, Straus, & Young, 1954.

This is one of several accounts of the school on Caney Creek (later Alice Lloyd College), which was founded by Alice Lloyd, a woman who was interested in mountain youth.

301. Edwards, Debbie. "Forum." *Youth Mag.* 27 (Sept. 1976): 76–77.

Edwards, a native of West Virginia, struggles to pay for her own college education. "Lots of young women go to work in sewing factories because they can't afford to go to college, or even finish high school, because their parents are so poor."

302. Frederickson, Mary. "The Southern Summer School for Women Workers." *Sou. Expos.* 4 (Winter 1977): 70–75.

A definitive article about the workers education program, begun in 1927 and run until World War II. The school began at Sweet Briar College but later moved to Asheville, North Carolina. The staff sought to provide young workers from textile, garment, and tobacco factories with the analytic tools for understanding the social context of their lives.

303. Fuson, H. H. "Why Educate the Mountain Woman?" *Mt. Educator* 1 (July 1903): 2–3, 5.

The author was superintendent of the Bell County, Kentucky, school system when he wrote this article. "There are no homes in the country that need wholesome instruction so much as the homes of the mountain people." He concludes the mountain woman definitely should be educated.

304. Gordon, Norma Baker. "The Discovery of the World." *Mt. Life & Work* 35 (Winter 1959): 39–41.

Gordon, raised in Cutshin, Kentucky, tells of how her discovery of the world of books led her to the discovery of the world. At the time of writing, she was a senior at Berea College.

305. Hall, Nora K. "What's Wrong with Our Schools?" *Mt. Rev.* 1 (Sept. 1974): 29.

The author, who taught in Eastern Kentucky schools for 40 years, says political control and poorly trained teachers are the main reasons schools in Appalachia are deficient. A look at the problem from a mountain teacher's viewpoint.

306. Hardin, Gail. *The Road from West Virginia*. Chicago: Children's Press, 1970.

The story of a school dropout, a coal miner's daughter, who tells about factory jobs she has held which make her value a high school diploma.

307. Hickey, Margaret, ed. "Forgotten Children: Miracle of Pilot Knob." *Ladies Home Journal* 65 (Jan. 1948): 23–24, 110, 112.

An article about a remote community in the Tennessee mountains, about the Save-the-Children Federation and their work of community development, and about mountain women and girls. The women in the community helped build a school and community center.

308. Hill, Jennie Lester. "Home Life in the Kentucky Mountains." *Berea Quarterly* 7 (Nov. 1902): 11–18.

The author, a teacher at Berea College, traveled extensively in the mountains visiting the homes of former Berea College students.

309. Hoffius, Steve. "I Expect I'll Get a Plaque." *Sou. Expos.* 7 (Summer 1979): 74–76.

Septima Poinsette Clark has acquired a mythic reputation. A black woman, she taught school in South Carolina and worked for a period at the Highlander Folk School in Monteagle, Tennessee.

310. Hoffman, Mary Lindsey. "Adult Schools in the Mountains." *Survey* 61 (Jan. 1929): 499–501.

Before organizing the Opportunity School for Adult Education at Berea, Kentucky, Helen Dingman spent four months in Denmark studying the folk-school system of adult education.

311. Holderman, Elizabeth S. "Out of the Beaten Path." *Berea Quarterly* 17 (Jan. 1914): 21–29.

The author was an extension worker at Berea College at the time this article was written. Good insight and sensitive portrayal of girls and women she met while traveling in the mountains.

312. Hurst, Taylor. "Marryin' Doesn't Excuse Her." *Mt. Life & Work* 3 (Oct. 1927): 21–24.

An article by a mountain doctor who was also serving as truant officer for Perry County, Kentucky. It reveals the very young age at which mountain girls married then and the attitude of some of the mothers.

313. James, Oleona. *My Colorful Days*. Boston: Christopher, 1940.

The author spent years as a social worker and teacher among women and their families in the mountains.

314. Janison, Elsie S. "A School for Women Workers in Industry in the South." *School and Society* 36 (Oct. 8, 1932): 473–75.

This educational experiment was undertaken for the women employees in North Carolina mills, and was housed at Fruitland Institute near Hendersonville. A worthy project and successful for the most part.

315. Justus, May. *The House at No-End Hollow*. New York: Doubleday, Doran, 1938.

A book for junior high level readers about Becky, who lives in the mountains with her grandmother, brother, and sister. It tells of their struggle to keep their family together and build a new school.

316. Kinder, Alice J. "Brave Candle in the Dark." *Mt. Life & Work* 37 (Winter 1961): 53–56.

Kinder tells about her aunt, a native of the Kentucky mountains, "who had acquired only a sprinkling of education in a country school, but in the school of experience she . . . mastered a course not offered in a college curriculum."

317. Lewis, Claudia. *Children of the Cumberlands*. New York: Columbia Univ. Press, 1946.

The author taught in a nursery school for two and a half years at the Highlander Folk School in Tennessee. A portrayal of mountain children and their mothers as perceived by a woman from outside the region.

318. McBain, Anna D. "What It Means to Be a Teacher." *Berea Quarterly* (May 1901): 19–21.

The author, a black girl who attended the Normal School division of Berea College, writes about her personal experiences teaching school in Garrard County, Kentucky.

319. McVey, Frances Jewell. "The Blossom Woman." *Mt. Life & Work* 10 (Apr. 1934): 1–5.

Weavers, basket makers, and former Pine Mountain and Hindman Settlement pupils gather at a mountain home and tell stories of Katherine Pettit and May Stone, who worked hard to establish the schools. We get insights into some of the women as they talk.

320. Matthews, Aaron, and Matthews, Mary. "He said nobody should keep no dam' books on his place. . . ." *Such As Us: Southern Voices of the Thirties*. Chapel Hill, Univ. of North Carolina Press, 1978.

Both husband and wife talk about sharecropping in the early 1920s and the desperate poverty of their lives.

321. Matthias, Virginia. "Alice Slone: Mountain School Builder." *Mt. Life & Work* 33 (Winter 1957): 5–10.
    How a teacher helped a community build its own school.

322. Myers, Elizabeth P. *Angel of Appalachia: Martha Berry*. New York: Messner, 1968.
    What can one woman do in Appalachia to make life better for many people? Martha Berry, a southern belle, established a school and gave new opportunities to those she called "my thousands of children."

323. Phelan, Mary Kay. *Martha Berry*. New York: Crowell, 1972.
    Martha Berry founded a school for mountain children which in later decades became Berry College.

324. Ridgway, Florence Holmes. "A Charge to Keep: Narratives and Episodes Devoted to the Women Who Helped Build a Place for Worship and for Learning on the Berea Ridge." Berea, Ky.: Berea Woman's Club, 1954. Typescript in Berea Coll. Archives.
    This drama articulates the special courage and devotion of the women who helped found Berea College. The personal stories of Matilda Fee and Elizabeth Rogers support the author's contention that "there were mothers of Berea as well as fathers." The church, the college, the town, all owe their existence to the labors and sacrifices of these women.

325. Rogers, Lucille. *Light from Many Candles*. Nashville: McQuiddy, 1960.
    A history of pioneer women in education in Tennessee.

326. Sexton, Daveena. "Mattie Profitt: An Interview." *Mt. Rev.* 1 (Sept. 1974): 27–28.
    An Eastern Kentucky schoolteacher describes her experiences, the political control of the schools, and her present life.

327. Stewart, Cora Wilson. "Moonlight Schools." *Survey* 35 (Jan. 8, 1916): 429–31.
    The author founded the moonlight schools for adult education in the mountains. This article relates how she came to be involved in this work.

328. Stuart, Jesse. "A Woman of Stature." *Appalachia* 7 (Oct./Nov. 1973): 35–40.
    An account of a student in Jesse Stuart's school when he was a young teacher. Anne worked hard to secure an education and walked 104 miles in two days to take state examinations.

329. Tucker, Emma Curtis. "The Little Lady of the Transformation." *South Atlantic Quarterly* 21 (Oct. 1922): 327–34.

An article about Alice Lloyd and her work at Caney Creek, Kentucky.

330. White, Alma. *The Story of My Life.* New Jersey: Pillar of Fire, 1919.

White, one of seven sisters, was born in 1862 at Kinnikinneck in Lewis County, Kentucky. Her mother and sisters were typical mountain women. She yearned for an education, was later converted, became a minister, and founded the Pillar of Fire Church.

Fiction & Drama

331. Addington, Luther F. *The Little Fiddler of Laurel Cove.* Indianapolis: Bobbs-Merrill, 1960.

Written primarily for children, this book tells of the efforts of a young girl and her brother to attend high school.

332. _____. *Sugar in the Gourd.* Indianapolis: Bobbs-Merrill, 1961.

The title of the book is also the title of a mountain fiddle tune. A young girl wants to help her family in a special way.

333. Agee, James. *A Death in the Family.* New York: Avon, 1938.

This novel deals with death and how different members of the family handle the loss of a loved one. Mary Follet, a Tennessee woman, is portrayed convincingly and with sensitivity.

334. Alves, Juliet. *Hulda.* New York: Scribner, 1942.

The Kentucky frontier of the 1790s is seen through the eyes of a robust girl from North Carolina. Hulda epitomizes the spirit of the strong women who followed their men into the lawless wilderness to create a commonwealth.

335. Anderson, Sherwood. *Kit Brandon.* New York: Scribner, 1936.

Kit, raised on a poor mountain farm, works in the cotton mills in North Carolina and later marries the son of a man involved in organized crime.

336. Anthony, Ivan Blair. *The Potters o' Skunk Hollow.* Boston: Humphries, 1946.

Lowisa Potter starts life as a juvenile delinquent. When World War II comes along, she contracts to marry eight different mountain men to draw their allotment checks. Eventually her sins catch up with her. This story reminds one of Jesse Stuart's

Taps for Private Tussie, though not as strong, engaging, or believable.

337. Armstrong, Anne. *This Day and Time.* New York: Knopf, 1930; Johnson City: East Tennessee State Univ., 1974.

Ivy's husband has deserted her, leaving behind a young son, a ramshackle cottage, and very little else. Ivy survives by hard work and the determination to make a good life for her son, and by the dream that her husband will return one day.

338. Arnow, Harriette S. *The Mountain Path.* New York: Corici, Friede, 1936; Berea, Ky.: Council of the Southern Mountains, 1963.

An exciting story, full of the woes and hardships common to Kentucky mountain people. The story is about a young teacher in the Cumberland Mountains who boards with Lee Buck's family. Buck's wife, Corie, is delightfully ingenious—imaginative, sincere, and not above using devious means to get her own way.

339. _____. *The Dollmaker.* New York: Macmillan, 1954.

This modern classic reveals the characteristics of mountain women in a clear, forceful, and honest manner. Gertie Nevels is forced to move to industrial Detroit during World War II, and finds living conditions much worse than in the mountains. This book shows the mountain woman's inability to speak up for herself against her husband's wishes.

340. _____. *Hunter's Horn.* New York: Macmillan, 1954.

Nunnely Ballew half starves his family, makes illegal liquor, and sells his livestock to buy expensive hounds in his efforts to capture a near-legendary fox. While the novel is primarily about the man and his fanaticism, his wife and daughters play very important roles. Arnow is one of the best of the Appalachian writers in her portrayal of mountain women.

341. Bailey, Janice. "The Artificial Wreath." *Mt. Rev.* 3 (Winter 1978): 9–11.

An old mountain woman's last hours are depicted in this short story. Her daughter wants her to come to the city and live.

342. Baker, Louise R. *Cis Martin.* New York: Eaton & Mains, 1898.

Cis, the narrator, has been educated in New York. Her father loses his job and decides to return to his native southland and go into the lumber business. The story is primarily about Cis and her job teaching in a mountain school, but we get impressions of young girls and women as she sees them.

343. Banks, Gabriel Conklyn. *The End of the Day.* New York: Pageant, 1966.

This romantic tale is reminiscent of Shakespeare's *Romeo and Juliet.* Two young lovers become engaged at a Kentucky mountain

inn and the boy goes off to war. Letters produce misunderstand-
ings, and two deaths result.

344. Banks, Nancy Huston. *Round Anvil Rock*. New York: Macmillan,
1903.

A romance set in the Appalachian hills. Anvil Rock, Cedar
House, and the Sisters of Charity all figure in the book; the main
character is a young woman.

345. _____. *The Little Hills*. New York: Macmillan, 1905. (Autho-
rized facsimile made by Xerox University Microfilms, Ann Arbor,
Michigan, 1975.)

The widow of a village minister has to go live with her in-laws in
Eastern Kentucky after her husband dies. Her relationships, especially with the women, are revealing.

346. Barnes, Annie Maria. *The Ferry Maid of the Chattahoochee: A
Story for Girls*. Philadelphia: Pennsylvania Publishing Co., 1899.

Romantic events in the life of a shy hill girl.

347. Bartlett, Frederick Orin. *Big Laurel*. Boston: Houghton Mifflin,
1922.

Includes all the fictional stereotypes about mountain people: a shy
mountain girl, a handsome flatland visitor, a gun-toting
mountain man, and a gentle lady. The setting is the Blue Ridge
Mountains.

348. Barton, William Eleazer. *Sim Galloway's Daughter-in-Law*. Boston: Pilgrim, 1897.

Margaret, Sim's daughter-in-law, has been wild in her life style,
deserting her daughter and equally wild husband. She repents and
returns to the Kentucky mountains to save Sim's farm from fore-
closure and her daughter from disgrace. The scapegrace son, Bill
Galloway, turns up opportunely and all ends well.

349. _____. *Pine Knot: A Story of Kentucky Life*. New York: Appleton,
1900.

Barbara Buzbee, daughter of an abolitionist schoolteacher, becomes engaged to a Confederate officer from the Bluegrass instead
of to her mountain admirer, a chaplain in the northern army.
Complications beset her until she gains strength and insight to set
her affairs in order.

350. Baxter, Tamara R. "The Curin." *Appal. Heritage* 7 (Spring 1979):
13–17.

A short story narrated by a young girl. She and a friend hide in the
friend's house to watch Granny heal a sick child.

351. Begley, Nancy. *Strange Lady*. Ashland, Ky.: Economy Printers,
1972.

The author is a native of Breathitt County, Kentucky. A baby is left in a cabin which houses husband, wife, and six children. Where the baby came from, who brought it there, and why, perplex the community for years. As the mystery unravels, mountain women are seen in their many and complex likenesses and differences.

352. Belcher, Margaret Crowder. *Sunday Shoes*. New York: Pageant, 1955.

A native of West Virginia, the author writes with depth and keen perception about two families. The main character is Becky, a mountain girl. We are introduced to other women and girls through Becky's acquaintance with them.

353. Bennett, Emerson. *The Bride of the Wilderness*. Philadelphia: Peterson, 1854.

This book is set in the last quarter of the eighteenth century. A man, his wife, his wife's unmarried sister, and various other people settle in Laurel Ridge, Virginia. The main character is Gertrude, who has various exciting adventures in the wilderness and with her suitors.

354. Bledsoe, Mary. *Shadows Slant North*. Boston: Lothorp, Lee, & Shepard, 1937.

A story about a mountain woman and her struggle to get an education. She loses her man to another women through a typographical error. Accuracy and naturalness make up for the lack of sustained excitement.

355. Bolton, Ivy Mae. *Tennessee Outpost*. New York: Logmans, Green, 1939.

Though a sixteen-year-old boy is the hero, a brave girl plays an important part in this historical tale about Tennessee when it was claimed by the Spanish.

356. Bonner, Sherwood. "The Case of Eliza Bleylock." *Harper's Weekly* 25 (Mar. 5, 1881): 155–56.

A revenue agent goes into the Cumberland Mountains disguised as a peddler. He stays at Eliza's home and courts her, falsely, to get information about moonshine stills. He arrests Eliza's father and brothers; when they return they revile and persecute her and refuse to hear her pleas of innocence. Eliza dies.

357. Boykin, Elizabeth Jones. *The Call of the Mountains*. Philadelphia: Dorrance, 1928.

Amanda, a New York girl, marries a young man from Appalachia and comes home with him. After five years of wedded bliss he dies, leaving her with two small sons to support. The book deals with her life as a young mother struggling to become a writer. Sarah, a native mountain woman, befriends her. All ends well.

358. Brewer, Mary T. "I Ain't Never Been So Scairt." *Mt. Life & Work* 32 (Autumn 1956): 37–39.

It takes them all night to bury the dead chickens and turkeys. "Hit must a been a dog," Pa says. They try to find the dog but end up tearing down the mountain in fear.

359. Brice, Marshall Moore. *Daughter of the Stars*. Verona, Va.: McClure, 1973.

A novel based on historical figures and events. Jean McGreal was born at sea and lived in Western Pennsylvania and the Shenandoah Valley of Virginia. Captured by the Indians in 1745, she escaped and lived to have two husbands and many descendants.

360. Brodhead, M. Eva Wilder McGlasson. *Diana's Livery*. New York: Harper, 1891.

This story is set in the lovely little community of Shakertown at Pleasant Hill, Kentucky. Laura is a foundling left to be raised by the Eldress and the other Shaker women. When she is of age, they send her away to be educated in a secular school. When she returns, all sorts of emotions and tensions are unleashed.

361. _____. *An Earthly Paragon*. New York: Harper, 1892.

A girl from the city meets and falls in love with a mountain man. They find happiness in the Kentucky hills.

362. Buck, Charles Neville. *The Call of the Cumberlands*. New York: Grosset & Dunlap, 1913.

A flatland artist manages to get himself involved in a full-blown Kentucky mountain feud and barely escapes with his life. He marries a mountain girl, the heroine of the story.

363. _____. *The Battle Cry*. New York: Wyatt, 1914.

A graduate of Bryn Mawr moves to the Kentucky mountains to teach school. Her encounters with mountain women and girls are interesting, though the main plot deals with her determination to marry a feud leader and become a mountain woman.

364. _____. *A Pagan of the Hills*. New York: Grosset & Dunlap, 1919.

Because of many factors, a mountain girl learns the lumbering business at a time when women stayed home and took care of the home and family.

365. _____. *Flight to the Hills*. New York: Doubleday, 1926.

A young woman, Cynthia Meade, leaves Asheville under suspicion in the death of Jack Harrison. She goes to Kentucky but is soon involved in a family feud. Harrison eventually turns up again and the heroine must decide between two lovers. A mystery story told in mountain dialect.

366. Burgwyn, Mebane Holoman. *Penny Rose*. New York: Oxford Univ. Press, 1952.

A young woman who lives on a North Carolina farm must make a living for her fatherless family. She has to choose between handsome Jeffrey and the realities of wresting food from the soil.

367. _____. *True Love for Jenny*. Philadelphia: Lippincott, 1956.

Living in the peanut-growing country of North Carolina, 15-year-old Jenny Stewart faces many problems: her love for handsome Charlie, a disagreement with her mother, and chairmanship of the Harvest Ball.

368. Burman, Ben Lucien. *The Four Lives of Mundy Toliver*. New York: Mesner, 1953.

As many mountain women did during World War II, Mundy leaves the mountains to do war work. She eventually comes home, however, and settles down to life at Coal Creek, Kentucky.

369. Burnett, Frances Hodgson. *Louisiana*. New York: Scribner, 1880.

The few days which Louisiana Rogers spends at a fashionable resort cause her to become dissatisfied with her North Carolina mountain home and environment.

370. _____. *"Jarl's Daughter" and other Novelettes*. 1881. Reprint: Short Story Index Reprint Series. Freeport, N.Y.: Books for Libraries Press, 1969.

A story about a mountain girl: how she faces life and what she extracts from it day by day.

371. _____, and Gillette, William H. *Esmeralda*. New York: French, 1881.

A comedy drama in four acts, this play was presented at Madison Square Theatre and was performed 850 times during the first run. An entrepreneur from the East buys the Rogers family's farm because he thinks there is iron ore on the property. Ma Rogers sweeps the family off to France, against their wishes, to hunt a titled husband for Esmeralda, who wants to stay in the mountains and marry her sweetheart, Dave. Ma Rogers gets her just desserts in the end and Esmeralda gets the man she loves.

372. Burr, Amelia Josephine. "The New House." *Mt. Life & Work* 2 (Jan. 1927): 15–16.

A young girl's determination to attend school changes her family's appearance and also their appreciation for the "pretties" in life.

373. Burt, Nellie. "A Home for Nellie." *Mt. Life & Work* 8 (Apr. 1932): 16–18.

Nellie, a mountain girl, and her two young brothers are put on a train by their mother in West Virginia and shipped to their father in Kentucky. The father, who does not want them, places the boys in foster homes and takes Nellie to Bethany Orphanage in Jackson, Kentucky. Nellie is a lively, intelligent, delightful girl, representative of many mountain girls and women.

374. Burton, Carl D. *Satan's Rock*. New York: Appleton-Century-Crofts, 1954.

A young man becomes obsessed with a wild young mountain girl who is reputed to have supernatural powers.

375. Bush, Isabel Graham. *Goose Creek Folks: A Story of the Kentucky Hills*. New York: Revell, 1912.

Young country girls are sent off to various kinds of missionary and settlement schools to learn cooking and cleaning and reading and writing. A sensitive portrayal of how girls were often overwhelmed by glimpses of the outside world.

376. Byars, Betsy. *The Summer of the Swans*. New York: Viking, 1974.

A sensitive story of a 14-year-old Appalachian girl and her mentally retarded brother. It shows how a girl approaching womanhood faces reality.

377. Cadle, Dean. "Cry in the Wilderness." *Appal. Heritage* 7 (Summer 1979): 42–48.

A short story told from the viewpoint of Birdie Walker, who has his own reasons for wanting the new preacher run out of town. He gets Alice Rowe, "that woman on the hill," to play a trick on the preacher and the people at the revival. The trick backfires on Birdie when Alice is converted and becomes a changed woman.

378. Cain, James Mallahan. *The Butterfly*. New York: Knopf, 1947.

A young woman comes back to the West Virginia-Kentucky border mine camp where she was born. The story deals with moonshining practices and coal-camp life styles.

379. Cann, Marion Stuart. *On Skidd's Branch*. Scranton, Penn.: Republican Job Rooms, 1884.

An outlaw kidnaps a young girl and holds her for ransom. None is paid, however, and the outlaw's common-law wife raises the girl. The outlaw falls in love with the teenage girl, who violently resists his advances. A revenuer from outside the mountains rescues her.

380. Cather, Willa Sibert. *Sapphira and the Slave Girl*. New York: Knopf, 1940.

A good character sketch of a Virginia lady who is considered to have married beneath her, and her husband, who runs a mill in the Blue Ridge Mountains. Cather wrote this novel from stories her parents told her about their relatives in Virginia.

381. Caudill, Harry M. *Dark Hills to Westward*. Boston: Little, Brown, 1969.

This book is based on legendary accounts of Jenny Wiley, a white woman and Kentucky pioneer who was captured by Indians.

382. Caudill, Rebecca. *Barrie & Daughter*. New York: Viking, 1943.

The story is set in Poor Fork Valley, Harlan County, Kentucky. Fern, the elder daughter of Peter Barrie, helps her father run a store which charges fair prices to the poverty-stricken mountain people.

383. _____. *Happy Little Family*. Philadelphia: Winston, 1947.

A story about two little Eastern Kentucky girls who are four and six years old.

384. _____. *Tree of Freedom*. New York: Viking, 1947.

A story about a teenage girl who finds herself alone on the frontier in the eighteenth century.

385. _____. *Schoolhouse in the Woods*. New York: Holt, Rinehart & Winston, 1949.

The main character is a girl named Bonnie. The book describes her experiences in her first year of school.

386. _____. *Saturday Cousins*. New York: Holt, Rinehart & Winston, 1953.

A group of six cousins meet at one of their homes every Saturday afternoon. The two oldest are Laurel and Julie; they make many decisions about what the group will plan and do.

387. _____. *Susan Cornish*. New York: Viking, 1955.

A young woman assumes her first position, teaching school in a poor mountain community.

388. _____. *Time for Lisa*. New York: T. Nelson, 1959.

A sensitive story about a lonely girl who longs for time and attention.

389. _____. *The Best-Loved Doll*. New York: Holt, Rinehart & Winston, 1962.

A story of a child and a doll in Appalachia, a land where there are few dolls for little girls.

390. Chapin, Anna Alice. *The Eagle's Mate*. New York: Grosset & Dunlap, 1914.

The story of Anemone Breckenridge, a sheltered little valley girl, who is carried off by the wild feuding family of Marne. She is forced to marry Lancer Marne and become part of the clan.

391. _____. *Mountain Madness*. New York: Wyatt, 1917.

This story is set in the warm sulphur springs area of western Virginia. Edith Forsythe gets lost in the forest and is rescued by

Martin Gale, a mountain man. A love triangle complicates the plot.

392. Chaplin, J.D. "Bashful Am'line." *Youth's Companion* 58 (Jan. 22, 1885): 26.

A short story about an abandoned young woman who hides in the mountains, has a baby girl, and dies. Young Am'line grows up painfully shy but showing traces of good breeding. The mountain women are presented in the stereotype of the day: bare-footed, gap-toothed, pipe-smoking, crude, illiterate. Worth reading for a glimpse of how mountain people were portrayed in 1885.

393. Chapman, Maristan. *The Happy Mountains*. New York: Viking, 1928.

The novel is set in the Tennessee mountains. Rashe and Barsha Lowe are sad because their son, Wait-Still-On-The-Lord, is itching to go beyond the mountains to see what the world is like. Barsha, Dena Howard and her sister Bess are well-characterized mountain women.

394. _____. *Homeplace*. New York: Viking, 1929.

This continues the story of Rashe and Barsha Lowe, their son "Waits," and Dena Jones. There is a mystery and great violence before everything is untangled. The women are portrayed in a convincing fashion.

395. _____. *Glen Hazard*. New York: Knopf, 1933.

A man is shot in Sheriff Marks's office while he is out of town. While told from the point of view of Marks and other men in this Tennessee community, several women are portrayed at length and in depth: Barsha Lowe, better at detecting than the sheriff; Liz Woody, widow of the murdered man and herself marked for murder; Dena Lowe, Barsha's daughter-in-law; and Veda Maynard, whom Dena alternately pities and despises because Veda is a "poorlander."

396. _____. *Clue of the Faded Dress*. New York: Appelton-Century, 1938.

A book about a group of young women in the Tennessee mountains. One of them is accused of stealing from the rich new girl in the community. The clue of the faded dress is the key which unlocks the mystery.

397. Chevalier, Elizabeth Pickett. *Drivin' Woman*. New York: Mac-Millan, 1942.

A story of a woman from Virginia, America Collier, whose family lost everything during the Civil War and in a fire afterward. The novel tells of her travels and her struggles to live. For a time she lives in the Kentucky mountains.

398. Childers, Beulah Roberts. "Sairy and the Young 'uns." *A Southern Harvest: Short Stories by Southern Writers.* Robert Penn Warren, ed. Boston: Houghton Mifflin, 1937.

A short story depicting two kinds of mountain women: the hard-working, thrifty woman, scrupulously clean in both her person and her home; and the aimless, shiftless woman, mother of many children, letting her oldest daughter assume most of the burden of the smaller children.

399. Clarke, Kate Upson. "For Looly." *Harper's*, Feb. 1886, pp. 429–43.

A short story about a mountain girl, her attempt to save up money for her younger sister's education, and her relationship with a man from a nearby town.

400. Cleaver, Vera. *Where the Lillies Bloom.* Philadelphia: Lippincott, 1969.

A family of children are orphaned and a brave young girl struggles to keep her brothers and sisters together in the Great Smoky Mountains of Tennessee.

401. Comak, David English. *June of the Hills: The Junaluska Prize Novel, a Story of the Southern Mountains with Lake Junaluska, North Carolina, as the Center of Action.* Lake Junaluska, N.C.: Literary Department, Junaluska Woman's Club, 1927.

June Adair, beautiful and deeply religious, gives up an operatic career to teach in the mountains.

402. Compton, Hannibal Albert. *A Moonshiner's Folly and Other Stories.* Boston: Roxburgh, 1915.

Born and raised in log cabins in the hills, the women found in these stories are strong and robust, gentle and tender, loving and forgiving.

403. Comstock, Harriet Theresa Smith. *The Man Thou Gavest.* New York: Doubleday, 1917.

The protagonist goes to the mountains to recuperate from an illness. He hears gossip about a no-account girl, Nella-Rose, and entices her into marriage without a preacher. Later he abandons her to go home and marry his fiancee.

404. Connell, Evan S. "I Come From Younder Mountain." *Prize Stories of 1951: The O. Henry Awards.* New York: Doubleday, 1951.

A story about a North Carolina hill girl who walks from her home to the nearest town, carrying her dead baby to the doctor.

405. Cooke, Grace MacGowan. *The Power and the Glory.* New York: Doubleday, Page, 1910.

A Tennessee mountain girl moves to a nearby mill town. There are socialite do-gooders and those genuinely interested in, and working hard for, improvement in the working girl's condition. Several subplots make for exciting reading.

406. Cooke, John Esten. *My Lady Pokahontas*. Boston: Houghton Mifflin, 1885.

This narrative, supposedly written by Amos Todkill, relates the story of Captain John Smith and the Indian princess Pokahontas. The book is a first-person account of Todkill, told from the perspective of the princess.

407. Credle, Ellis. *Janey's Shoes*. New York: Grosset & Dunlap, 1944.

Three children make the journey up the steep, rocky road to Granny's house on a North Carolina mountain. There they hear the story of Granny's first trip up the trail as a little girl. Good characterizations of the children and especially of Granny as she tells of her parents and the fortitude they had to undertake the journey.

408. ———. *Big Doin's on Razorback Ridge*. New York: Nelson, 1956.

A book written for young people, set in the Tennessee hills during the time of the TVA construction of Norris Dam. The mountain people plan to participate in the dedication. The girls piece a quilt to present to the president, and Nancy's wildest dreams come true when she and Jodey get to do a clogging dance and win first prize.

409. Crim, Matt. "S'phiry Ann." *Century* 33 (Feb. 1887): 606–16.

S'phiry Ann is in love with Gave, who makes moonshine liquor. He asks her to marry him but she says no, not unless he gives up his illegal business. He does not listen to her, and it takes a near capture by government men to convince him.

410. ———. "The Strike at Mobley's." *Century* 50 (July 1895): 378–84.

The men on Deer Creek spend far too much of their time at the local store, according to their wives. In a vain attempt to assert women's rights, Mrs. Mobley goes on strike.

411. Cunningham, Albert Benjamin [pseud. Garth Hale]. *Strait Is the Gate*. New York: Dutton, 1946.

A novel about Leona Maden, her husband Curt, her furtive fling with a happy-go-lucky neighbor, and the death of her young son. More sophisticated writing than one finds in Cunningham's Jess Roden mysteries.

412. Danforth, Harry Edmund. *The Trail of the Gray Dragoon*. New York: H. Vinal, 1928.

A love story of a Yankee soldier and a fiery Rebel girl. It takes place at an old inn on the Kanawha Turnpike on Gauley Mountain in West Virginia.

413. Daniel, James Walter. *The Girl in Checks: Or, The Mystery of the Mountain Cabin*. Nashville: Publishing House of the Methodist Episcopal Church, South, 1890.

A mystery story concerning a girl in a checked dress. The events take place in a mountain setting; there are religious overtones.

414. Dargan, Olive Tilford. *From My Highest Hill*. With 50 photographs by Bayard Wootten. New York: Scribner, 1925 (as *Highland Annals*). Revised ed., Philadelphia: Lippincott, 1941.

Sensitive characterizations of mountain women. The story is set in the North Carolina mountains, "not far from the Great Smoky Mountains at any time." Quite a bit of dialect is used and, although the writer is from outside the area, it is surprisingly authentic.

415. _____. [pseud. Fielding Burke]. *Call Home the Heart*. New York: Longmans, Green, 1932.

Ishma Waycaster, a sturdy, intelligent young North Carolina girl, sensitive to both the beauty and the squalor of her mountain home, leaves her husband and family and runs away with another man to a mill town. After two years, she returns to the hills and the husband she really loves.

416. _____. *A Stone Came Rolling*. New York: Longmans, Green, 1935.

Ishma Waycaster (of *Call Home the Heart*) and her family come to live on a farm near a mill town. She gets a job in the mill and becomes involved in the fight for better working conditions and better pay for the laborers. A strong character.

417. _____. *Innocent Bigamy*. Winston-Salem: Blair, 1962.

A collection of short stories, in several of which women are the main characters: "Love and Wardrift," "She Walked in Beauty," "Gangway!" and "River Joy."

418. Daviess, Maria Thompson. *The Melting of Molly*. Indianapolis: Bobbs-Merrill, 1912.

This novel set in Eastern Tennessee is a strange combination of romance and dieting.

419. Davis, Harold Lenoir. *Beulah Land*. New York: Morrow, 1949.

A young Cherokee girl from Crowtown in Western North Carolina is involved in the Civil War and the westward movement.

420. DeLeon, Thomas Cooper. *Juny: Or, Only One Girl's Story; A Romance of the Society Crust—Upper and Under*. Mobile, Ala.: Gossip Printing Co., 1890.

Juny, of unknown parentage, is being raised by moonshiners. She is rescued from them and is adopted by people in high society. Her entry into high society is an awkward and heart-rending process.

421. Dent, Thomas Lee. *Ludlow on the Kanawha*. New York: Comet, 1959.

An orphan girl in the West Virginia hills is told she is the long-lost granddaughter of a wealthy business woman. This brings her problems and complications as well as an expanded horizon.

422. Dickson, Sally O'Hear. *The Story of Marthy*. Richmond, Va.: Presbyterian Committee of Publications, 1898.

A young minister lives and works in the mountains of North Carolina. This is a novel about his wife.

423. _____. *Reuben Delton, Preacher*. Richmond, Va.: Presbyterian Committee of Publications, 1900.

A sequel to *The Story of Marthy*, beginning four years after the close of the first book. Reuben Delton is Marthy's husband.

424. Dobbins, Nancy Carol. *The Happy Appalachian*. Detroit: Harlo, 1978.

A three-act play about the Bragg family. The main character is Regina Bragg (Mom), a very active, domineering woman in her sixties. There is also a daughter, Maribeth. The play covers a few days in their lives leading up to Mom's going into the hospital.

425. Dos Passos, John. *Adventures of a Young Man*. New York: Harcourt, Brace, 1938.

The novel is set in Slade, Harlan County, Kentucky, where Glenn Spotswood spends some time assisting the striking miners of the Muddy Fork Local. Children and women are portrayed. Wheattey Napier is especially well characterized.

426. Dromgoole, Will Allen. *Cinch, and Other Stories: Tales of Tennessee*. Boston: Estes, 1898.

Most of the short stories deal in some way with the hardships of mountain women.

427. Dyer, Diana Smith. *Before I Sleep*. New York: Pageant, 1958.

Vena grows up in the mountains, an only child, allowed a great deal of independence by her father. She is unprepared for the role she must play as a mountain woman dependent upon men for survival and happiness.

428. Dykeman, Wilma. *The Tall Woman*. New York: Holt, Rinehart & Winston, 1962.

A truly heroic mountain woman is Lydia McQueen: strong, courageous, creative, and with a lot of natural ability and native intelligence as well as a loving heart. Her story is told from her marriage in 1864 to her death 30 years later.

429. _____. *The Far Family*. New York: Holt, Rinehart & Winston, 1966.

    Members of the Thurston family return to the old homeplace when one of their brothers is accused of murdering a Negro. The older sister, who never left home, is the strong one who helps her family through this difficult period.

430. _____. *Return the Innocent Earth*. New York: Holt, Rinehart & Winston, 1973.

    A story about a family of strong people. The women are especially well characterized. Dykeman portrays mountain women as they truly are.

431. Ebbs, Eloise Beckner. *Carolina Mountain Breezes*. Asheville, N.C.: Miller, 1929.

    A young girl, educating herself in what she thinks of as the "wicked city," amuses herself by telling her new friends of the virtues of mountain living.

432. Eggleston, George Cary. *Irene of the Mountains*. New York: Grosset & Dunlap, 1909.

    Set in the hills of Virginia, this book has two women as main characters. Irene is young, pretty, innocent; she falls in love with the right man. Judy Peters, middle-aged, large-girthed, flamboyant, is called the "Queen of the Mountains." She is head of her family and a political "boss" to be reckoned with every year at election time.

433. Ehle, John. *Move Over, Mountain*. New York: Morrow, 1957.

    The story of Jordan, who drives a coal truck in North Carolina. He and his wife, Annie, face the problems of being black and poor. He is also involved with another woman, Mona, from the North.

434. _____. *The Land Breakers*. New York: Harper & Row, 1964.

    A novel about a few families in the area around Morganton, North Carolina, between 1779 and 1783. One of the main characters is a woman named Lorry. The author writes a great deal about the relationships between families and between men and women.

435. _____. *The Road*. New York: Harper & Row, 1967.

    This book is primarily about Weatherby and his crew of convicts who cut the tunnel through Old Fort Mountain, thus opening up the Swannanoa Valley and Western North Carolina. Henryanna, a tall, blond mountain girl, several mountain women, and a freight carload of women convicts are portrayed.

436. _____. *The Journey of August King*. New York: Harper & Row, 1971.

A Western North Carolina farmer (circa 1850) risks his life, his property, and his reputation for the sake of a slave girl who is trying to escape.

437. Elliott, Sarah Barnell. *The Ducket Sperret*. New York: Holt, 1898.
Hannah Warren marries Si Ducket but a streak of independence shows up and she decides she would rather peddle apples and potatoes and have her own money than be dependent on any man for support.

438. Ellis, Edward Sylvester. *The Frontier Angel: A Romance of Kentucky Rangers' Life*. Beadle's Half Dime Library, no. 21. New York: Beadle & Adams, 1877.
In the 1790s a young girl immigrates to Kentucky with her family. She is abducted by a renegade, but her lover is able to rescue her with the help of a demented white girl who was captured by Indians as a child.

439. Erskine, Emma Payne. *The Mountain Girl*. Boston: Little, Brown, 1912.
A victorian novel in which a North Carolina mountain girl marries a Canadian doctor. The first part of the book gives a good picture of mountain life.

440. _____. *A Girl of the Blue Ridge*. Boston: Little, Brown, 1915.
When Lucy Babb, scarcely more than a child herself, has to assume responsibility for her newborn brother after her mother's death, the burden seems more than she can bear. With the help of Peg Kitchel's school and Daniel McEven, Lucy's life changes.

441. Evans, Willis F. *Isabella Stockton*. Boston: Christopher, 1929.
Most of this story takes place in the mountains of Virginia and West Virginia during the French and Indian War. Isabella is captured by the Indians as a small girl, raised by them, and later sold to a French trader. Other women are also portrayed.

442. Fairfax, Lina Redwood. "Hickett's Hollow." *Century* 20 (Sept. 1880): 758–66.
A mountain woman is cruelly punished because she is jealous of her wandering husband.

443. Farr, Sidney. "Salty and Apple Blossoms." *Visions of Tomorrow's Yesterday*, pp. 63–66. A publication of the Twenty Writers Club. Berea, Ky.: Berea Coll. Press, 1973.
A short story told in the first person by an old, old woman who remembers when she was a young mountain girl and had a dog she loved and lost. Reveals strength of character and courage as well as sensitivity and deep emotions as a girl struggles to adapt to a male-dominated way of life.

444. _____. "Don't Cry Now, the Baby's Sleeping." *Mt. Rev.* 1 (Summer 1975): 14–15, 44.

A story about a young mother in Appalachia who takes her baby up to the ridges to pick huckleberries, against her husband's wishes. The tragedy which takes place is inevitable. Good character study of a stubborn, independent woman and of the mother-in-law, a hypochondriac.

445. Field, Hope. *Stormy Present.* New York: Dutton, 1942.

Sherrill Poague is the only female in a household of boys. Though she was raised in a cabin in the Appalachian mountains and members of her family are not educated, she has a thirst for knowledge. She marries and moves to Cincinnati and continues to read and learn as she absorbs elements of her new environment.

446. Fields, Jewell Cardwell. "Why Not Tonight?" *Mt. Life & Work* 50 (Apr. 1974): 17–20.

A short story in which a young girl is taken to a revival meeting by her mother. A good portrayal of mountain women and girls and the role religion plays in their lives.

447. Fletcher, Inglis Clark. *The Scotswoman.* Indianapolis: Bobbs-Merrill, 1955.

Flora Macdonald leaves Scotland in 1774 and arrives on Cape Fear just before the Revolution. She becomes involved in political troubles and later rallies her Scottish Highlanders to the Loyalist side against the Patriots. The climax comes in the Battle at Moores Creek Bridge.

448. Ford, Jean. *I'll Walk to the Mountain.* New York: Greenberg, 1936.

A story of men and women in the Tennessee mountains and of a Greenwich Village girl who comes hitchhiking to the hills.

449. Ford, Jesse Hill. *Mountains of Gilead.* Boston: Little, Brown, 1961.

When her boyfriend becomes engaged to another woman, Patsie Jo turns the mountain code of honor to her benefit by goading her father into gunning for the boyfriend.

450. Ford, Leslie. *Burn Forever.* New York: Popular Library, 1963.

A story of young lovers in the Tennessee Valley caught up in violence, murder, and intrigue. As the young woman of Appalachia deals with fear and hate, her strength of character is revealed.

451. Fox, Genevieve May. *Mountain Girl.* Boston: Little, Brown, 1932.

The first of three novels about Sairy Ann. She goes from the Slone's Creek Settlement School to Clayburgh, a Bluegrass city, for nurse's training. She marries a doctor and they plan to build a clinic near Sairy's old home on Hollybush Creek.

452. _____. *Mountain Girl Comes Home.* Boston: Little, Brown, 1934.

In this sequel, Sairy Ann comes home with her husband and tries to get her people to accept this "fotched-on" doctor. When he cures a little orphan girl, Lona Allen, of her lameness, mountain people begin to accept him, and when Sairy has a little girl of her own, they become even more accepted and liked by community people.

453. _____. *Lona of Hollybush Creek.* Boston: Little, Brown, 1935.

In the last part of the trilogy about Sairy Ann, Lona Allen, the lame girl Sairy Ann's husband cured, is in school but does not do well in reading, writing, and arithmetic. But she is a skilled craftswoman and revives the almost forgotten art of weaving "kivers," teaches it to others, and finds a market for the products.

454. Fox, John, Jr. *A Cumberland Vendetta.* New York: Harper, 1895.

A collection of short stories set in the Cumberland Mountains of Eastern Kentucky. Mountain girls and women figure in almost every story.

455. _____. *Hell-Fer-Sartin.* New York: Harper, 1897.

A collection of short stories set in Eastern Kentucky, originally published in *Harper's Weekly, The Century,* and other periodicals. Most of them have pretty mountain girls as central characters.

456. _____. *The Trail of the Lonesome Pine.* New York: Scribner, 1908.

One of Fox's most famous books. The story is about a mountain-born girl, June Tolliver, who meets an outlander, Jack Hale. They fall in love and June is sent to the outside world to be educated and polished.

457. Furman, Lucy. *Mothering on Perilous.* New York: Century, 1910.

Furman came to the Hindman Settlement School in Kentucky in the early part of this century, lived and worked there, and was able to study at first-hand the women and girls of the mountains. In this novel a social worker attempts to educate mountain children at a settlement school. There is mutual cultural shock but they learn to overcome it.

458. _____. "Hard-hearted Barbary Allen." *Century* 83 (Mar. 1912): 739–44.

A mountain girl, on the pattern of Barbara Allen, allows two men to battle for her hand. When one is dead and the other in the state penitentiary at Frankfort, she returns to school.

459. _____. "The Scarborough Spoons: A Story of English and Americans." *Century* 85 (Nov. 1912): 126–35.

Emily Scarborough learns of long-lost relatives in the Kentucky hills. Heirloom spoons, etc., help establish facts.

460. _____. "Christmas Tree on Clinch." *Century* 85 (Dec. 1912): 163-71.

A short story about a feud and how the women help to settle it.

461. _____. "The Most Knowingest Child." *Century* 85 (Mar. 1913): 763-69.

A good presentation of the superstition and medical ignorance prevalent in the mountains early in this century. A young girl, a good scholar, dies of tuberculosis.

462. _____. *Sight to the Blind*. New York: Macmilan, 1914.

This story has the right proportion of sentiment and realism. A mountain woman believes her blindness is a curse from God because she rebelled against the loss of her child. At last she is helped to understand that her trouble is cataracts which can be removed.

463. _____. "Out by Ox Team." *Outlook* 133 (Apr. 1923): 655-58.

One of the teachers at the settlement school rides into a valley and finds a moonshine still. She is involved in a mountain funeral.

464. _____. *The Quare Women: A Story of the Kentucky Mountains*. Boston: Little, Brown, 1923.

A group of women camp out in Knott County, Kentucky, and set about efforts to bring civilization to the hills. The mountain women and their families help in many ways. The story is light and humorous at times.

465. _____. *The Glass Window: A Story of the Quare Women*. Boston: Little, Brown, 1925.

The story of the women who came to found the Hindman Settlement School in Hindman, Kentucky. There are anecdotes and events concerning mountain women.

466. Gehringer, Martha Gallion. "Want." *Mt. Rev.* 1 (Winter 1975): 5.

A short story about an adolescent girl saddled with three younger brothers to care for as well as an ailing mother. She contends with heat, flies, illness, and fatigue in a poverty-stricken setting.

467. George, Francis. *The Only Nancy*. New York: Revell, 1917.

Nancy was stolen from her family, who lived near Blowing Rock, North Carolina, and brought to the Kentucky mountains. An artist comes to the mountains, becomes interested in Nancy, and helps her locate her family.

468. Gielow, Martha S. *The Light on the Hill*. New York: Revell, 1915.

A young man falls in love with Sary, a mountain girl. Because their disapproving families will not consent to their getting married, they marry secretly. They are separated for a time, and during the time apart Sary dies.

469. Giles, Janice Holt. *The Enduring Hills.* Philadelphia: Westminster, 1950.

Good strong characterizations of Hod Pierce's mother, sister, and neighbors, and especially of Mary Hogan, who becomes his wife. Mary was raised in Texas and came to Louisville to teach school until she met Hod and moved to the hills with him.

470. _____. *Miss Willie.* Philadelphia: Westminster, 1951.

A sequel to *The Enduring Hills.* Miss Willie, Mary Hogan's aunt, comes to teach at a one-room school in the hills but finds her Texas background has not prepared her for this kind of life. She has a rough time for a while as she gets to know the women and girls and their families. After a few years she marries and settles in to be wife to a mountain man and mother to his teenage son.

471. _____. *Tara's Healing.* Philadelphia: Westminster, 1951.

Dr. Tara Cochrane, a friend of Hod Pierce during his army days, is found ill in the psychiatric wing of a Louisville hospital. Hod brings him home for a visit, and Mary's good cooking, the fresh air, sunshine, and the warmth of the people, all help in his healing.

472. _____. *Hannah Fowler.* Boston: Houghton Mifflin, 1956.

A mountain woman struggles with blizzards, wolves, capture by Indians, and the long journey back home. Set in the period in which Jennie Wiley lived, some events in this story are similar to what happened to Jennie—capture by the Indians, escape, etc.

473. _____. *The Believers.* Boston: Houghton Mifflin, 1957.

A young woman and her husband join the Shaker colony. He becomes a fanatical believer and forsakes her when she most needs him. A good strong story; all the women are well characterized.

474. _____. *Savannah.* Boston: Houghton Mifflin, 1961.

The story of a strong woman of great courage who lives in the Appalachian territory in 1829. Savannah fights hunger, cold, and fear of the Indians. But most of all she has to conquor her fierce pride to keep her children from starving.

475. _____. *Wellspring.* Boston: Houghton Mifflin, 1975.

This book is composed of chapters, each a short story. Three have women as main characters: "Dear Sir," "Tetch 'N Take," and "Wilderness Road."

476. Gill, George Creswell. *Beyond the Bluegrass: A Kentucky Novel.* New York: Neal, 1908.

The hero comes to the mountain territory and finds the women and men either the best or the worst he's ever met, according to his descriptions. The book mostly praises mountain people.

477. Gilmore, James Roberts. *Among the Pines: Or, South in Secession Time.* New York: Gilmore, 1862.

A man from New York visits southern friends in North Carolina. The story shows how he perceives the people.

478. _____. *A Mountain White Heroine.* New York: Belford, Clarke, 1889.

In addition to the usual characteristics given women of that time, this novel has several ingredients: violence, moonshine, feuds, and mountain laurel.

479. Givens, Charles G. *All Cats Are Gray.* Indianapolis: Bobbs-Merrill, 1937.

Most of the main characters are men in this story set in East Tennessee, but a few stalwart mountain women are portrayed. There are a 20-year-old murder mystery, Tennessee Valley politics, and men and women who retain some of the pioneer spirit of their ancestors.

480. Glasgow, Ellen. *Barren Ground.* New York: Doubleday, Page, 1925.

This powerful story, set in the Knobs country of Kentucky, is about a strange and lovely girl of the mountains.

481. _____. *Vein of Iron.* New York: Harcourt, Brace, 1935.

Ada Fincastle has always heard that the ancestors of the Virginia mountaineers were strong and had great dignity, but the present generation are not so strong. The portrayal of Ada and her people depicts physical and spiritual poverty. There are a number of women characters.

482. Goodwin, Maud Wilder. *White Aprons.* Boston: Little, Brown, 1899.

This story takes place in Virginia during the Revolutionary War. Penelope Payne falls in love with Major Fairfax, a rebel soldier, though her father is loyal to the king. She suffers much and travels the ocean to save her lover's life.

483. Gordon, Caroline. *Green Centuries.* New York: Scribner, 1941.

This story centers around two brothers, one of them a friend of Daniel Boone and the other captured by the Cherokee when the brothers accompany Boone on his first journey into the magical land called Kaintuck. There are a number of strong-willed, passionate, courageous women.

484. _____. *The Women on the Porch.* New York: Scribner, 1944.

Catherine Chapman leaves her husband and returns to her rural

Kentucky home. He follows her and they reconcile. The theme is unfaithfulness in modern marriages.

485. Govan, Christine Noble. *Sweet 'Possum Valley.* Boston: Houghton Mifflin, 1940.

A lighthearted book that follows the summer adventures of young mountain boys and girls, black and white, and their search for the famous Bell Witch of Tennessee. An unusual combination of races in a mountain situation.

486. Gowen, Emmet. *Mountain Born.* Indianapolis: Bobbs-Merrill, 1930.

The story relates Fate Shannon's efforts to patch up the feud between the Shannons and the Fieldses while he is hoping to win Nearme (Nearer-My-God-To-Thee) Fields for his wife.

487. Gray, Elizabeth Janet. *The Fair Adventure.* New York: Viking, 1940.

A North Carolina girl graduates from high school with a keen interest in dramatics and art. Her ambition is to go to a large northern college.

488. Green, Lewis W. *And Scatter the Proud.* Winston-Salem, N.C.: Blair, 1969.

A collection of short stories set in Asheville, North Carolina. Various women from different walks of life figure prominently in Books One and Two.

489. Green, Mary. *Honeysuckle Hill: A Hillbilly Makes the Grade.* New York: Exposition, 1961.

A mountain girl has a shotgun wedding and moves to Chicago. Later her marriage is annulled and she returns to the hills with a second husband.

490. Green, Paul. *Wilderness Road.* New York: French, 1956.

This outdoor drama, which has been performed at Berea, Kentucky, for nearly a decade, has a number of mountain women and girls in the cast of characters.

491. Greene, Nanci Lewis. *Nance: A Story of Kentucky Feuds.* Chicago: Neely, 1893.

This story sounds somewhat like the Hatfield-McCoy feud. Two Kentucky families are bitterly fighting each other. A girl from one side falls in love with a boy from the other. Told from the women's viewpoints for the most part.

492. Greer-Petrie, Cordia. *Angeline of the Hill Country.* New York: Crowell, 1921.

The author spent several summers in the Kentucky hills, where Angeline was one of her neighbors. "She was poor but proud—illiterate but shrewd—and scorned the futile amenities of conventional society." This story and its sequels are allegedly based on Angeline's monologues about her trips to Louisville.

493. _____. *Angeline at the Seelbach*. Louisville, Ky.: Angeline Publishing Co., 1923.

Angeline is the narrator of this stereotyped but nevertheless humorous piece, which is heavy with dialect. She and her husband accompany Judge Bowles to Louisville and have their first encounter with a big city hotel, with its plush decorations and gleaming bathroom fixtures.

494. _____. *Angeline Stepping Out*. Louisville, Ky.: Angeline Publishing Co., 1923.

Angeline talks about the time Judge Bowles took her and Lum to Louisville to testify in a lawsuit. While there, they are taken to see *Othello*. Angeline's comments about Shakespeare are worth reading.

495. _____. *Angeline Doin' Society*. Louisville, Ky.: Angeline Publishing Co., 1923.

Angeline continues her monologue about her trip to Louisville with Judge Bowles, their stay at the Seelbach Hotel, and their various experiences in the city.

496. _____. *Angeline Gets an Eyeful*. Louisville, Ky.: Angeline Publishing Co., 1924.

Angeline's impressions of the "idle rich," whom she meets when she and Lum spend a weekend at Senator Clark's home.

497. _____. *Angeline Hittin' On High*. Louisville, Ky.: Angeline Publishing Co., 1925.

Angeline and Lum go to Louisville to testify in a court case for Judge Bowles. On the way home, they stop to visit Judge Bowles's niece Betty, and her husband, Senator Clark. Angeline has much to say about the dilettante society she encounters.

498. _____. *Angeline Fixin' for the Queen*. Louisville, Ky.: Angeline Publishing Co., 1926.

A companion story to *Angeline Hittin' on High*. She tells about trips to Chicago and New York and gives her impressions of high society.

499. _____. *Angeline Tames Her Sheik*. Louisville, Ky.: Angeline Publishing Co., 1927.

After Judge Bowles introduces Angeline and Lum to the outside world, their days become a jumble of visiting high society. Lum decides he's going to "be a Sheik and go to Hollywood," but Angeline soon sets him straight.

500. _____. *Angeline Goes On Strike*. Louisville, Ky.: Angeline Publishing Co., 1928.

Angeline complains that while she does all the drudge-work around the place, Lum does only what he wants to do. He slips off to attend a circus in a distant city and she declares war.

501. Grey, Katharine. *A Little Leaven*. Philadelphia: Lippincott, 1922.
A typical story of a mountain girl who marries a man from outside the area and goes to live in the city. She is unhappy and he is often ashamed of her backwoods manners. They separate and she tries to make a life for herself.

502. Grubb, Davis. *The Night of the Hunter*. New York: Harper, 1953.
A book filled with suspense. A young boy and girl are hunted by their stepfather, who intends to kill them. Good characterizations of the children and especially of their mother, who is typical of a certain type of woman in Appalachia.

503. ———. *A Dream of Kings*. New York: Scribner, 1955.
Catherine loves Tom and bears his illegitimate child after Tom goes to fight in the Civil War. She is haunted by the memory of her father, who deserted her when she was a child, after telling her he would return one day as a king bringing her great treasures. A unique treatment of the Electra complex.

504. ———. *The Barefoot Man*. New York: Simon & Schuster, 1971.
A powerful story about the West Virginia coalfields during the Depression, and the old woman who leads the miners in their fight against company thugs.

505. Hall, Esther Greenacres. *The Here-to-Yonder Girl*. New York: Macmillan, 1932.
A book written for teenagers. Tassie Tyler is an orphan girl who wants an education but is too old to enter the first grade of the Singing Branch Settlement School. Instead, she makes a home for six orphan children. The Settlement School is threatened by fire and Tassie warns the people in time. In gratitude, the teacher offers free tuition for Tassie and her orphans.

506. Hall, Granville Davisson. *Daughter of the Elm*. Fairmont, W.V.: Arcuri Book Shop, 1946.
The story of crime and a gang who terrorize the countryside in Northern West Virginia prior to the Civil War. The heroine, Loraine Esmond, grows up with the crime but is not influenced by it.

507. Ham, Tom. *Give Us This Valley*. New York: Macmillan, 1952.
The story of Elizabeth Stonecypher, who marries at a young age. She and her husband travel from Pennsylvania to the southern mountains, where they make their home. A number of native mountain women are also featured.

508. Hamilton, Carl. *King of the Forest*. New York: Vantage, 1978.

While the main character is Kyle Mercer, a mountain youth who loves the forests and deplores the coming of coal companies and lumbering corporations, three mountain women play major roles.

509. Hamner, Earl, Jr. *Spencer's Mountain*. New York: Dial, 1961.
This book, on which "The Waltons" television series is based, has several mountain women and young girls in it. Especially well characterized are Olivia, the mother, and Grandmother Eliza.

510. Hannum, Alberta Pierson. *Thursday April*. New York: Harper, 1931.
A novel about a young girl, Thursday April, born and raised in the Blue Ridge Mountains, during the period 1897–1917. She is saved from an early marriage and given an opportunity for schooling. A restrained use of dialect and scenic background makes this a naturalistic piece of writing.

511. _____. *The Hills Step Lightly*. New York: Morrow, 1934.
The life story of a mountain woman, from her lonely pre-Civil War childhood to her old age. An interesting background of witch lore, mountain humor, and details of everyday life.

512. _____. *The Gods and One*. New York: Duell, Sloan, & Pearce, 1941.
A mountain girl is betrayed by a city visitor and is left with her woods-colt, shunned by the people in the community. She moves in with Squire Larks, his three wives, and 30-odd children at Lark's Gap. A fair amount of mountain lore and backwoods life are accurately portrayed in spite of the far-fetched plot.

513. _____. *Roseanna McCoy*. New York: Holt, 1947.
A fictional account of the famous Hatfield-McCoy feud. Roseanna is the main character and the story deals more with her love affair with Ance Hatfield and their flight to West Virginia than with the feudists' bloody battles.

514. Harben, William Nathaniel. *Mam' Linda: A Novel*. New York: Harper, 1907.
A story about a black woman in the Appalachians.

515. _____. *Dixie Hart*. New York: Harper, 1910.
Dixie Hart is a young, tomboyish mountain girl who works hard to hold her family together.

516. _____. *June Dawson*. New York: Harper, 1911.
Another poor, young mountain girl—pitted against uneven and greatly unjust odds—triumphs in the end.

517. Harris, Bernice Kelly. *Janey Jeems*. New York: Doubleday, 1946.
Janey is just 15 when she marries Jeems West, a man who has already been married once. She bears children, keeps house, and

helps Jeems scratch out a living from the soil of the Carolina hills. She teaches her children to fear God and shun evil.

518. Harris, Corra May White. *A Circuit Rider's Wife*. Philadelphia: Altemus, 1910.
A semiautobiographical novel about the trials and tribulations of a minister's wife. A gleam of humor and evidence of a strong, independent woman run through the book.

519. _____. *Eve's Second Husband*. Philadelphia: Altemus, 1911.
Autobiographical fiction from the North Georgia hills.

520. _____. *The Co-Citizens*. New York: Doubleday, Page, 1915.
One of the early women's liberation novels, with a setting in North Georgia.

521. _____. *A Circuit Rider's Widow*. New York: Doubleday, Page, 1916.
A semiautobiographical novel about the author's life in North Georgia as a Methodist minister's widow.

522. Harris, Credo. *Sunlight Patch*. Boston: Small, Maynard, 1915.
Jane is raised in the home of her father (a moonshiner and outlaw) in the Cumberland Mountains. Later she receives a certain amount of education at a convent in the valley and is sent to a school in the East. When she comes back to the hills it is to open a school.

523. Harris, Joel Chandler. "Trouble on Lost Mountain." *Century* 31 (Jan. 1886): 425–36.
A young girl is murdered in the North Georgia mountains.

524. Hatcher, Harlan. *Patterns of Wolfpen*. Indianapolis: Bobbs-Merrill, 1934.
The story is set in the upper Big Sandy Valley in Kentucky, and revolves about Cynthia, whose father sells land to a timber company. Cynthia hopes to go to the Pikeville Institute with some of the money, but things change with the advent of the logging crew.

525. Haun, Mildred. *The Hawk's Done Gone*. Indianapolis: Bobbs-Merrill, 1940.
An East Tennessee Granny woman sees many kinds of women in various situations as she goes up and down the creeks delivering their babies. Several stories reveal the strong, independent nature of mountain women.

526. _____. *The Hawk's Done Gone and Other Stories*. Nashville, Tenn.: Vanderbilt Univ. Press, 1968.
This edition includes all the material in *The Hawk's Done Gone* (above) plus 10 additional short stories.

527. Hay, James, Jr. *The Hidden Woman*. New York: Dodd, Mead, 1929.
A murder mystery in Asheville, North Carolina. Some native

women, black and white, are on the periphery, but three women from outside the area figure more prominently in the events.

528. Helmut, Jan [pseud.]. *Daisy's Fanny*. New York: Vantage, 1951.
A story about innocent Fanny, who has such a lush body as a young teenager that every man in the community wants to take her to bed. Her mother treats her harshly and she turns for comfort and friendship to Ishmel, a black boy near her own age.

529. Herbert, Mary. "A Mountain Wedding." *Mt. Life & Work* 40 (Fall 1964): 44–49.
A mountain mother is surprised when her son announces at breakfast that he is being married that day after church. She begins working frantically to prepare a feast for the crowd of people who are sure to come to the house.

530. Herrick, Huldah. *Ginsey Kreider*. Boston: Pilgrim, 1900.
A novel about a young girl whose father is feuding with the McCoy clan. Ginsey is kidnapped, raped, and shut up in a cave. Wonderful Aunt Theesta rescues her and restores her to her grieving family. The father welcomes her with open arms, but Ginsey's mother does not so easily receive her "ruint" daughter.

531. Heywood, DuBose. *Angel*. New York: Doran, 1926.
The daughter of a hell-fire-and-damnation preacher, pretty Angel falls in love with a handsome bootlegger, who is captured by revenue officers. The pregnant young girl has no choice but to marry the old man who wants her and takes her to a remote cabin to live.

532. Higbee, Alma Robinson. "Whistlin' Gal." *Amer. Mercury* 61 (July 1945): 66–71.
Higbee, a Kentucky native, characterizes Appalachian women and girls to a fine degree. In this short story, Lonie May is the youngest of five unmarried girls. Her mother tries to marry her to an old man but Lonie May has other plans. Throughout the story runs the old saying: "A whistlin' gal and a crowing hen, never come to no good end." Lonie May loves to whistle.

533. Hoffman, Marie E. *Lindy Lloyd: A Tale of the Mountains*. Boston: Marchall Jones, 1920.
Lindy is blackmailed into marrying a man who is put in jail that very day. Later he dies, and the young man she loves comes back. Some humor is scattered throughout this tale of the Tennessee mountains.

534. Holmes, Mary Jane. *Tempest and Sunshine; Or, Life in Kentucky*. New York: Appleton, 1854.
Julia Middleton (Tempest) is a mean-tempered, nasty young woman who nearly brings tragedy to herself and her noble sister,

Sunshine. But in the end, Julia repents and changes. Sunshine makes a happy marriage.

535. _____. *Marian Grey: Or, The Heiress of Redstone Hall.* New York: Carleton, 1863.

Marian's fortune is stolen by her unscrupulous foster-father. But eventually she is united with her true love and, even more fortunate, regains her fortune.

536. Hornsby, Henry Homer. *Lonesome Valley.* New York: Sloane, 1949.

Unmarred by sentiment, this book competently treats mountain life and customs. The main character is a boy, but several female characters play very important parts.

537. Hough, Emerson. *The Way Out: A Story of the Cumberlands To-day.* New York: Appleton, 1918.

The story of a young man, David Joslin, who leaves his wife and father to find another life away from the mountains. There are chapters about various women he meets during his travels, as well as his mountain wife.

538. Housekeeper, Mrs. William G. [pseud. Rose Batterham]. *Pleasure Piece: Or, Fair Ellender in His Arms.* New York: Harper, 1935.

Fourteen-year-old Celie has lived her whole life in a secluded North Carolina mountain cave with her father, who had been wrongly accused of murder by the valley people. When her father dies, she sets out to find the only other man she knows. Her long trek through the mountains is Gothic in its elements of terror. A family in the valley come to her rescue and she finds her true lover.

539. Huddleston, Edwin Glenn. *The Claybrooks.* New York: Macmillan, 1951.

The setting is the area around Knoxville, Tennessee. The story centers around the women in the Claybrook family: Miranda, the strong old woman, and Bella, Xavia, and Tabby, the latter an actress who has traveled the world and now comes home to live.

540. Hudson, Irene. "The Schoolma'am of Sandy Ridge." *Atlantic Monthly* 127 (Jan. 1921): 11–22.

A schoolteacher writes letters to various friends outside the Smoky Mountain area, describing the mountain people and their homes and life-styles. Good sketches of mountain women and girls.

541. Hurst, Samuel Need. *The Mountains Redeemed: The Romance of the Mountains.* Appalachia, Va.: Hurst, 1929.

"A true story of life and love in Southwest Virginia, interwoven with an exposition of... mountain life... the weird religion of the mountains... humorous, ridiculous, laughable, educational, industrial, and [the] political redemption of the mountains."

542. Hyatt, Rebecca Daugherty. *Marthy Lou's Kiverlid.* Morristown, Tenn.: Triangle, 1937.

Both a story and a book of instructions on weaving.

543. Jackson, Annis Ward. "The Pokeberry Sow." *Mt. Living* 9 (Autumn 1979): 39–41.

An autobiographical short story about the author's childhood and her grandmother, Annie. She relates an incident that happened when Annie was a young girl.

544. Jones, Madison. *A Buried Land.* New York: Popular Library. 1971.

A Tennessee Valley Authority dam floods the land and buries it completely. A mountain woman, victim of an unsuccessful abortion, dies, and two men, either of whom could have been father of the unborn child, bury her.

545. _____. *Forest of the Night.* New York: Popular Library, 1971.

A story set in the nineteenth-century Tennessee wilderness. Jonathan Cannon comes to teach school in the mountains. He and the ex-wife of a notorious local outlaw fall in love. A good picture of a mountain woman in this kind of situation.

546. Jones, Russell Bradley. *Uncle Sandy.* Dalton, Ga.: Showalter, 1946.

The story of a North Georgia woman who is known as an eccentric by family and friends.

547. Justus, May. *The Other Side of the Mountain.* Garden City, N.Y.: Doubleday, Doran, 1931.

A book for junior high level readers about Glory, who has never seen the other side of the mountain on which she lives and, never been to school. This book tells of the year she is ten and how she discovers the world beyond the side of the mountain.

548. _____. *The House at No-End Hollow.* New York: Doubleday, Doran, 1938.

A book for junior high level readers about Becky, who lives in the mountains with her grandmother, brother, and sister. It tells of their struggle to keep their family together and build a new school.

549. _____. "That Makes Home." *Mt. Life & Work* 15 (July 1939): 26–30.

A short story about a grandmother and nine orphaned grandchildren who are fighting to keep their home. Strong characterizations of grandmother and her granddaughter Becky.

550. Kaler, James Otis [pseud. James Otis]. *Hannah of Kentucky: A Story of the Wilderness Road.* New York: American Book Co., 1912.

Fourteen-year-old Hannah begins writing her story at Boones-borough in August 1777. She describes the struggles in establishing the fort, and the manners and customs of the day. A good portrayal of pioneer life from a woman's viewpoint.

551. Keathly, Laura. "Miz. Cindy." *Mt. Life & Work* 42 (Summer 1966): 32–34.

A short story about a hard-working mountain woman who constantly nags her husband, who has "retired to the rocking chair on the front porch." She goes "on strike" to try to make him see the necessity of helping with the garden and household chores. In the process, she develops a new concept of herself and her role as a woman.

552. Kelley, Edith Summers. *Weeds*. New York: Harcourt, Brace, 1923; Carbondale: Southern Illinois Univ. Press, 1972.

This novel is set in the tobacco-farm region of Central Kentucky. While not located specifically in the Appalachian part of the state, there is little difference to be found in the women, their lifestyles, husbands, families, poverty, education, and so forth. This book contains strong, realistic portrayals of women.

553. Kelley, Eleanor. *Kildares of Storm*. New York: Century, 1916.

Beautiful Kate Leigh, widowed mistress of Storm, a grim house between the Bluegrass and the mountains, waits a generation to find husbands for her daughter and herself. Ultimately she settles in a backward section of the mountains to devote herself to social work.

554. _____. *Mixed Company*. New York: Harper, 1936.

A collection of short stories about strong women in the mountains.

555. Ketchum, Annie Chambers. *Nelly Bracken: A Tale of Forty Years Ago*. Philadelphia: Lippincott, 1855.

A novel about Nelly Bracken, whose father, Roger Bracken, emigrates from Virginia to Kentucky in 1780. Nelly is born in Kentucky and lives as many pioneer women of the times lived.

556. Kidd, Robert H. *Mountain Stories and Editorial Extracts*. Grafton, W.V.: Grafton Press, 1931.

The escape of a prisoner being tried for drinking "mountain dew," and the trial of a mountain scarlet woman are but two of the scenes from the West Virginia hills. The stories are told in a rollicking, journalistic style.

557. King, E. Sterling. *The Wild Rose of the Cherokee*. Nashville, Tenn.: University Press, 1895.

A semibiographical book about Nancy Ward, the girl born to an

English woman and a Cherokee Indian. Nancy was instrumental in promoting peace and good will between the Cherokee and white races. She has been called the "Pocahontas of the West."

558. King, Richard. "The Last Vigil." *Appal. Heritage* 6 (Spring 1978): 41–45.

A poignant story about a Confederate soldier's young wife living near Asheville, North Carolina. Aldecha tries to keep the farm chores done and take care of three boys while waiting and grieving for a husband who may never return.

559. Kirk, Charles D. *Wooing and Warring in the Wilderness.* New York: Derby & Jackson, 1860.

A series of sketches about the early settlers of Canetucky (Kentucky). A number of them are about women, young and old.

560. Knox, Joe. *Little Benders.* Philadelphia: Lippincott, 1952.

A collection of short stories featuring mountain women.

561. Kornfeld, Anita Clay. *In a Bluebird's Eye.* New York: Holt, Rinehart & Winston, 1975.

Honor's family live in the Tennessee mountains, though her mother comes from a fine home on a southern plantation—of which she never fails to remind people. Honor is 12 years old, struggling to grow up, seeing life in all its glaring reality at times, and loving her family, especially her father, an alcoholic.

562. Kroll, Harry H. *The Mountainy Singer.* New York: Morrow, 1928.

Set in the Tennessee mountains south of the Virginia border, the story is about Danny Hubbard, his father, aged Jake Hubbard, his young dark-skinned wife (Danny's mother), and Shoon, the girl Danny loves. Gossip says Danny's mother was forced to marry Old Jake and Danny agonizes over the possibility that he is a woods-colt.

563. _____. *Three Brothers and Seven Daddies.* New York: Long & Smith, 1932.

A book filled with witches, ogres, prophets, sinister villains, etc. A number of women are portrayed: Tennsy Obids, young and beautiful; Granny Pigeon, the witch of the community; a stepmother who keeps trying to crowd into her stepson's bed; and others.

564. _____. *Their Ancient Grudge.* Indianapolis: Bobbs-Merrill, 1946.

The author made a careful study of the Hatfield-McCoy feud. His device is to have six of the Hatfield and McCoy women tell their own stories—to relate the horror of both the setting and the events of this conflict between two families.

565. _____. *Summer Gold.* Philadelphia: Westminster, 1955.

A young mountain woman starts a summer camp on recently inherited land in North Carolina. She almost loses her land through wily lawyers.

566. Lambert, Stella Wilson. *Along Came the Other Girl: A Story of Love and Adventure in Pre-Revolutionary Virginia.* New York: American Press, 1961.

Anne Hennis from Liverpool, England, reaches the New World in 1761. She starts for western Virginia, crosses the Blue Ridge, encounters Indians, and meets Dick, her future husband.

567. Larson, Ronald M. "A Tragedy at Hillsville." *Appal. Heritage* 7 (Winter, Spring, & Summer 1979): 68–79, 62–79, 59–80.

This three-act play is based on an actual happening in the Carrol County, Virginia, courthouse. A number of women are involved in the events surrounding the shootout between the Allen family and county officials.

568. Lawrence, Mildred. *Walk a Rocky Road.* New York: Harcourt, Brace, Jovanovich, 1971.

An unexpected opportunity opens up to an Appalachian girl who cannot afford a college education.

569. Lawson, Laura Bennett. *Leonora: A Tale of the Great Smokies.* New York: Neale, 1904.

An abandoned woman stumbles into the North Carolina mountains near Asheville and dies of childbirth and grief. The daughter, Leonora, is brought up by a mountain family.

570. Lawson, Sidney. "The Worry Mouse." *Mt. Life & Work* 36 (Winter 1960): 30–34.

A short story about Jane, a young mountain girl, and her fears that there will be no money for Christmas. Jane's mother and Aunt Mossie are very creative in providing for their families. Good characterization of young girls and wives and mothers in Appalachia.

571. _____. "A Christmas Song." *World Evangel* 85 (Dec. 1966): 376–77.

A short story which reveals the courage and ingenuity of a young mountain mother, a widow left to raise a crippled son. Based on a true story related to the author by her grandmother.

572. _____. "Hetty, the Quare One." *Friends* 114 (Jan. 1967): 15–17, 50–52.

A young mountain girl struggles with the reality of her father's death in the coal mines, her responsibility for her younger brother, and her grief-stricken mother. She tries to understand and be tolerant of the manner in which neighbors and friends deal with death. In the process she grows up a little.

573. _____. "A Hill Country Christmas." *Teen Magazine* 12 (Dec. 1968): 72, 84–85.

In this story with an Appalachian setting there is no abundance of things, but in spite of poverty, the young girl, her mother, and aunt manage to capture the Christmas spirit. Good presentation of mountain women.

574. Lay, Elery A. *That Reek of Sin*. New York: Vantage, 1951.

This story is set in the period 1774–1788 in what is now Kingsport, Tennessee. Told from the point of view of Mary Webster, many of the events are based on historical facts, but the details are often altered.

575. LeGrande, W. Ames, III. "The Woman at the Well." *Mt. Life & Work* 37 (Fall 1961): 49–53.

An encounter between a young West Virginia mountain girl and a Confederate soldier during the Civil War.

576. Lesesne, Mary Richardson. *Torpedoes; Or, Dynamite in Society*. Galveston, Tex.: Shaw & Blayloc, 1883.

A North Carolina girl is the heroine of this story of love, tragedy, and triumph.

577. Lewis, John. *New Hope: Or, The Rescue*. New York: Bunce, 1855. Originally published in 1844 as *Young Kate*.

This story is set in 1798, near the Great Kanawha in western Virginia. It relates the adventures of Matilda Ballenger, her brother Henry, Helen Templemann, and others. Young Kate is a dog who plays an important role in the story. While the book is not primarily about women, they are portrayed throughout.

578. Litsey, Edwin Carlile. *A Maid of the Kentucky Hills*. Chicago: Browne & Howell, 1913.

Nicholas Jard, a city man, goes to the mountains in Kentucky for his health, and encounters a wild nature-girl, whom he courts and wins. There is a great deal of symbolism, with druids and satyrs.

579. Lumpkin, Grace. *To Make My Bread*. New York: Macaulay, 1932.

Emma Kirkland McClure, a widow lives in the mountains of North Carolina. This book chronicles the destinies of Emma and her children as they are forced to leave the mountains and seek work in a mill in South Carolina.

580. Lyle, Katie Letcher. *Fair Day, and Another Step Begun*. New York: Dell, 1974.

This book has Jungian overtones which are skillfully presented. Ellen Burd, an educated mountain girl, falls in love with John Waters, an outsider. She becomes pregnant and sets her heart and mind on marrying him, but he has other ideas and leaves the community. She follows him and all ends well. The story is told in lyrical prose that is delightful.

581. Maben, Charlotte. *Romance of the Cumberlands*. New York: Vantage, 1953.

A short novel of the backwoods country, of moonshine stills, feuds, kidnappings, love and marriage, birth and death. Several women figure prominently in the story.

582. McAfee, Nelly Marshall. *As By Fire*. Harrodsburg, Ky.: The Author, 1968.

Seventeen-year-old Electra Dudley runs away from her stern grandmother, and after many fantastic adventures discovers she is an English heiress and marries an admirer whose wife has recently died.

583. McCarthy, Cormac. *Outer Dark*. New York: Random House, 1968.

A Gothic novel about a child born of incest in a mountain cabin. His father/uncle takes the child out and abandons him, but a passing tinker rescues the infant. The mother, in great anguish, suspects the child is not dead and goes on a search for him.

584. McClelland, Mary Greenaway. *Oblivion: An Episode*. New York: Holt, 1885.

A flood in the North Carolina mountains is greeted with stoicism on the part of the mountaineers. A woman and her child are stranded as they attempt to cross the mountain. The child drowns and the woman loses her memory. The mountain people take her in and eventually she marries one of the men.

585. McComb, Joyce. "Cora." *Mt. Rev.* 4 (Sept. 1978): 8–11.

A powerful short story about a mountain woman and her deaf-and-dumb child. Cora is afraid of her stern husband, who rules his children and his wife with iron discipline. The death of the child brings freedom to Cora.

586. McElroy, Lucy C. *Juletty: A Story of Old Kentucky*. New York: Crowell, 1901.

A romantic story of a revenue agent who comes to the mountains and meets a mountain girl. He is sure there's an illegal still in the mountains and hunts until he finds it. To his dismay Juletty is the moonshiner.

587. _____. *The Silent Pioneer*. New York: Crowell, 1902.

In pioneer Kentucky, Esther Irvine is captured by the Shawnee, and Major John Armstrong, the man she loves, hunts for her. He is captured by Simon Girty and a band of Indians, but escapes and rescues Esther.

588. MacGowan, Alice. *Judith of the Cumberlands*. New York: Putnam, 1908.

> The story of a young mountain girl. Judith falls in love with a young justice of the peace who comes to the area, but they face attacks from a group that does not want him there.

589. ———. *The Wiving of Lance Cleaverage*. New York: Putnam, 1909.

> The story of Lance Cleaverage and his marriage to Callista Gentry, the problems they face, and their life together in the Cumberland Mountains.

590. ———. *The Sword in the Mountains*. New York: Putnam, 1910.

> The author was born in the North but raised in Tennessee. This story is about people and events of the Civil War. Young girls and women are portrayed throughout the story.

591. McMeekin, Isabel McLennan. *Journey Cake*. New York: Messner, 1942.

> Juba, a free black woman in the Yadkin Valley of North Carolina in 1793, is the heroine. Her mistress dies and she starts on a journey to take the Shadrow children over the mountains to Kentucky so they can join their father.

592. ———. *Juba's New Moon*. New York: Messner, 1944.

> A sequel to *Journey Cake*. The Shadrow children, their father, and Juba and her husband struggle to build a home in the wilderness near Fort Boonesboro, Kentucky.

593. McNamara, Mary C. *Glory of the Hills*. Covington, Ky.: The author, 1930.

> A young woman of the hills is ambitious and anxious to preserve her hills and her country. She is a student in one of the settlement schools for a while, and then works recruiting mountain men for the navy. Portrays strong patriotism.

594. McWhirter, Millie. *Hushed Were the Hills*. Nashville: Abingdon, 1969.

> The story of a widow and her two daughters in the Tennessee hills during the Depression.

595. Madden, David. *Cassandra Singing*. New York: Crown, 1969.

> A novel of modern Kentucky with stripmining, the motorcycle culture, poverty, and sickness, and through it all Cassandra singing. Powerful presentation of young Cassandra, her mother, and their relationships to the men in their family.

596. Maggard, Ella. *Weep for the Dawn*. New York: Carlton, 1969.

> This story is set in Eastern Kentucky. There are a number of women in the plot, including especially Emily, whose children were taken away from her because she signed a paper giving up all

rights to them. She was tricked into doing so because she was unable to read or write.

597. Malone, Joseph. *Sons of Vengeance*. New York: Revell, 1903.
This novel set in the Kentucky mountains centers around Mary Finley, whose husband has just been killed in a feud, and her daughter Sis, who eventually gets a chance to attend a mission school and secure an education.

598. Manley, Marline. *Kentucky Kate: Or, The Moonshiner's League*. Log Cabin Library, no. 366. New York: Street & Smith, 1896.
Harry Morgan is supposedly an artist, but in reality he is a revenue agent in disguise. Kate, daughter of an Eastern Kentucky moonshiner, falls in love with him and stands by him in all his fights with the moonshiners. At the end she is killed as she tries to protect him.

599. Marius, Richard. *The Coming of Rain*. New York: Knopf, 1969.
A novel about love and violence, family pride and murder in post-Civil War times in East Tennessee. The women and girls, including some black women, are strong and well characterized.

600. Marler, Martha Griffis. *Kentucky Jane*. San Antonio: Naylor, 1962.
The life of a young mountain girl told in a number of sketches.

601. Marshall, Catherine Wood. *Christy*. New York: McGraw-Hill, 1967.
Partly a biography of the author's mother, a North Carolina native, presented as fiction. A young girl accepts a teaching post in East Tennessee, where she finds love and a vocation, and where she relates on a deep level with the mountain women.

602. Marshall, David Edward. *In Old Kentucky: A Story of the Bluegrass and the Mountains*. Founded on Charles T. Dazey's play. New York: Dillingham, 1910.
A mountain girl works hard to learn to read and write and is accused of trying to be like the Bluegrass aristocrats. An outlander comes to the mountains, falls in love with her, and she learns she is descended from a very aristocratic family in the Bluegrass.

603. Marshall, Robert K. *Little Squire Jim*. New York: Duell, Sloan & Pearce, 1949.
Left an orphan after his mother dies and his father, Big Squire, is killed by a jealous husband, Little Squire's life is influenced by a midwife, a mountain shrew, and a wanton woman. All does not end well for Little Squire.

604. _____. *Julia Gwyan*. New York: Duell, Sloan & Pearce, 1952.
A Gothic story of murder and family secrets. The heroine is an

older woman, but one who is still called "the first lady of Tatesboro."

605. Mayhall, Jane. *Cousin to Human*. New York: Harcourt, Brace, 1960.

Cleanth Cole has been raised on a farm in Eastern Kentucky. Now she is married, has children, and lives with her husband in Louisville. A major portion of the book deals with Cleanth's relationship with Lucy, her college-age daughter.

606. Melton, Frances Jones. *A Daughter of the Highlanders*. Boston: Roxburgh, 1910.

Ruth MacKenzie is a young orphan descended from a Scottish family who came to North Carolina in the time of Flora Macdonald. Three lovers complicate Ruth's life for a while.

607. Miles, Emma Bell. *The Spirit of the Mountains*. New York: James Pott, 1905; Knoxville: Univ. of Tennessee Press, 1975.

This book has been reprinted and is stirring a revival of interest never accorded the original printing. Miles describes a typical school in the mountains, sketches an old couple and a young one, and shows the relations between men and women, and the peculiar respect given to old women in the mountains.

608. Miller, Mrs. Alex McVeigh. *Lynette's Wedding*. New York: Street & Smith, 1896.

A Greenbriar County, West Virginia, girl is in love with one man, who is accused of murder, and engaged to be married to another, older and richer than she.

609. Miller, Heather Ross. *The Edge of the Woods*. New York: Atheneum, 1964.

In a fight for her sanity, a North Carolina woman searches for her past in the Uwharrie hills.

610. Miller, Helen Topping. *Sharon*. Philadelphia: Penn, 1931.

Sharon's days have drifted by, filled with hazy daydreams. At the end of one day, a plane falls from the sky. She helps nurse the crippled pilot and later marries him. Suddenly she finds herself responsible for five people. She leaves North Carolina and returns to the farm in the Smoky Mountains her family had left years ago. Her Aunt Hattie is a wonderfully characterized old mountain woman with all her gossip, folklore, and folk medicines.

611. ———. *Splendor of Eagles*. Philadelphia: Penn, 1931.

A Western North Carolina girl's mother remarries and she has to make her home with her father, a pulp-mill owner.

612. ———. *The Flaming Gahagans*. Philadelphia: Penn, 1933.

Abby is the attractive, red-headed daughter of the clannish Gahagans. She narrowly escapes sacrificing her own happiness to save her father and brother.

613. _____. *Hawk in the Wind*. New York: Appleton-Century, 1938.
A mountain woman becomes a widow and has to run a pulp mill to keep her family solvent. Accidents, labor trouble, and speculators from outside the North Carolina mountains who buy up the timberland almost bring the mill to bankruptcy. But the woman is strong, courageous, and ingenious, and all is saved.

614. Miller, James Wayne. "The Lily." *Mt. Life & Work* 34 (Autumn 1958): 54–56.
Walking to a tomb. an older woman tells a younger woman that you do not weep when you get old, and death is the day the lily blooms and fills the air with sweetness. The two women find the tomb empty and weep with joy.

615. Mills, Mary Hampton. *Be Ye Beggar or King*. Asheville: Advocate, 1925.
A simple and beautiful Western North Carolina girl, Audrey Ross, falls in love with an outlander who has come to the mountains for his health.

616. Montague, Margaret P. *The Poet, Miss Kate, and I*. New York: Baker & Taylor, 1905.
A story about city people and their confrontations with the natives of an Allegheny resort area.

617. _____. *In Calvert's Valley*. New York: Baker & Taylor, 1908.
Hester Rymal returns to Willoughby, West Virginia, because that is where she finds "life." Soon she is involved in a murder to which an innocent man confesses. Only Hester knows he is innocent.

618. _____. *Linda*. Boston: Houghton Mifflin, 1912.
At 16, Linda is forced to marry a man twice her age. She does not love him but must obey her parents. Though she later falls in love with someone else, she stays with her husband until his death.

619. _____. *Deep Channel*. Boston: Atlantic Monthly Press, 1923.
Julie Rose grows up, goes to Richmond, and falls in love with a World War I army deserter. Then his wife turns up and Tim leaves Julie, saying he is going to turn himself in. Julie goes back to the hills and finds it possible to start life anew.

620. Moore, Bertha Belle. *The Girl of the Listening Heart*. Grand Rapids, Mich.: Eerdmans, 1937.
Elizabeth Ann Ellison is ambitious to become a writer and leave her North Carolina farm home. She gets in with a sophisticated group in Charlotte. After some unpleasant experiences, she realizes her true happiness is to be found in her homeplace.

621. _____. *As By Fire*. Grand Rapids, Mich.: Eerdmans, 1939.
A book for young people about Peggy Tavenner, who has to leave her North Carolina home to realize how little meaning her life has because of her un-Christian behavior. She finds happiness by marrying Martin Poe.

622. _____. *Ordered Steps*. Grand Rapids, Mich.: Eerdmans, 1940.
A Tar Heel mountain girl, Caroline Wynn, loses her sight and is taken to Philadelphia by wealthy vacationers, who give her an opportunity for a singing career and medical attention to restore her sight. A pleasant, surprise ending.

623. Morehouse, Kathleen Moore. *Rain on the Just*. New York: Furman, 1936.
The setting is Brushy Mountain in North Carolina. A well-written Gothic story of Dolly Allen, a fictional mountain woman.

624. _____. "With the Fog." *Story Survey*. Harold William Blodgett, ed. Philadelphia: Lippincott, 1939.
The story of a childbirth in an already crowded, underfed North Carolina family.

625. Murdoch, Louise R. Sanders. *Almetta of Gabriel's Run*. New York: Meridian, 1917.
A perceptive novel about a lively, chatty girl who must make her home with friends and relatives, turn-and-turn-about. Through her conversations many mountain folkways are brought to light.

626. Murfree, Mary Noailles [pseud. Charles Egbert Craddock]. *In the Tennessee Mountains*. Boston: Houghton Mifflin, 1884.
A young man in the mountains of Tennessee is convicted of a crime. This is the story of Cynthia Ware, who makes it her mission to prove his innocence.

627. _____. *In the "Stranger People's" Country*. New York: Harper, 1891.
An archaeologist goes into the mountains of Tennessee to study prehistoric burial grounds. One mountain family becomes involved with the study. Many problems arise because the wife, Adelaide, does not agree with what goes on.

628. _____. *A Spectre of Power*. Boston: Houghton Mifflin, 1903.
A curious Cherokee girl brings grief not only to the town of Great Tellico but to her nation.

629. _____. *The Amulet: A Novel*. New York: Macmillan, 1906.
The end of the Seven Years' War finds an English girl in the Cherokee country of the Smoky Mountains, where she has adventures with mountain women and others.

630. Myers, Elizabeth P. *Rock of Decision*. Grand Rapids: Eerdmans, 1931.

A Blue Ridge Mountain girl, Phoebe Bradford, cannot understand at first why Christians have to suffer. She almost hates God, but through experience learns God's place in her life.

631. _____. *The Touch of Polly Tucker*. Grand Rapids, Mich.: Eerdmans, 1952.

A moralistic fiction for young people, with a mountain setting.

632. Nisbet, Alice. *Send Me an Angel*. Chapel Hill: Univ. of North Carolina Press, 1946.

The setting is the foothill countryside of Western North Carolina. A young girl struggles to manage a plantation.

633. Norman, Gurney. "The Tail End of Yesterday." *Mt. Life & Work* 43 (Spring 1967): 20–22.

Granddad is in the hospital and the rest of his family thinks he is crazy and full of drugs. Poor Granddad—no one seems to understand he is just old. Good characterizations of the narrator's grandmother and two aunts as they face the crisis.

634. _____. "The Colliers, Home for the Weekend." *Mt. Life & Work* 45 (Aug. 1969): 12–16.

The author has a deft hand in characterizing mountain women. This story of aunts, grandmothers, and sisters is well done.

635. _____. *Divine Right's Trip*. New York: Dial, 1972.

While most of this book is about a young man, his friends from the drug culture, and the "culture shock" of the West Coast people in face-to-face meetings with Appalachians, there is a wonderfully typical mountain character in the book—Mrs. Godsey.

636. _____. *Kinfolk*. Lexington, Ky.: Gnomon, 1977.

This book has a series of chapters, each a short story in itself, several of which have women as main characters: "The Fight," "Home for the Weekend," "Maxine," "The Wounded Man," and "A Correspondence."

637. Nourse, James Duncan. *The Forest Knight: Or, Early Times in Kentucky*. New York: Ferreth, 1946.

Mary Shelbourne is seized by Indians and taken from her home on the banks of the Elkhorn. Her foster father and her lover rescue her.

638. Obenchain, Eliza Caroline Calvert. *Aunt Jane of Kentucky*. Boston: Little, Brown, 1908.

A collection of short stories with Kentucky mountain settings.

639. _____. *Sally Ann's Experience*. Boston: Little, Brown, 1910.

A short story separately published; also found in *Aunt Jane of Kentucky*.

640. _____. *To Love and to Cherish*. Boston: Little, Brown, 1911.

Mountaineer Reuben Ward educates himself and is finally offered the Democratic nomination for governor; he turns down the offer, however, because the little mountain girl he married, a perfect homemaker and mother, is not up to the society which would surround the first lady of the state.

641. Olmsted, Stanley. *At Top of Tobin*. New York: Dial, 1926.
Mollie Donbrook wants to leave the North Carolina mountains and raise her young son in Florida.

642. O'Neill, Jean. *Cotton Top*. Lee & Shepherd, 1953.
A young mountain girl counts up her blessings and decides she has everything she could ever want or need right in the hills. Then she encounters a girl from the city and learns many lessons.

643. Ormsby, Virginia H. *Mountain Magic for Rosy*. New York: Crown, 1969.
A guitar-playing girl in the North Carolina mountains has a problem which is solved through Granny's magic.

644. Pace, Mildred Mastin. *Home Is Where the Heart Is*. New York: McGraw-Hill, 1954.
A young girl's father leaves her with a well-off family to work her way. She learns to be independent and take happiness where she can find it.

645. Page, Isaac Marshall. *The Kentuckians: Or, A Woman's Reaping*. Cincinnati: Page, 1917.
A moral tale about a young wife who, through selfishness and lust, degrades herself, causes the death of her son, and runs away with the town doctor. She repents at the end of her life.

646. Page, Myra. *Daughter of the Hills*. New York: Persea 1977 [1950].
A novel that shows the pride and love one woman feels for the mountains. She tells of falling in love, getting married, and having children, and of her work in promoting better working conditions in the mines.

647. _____. *With Sun in Our Blood*. New York: Citadel, 1950.
Dolly and her brother and sisters take a stranger in out of a storm. This proves to be the beginning of an adventure set in the Cumberland Mountains of Kentucky.

648. Paine, Dorothy Charlotte. *A Maid of the Mountains*. Philadelphia: Jacobs, 1906.
A poor North Carolina mountain girl meets a rich girl who comes to the mountains for the summer. The society girl plans to help her get an education.

649. Pearson, Cora Wallace. *The Double Standard*. North Wilkesboro, N.C.: Pearson, 1966.
A Western North Carolina girl becomes pregnant and has to leave her home in disgrace.

650. Peattie, Donald Culross. *Up Country: A Story of the Vanguard.*
New York: Appleton, 1928.

A young girl journeys from England to her new home in the Blue
Ridge mountains. Many impressions of mountain people.

651. Peattie, Eliza Wilkinson. *The Azalea: The Story of A Girl in the
Blue Ridge Mountains.* Chicago: Reilly & Britten, 1912.

After her mother, a circus performer, dies, Azalea is befriended by
two families and has to choose between the McBirneys, who live
high up in the Blue Ridge, and the Carsons on their plantation-
like home in the valley.

652. ———. *Annie Laurie and Azalea.* Chicago: Reilly & Britten,
1913.

The story of two Western North Carolina girls. Annie Laurie and
her family lose their hard-earned savings to a thief, and Hector
Dishbrow, a suspect, leaves town. He returns later to help resolve
the whole thing.

653. ———. *Azalea's Silver Web.* Chicago: Reilly & Britten, 1915.

Azalea, now 18, finds that she is the missing granddaughter of the
wealthy Knox family in South Carolina, and again must make a
choice between the mountains and plantation life.

654. Peel, Alfreda Marion. *Witch in the Mill.* Richmond: Dietz, 1947.

Several stories composed from gossip, folklore, and witchcraft
materials. It is interesting to note that those with occult powers in
the mountains are always portrayed as women.

655. Peercy, Ernestine. "Too Old to Cry." *Mt. Life & Work* 42 (Spring
1966): 20–22.

A short story about Rosie, whose parents do not see the value in
an education for their little girl. They keep her out of school so
much some years that she fails to pass to a higher grade.

656. Pepper, Nellie Whan. *The Young Mrs. Blennerhasset: A Novel of
Early Days in West Virginia.* New York: Exposition, 1964.

A novel which is plotted around the Burr conspiracy in West
Virginia.

657. Philipps, Louise. *Land of Tomorrow.* Jericho, N.Y.: Exposition,
1974.

A novel about the Walton family, who live in the Cumberland
Mountains of Kentucky. A very wealthy family, they suffer much
loss during the Civil War. Laurabelle Mullins attracts two of the
Walton brothers and the whole family is plunged into trouble.

658 Pierson, Edna Church. *The Witch of Turner's Bald.* Banner Elk,
N.C.: Grandfather Home for Children, 1971.

Bluebelle Barney is as wild as the creatures frequenting the
wooded hillsides. The valley people call her a witch. Matthew

Friend, come to pastor a church in this remote valley, befriends Bluebelle. Annie O'Doone, a typical mountain woman, is also a friend of the lonely girl.

659. Pifer, Albert Donald. *The Daughter of the Smokies.* Punta Gorda, Fla.: Eternal Lights, 1966.

A novel set in the Smoky Mountains, concerning a young girl struggling to find her place in the world and among its people.

660. Pleasant, John. *Swing the Big-Eyed Rabbit.* Philadelphia: Blakiston, 1944.

The story of Cumberland Mission School under the leadership of fanatical Dr. Peabody. Among the women and girls are Millie Darnell, Stella Varney, and Dr. Peabody's sister.

661. Pleasants, Lucy Lee. "Hannah Dawston's Child." *Atlantic Monthly* 4 (Mar. 1880): 362–74.

A mountain woman resists attempts by a childless city woman to buy her baby.

662. Pool, Marie Louise. *Dally.* New York: Harper, 1891.

Dally, an untutored mountain girl, goes north to live with a Massachusetts widow. The resultant clash of cultures is an interesting commentary on how well mountain women adapt to different environments.

663. _____. *Against Human Nature.* New York: Harper, 1895.

A mountain woman dies leaving an orphaned daughter, and a New England spinster travels to North Carolina to care for her. When New England provincialism meets southern mountain provincialism, the results are humorous.

664. _____. *In Buncombe County.* Chicago: Stone, 1896.

Two northern ladies visit the North Carolina mountains near Asheville. Their impressions of the mountaineers, especially the women, are interesting to a certain degree.

665. Preston, Nelly. *Paths of Glory.* Richmond: Whittet & Shepperson, 1961.

A fictional account of the life of Elizabeth, sister of Patrick Henry, and her two marriages on the Appalachian frontier.

666. Preysz, Louisea Rosalie. *Larning.* Boston: Mead, 1939.

A tale of an old-maid schoolteacher in the West Virginia mountains.

667. _____. *Dear Teacher.* Boston: Mead, 1942.

An old-maid schoolteacher in West Virginia has many hilarious adventures.

668. Price, Edith Ballinger. *My Lady Lee.* New York: Greenberg, 1925.

A blind girl leaves her native mountains to live in an institution for the blind in the north. Not much of the action takes place in the mountains.

669. Putzel, Mary Ellison. "The Song Giver." *Appal. Heritage* 7 (Summer, 1979): 3–8.

A short story of death in a family as perceived by Ruby, one of the daughters. In order to make things a little better for them economically, the widowed mother agrees to let Ruby live with a relative.

670. Quigley, Michael J. *April Is the Cruelest Month.* New York: McGraw-Hill, 1971.

A sensitive account of a young girl in a coal camp in West Virginia who is dying of cancer, and the people who try to care for her.

671. Quillen, Bess B. *In the East Kentucky Hills.* Philadelphia: Dorrance, 1970.

A "simple narrative" of the life of a representative family in the early twentieth century in Eastern Kentucky.

672. Ralph, Julian. "Where Time Has Slumbered." *Harper's* 89 (Sept. 1894): 613–30.

A story of West Virginia mountain characters around the turn of the century—hunters, circuit riders, and women.

673. Rayner, Emma. *Visiting the Sin: A Tale of Mountain Life in Kentucky and Tennessee.* Boston: Small, Maynard, 1900.

A mountain girl plots revenge upon those who caused her father's death. She relies on superstition and biblical direction to guide her. There are scenes in a Kentucky log mill and at religious services.

674. Read, Opie. *The Wives of the Prophets.* Chicago: Laird & Lee, 1894.

Up the Cumberland River in Tennessee is an old settlement called Bolga, said to have been settled in 1697 when a new religious order arrived from England. This novel is about five women chosen to serve three years each as wife of the prophet, and the intruder from outside who brings heartaches and trouble to the people.

675. Reece, Herbert Byron. *Better a Dinner of Herbs.* New York: Dutton, 1950.

Some Georgia mountain natives are gathered at the wake of the preacher, who was killed when his horse ran away with him. Through flashbacks we learn a story of seduction, guilt, and betrayal.

676. Reed, Jacqueline. *The Morningside of the Hill.* New York: Dodd, Mead, 1960.

Robbie Leighton Calhoun lives with her grandparents in the foothills of the Cumberlands. She has grieved for her dead parents for most of her young life. There is a mystery connected with her parents that no one will talk about. When Robbie most needs help an unexpected legacy comes to her and the mystery is revealed.

677. Reed, Rufus Mitchell. *Conquerors of the Dark Hills.* New York: Vantage, 1979.

A story set in Martin County, Kentucky. The author writes about his family and the people in the area. There are chapters dealing with topics related to women.

678. Rice, Laban Lacy. *A Mountain Idyll.* Nashville: Baird Ward, 1921.

The heroine of this story set in the Tennessee mountains proves that right triumphs in the end against perverse odds.

679. Richter, Conrad. *The Grandfathers.* New York: Knopf, 1964.

A story about a young girl growing up in the mountains of Maryland, and her search for the identities of her father and grandfather.

680. Ridenbaugh, Mary Young. *Enola: Or, Her Fatal Mistake.* St. Louis: Woodward & Tiernan, 1886.

Enola (alone spelled backwards) is the story of Beatrice Baring of Meadowville, Kentucky. Her husband deserts her while serving in the Confederate army. She remarries but loses her second husband. Eventually her life changes when she receives a large inheritance from Scotland.

681. Roberts, Bruce, and Roberts, Nancy. *Sense of Discovery: The Mountain.* Richmond: Knox, 1969.

A story about a young girl, a stranger in buckskin, and life and adventure in the mountains. A beautifully illustrated book.

682. Roberts, Dorothy J. *The Mountain Journey.* New York: Appleton Century, 1947.

There is a landslide at Flamecreek, West Virginia. Laurel is in labor and needs to be taken to the hospital but the road is impassable. She is deathly afraid of water and therefore cannot be taken in a boat. She is determined not to have the baby in her isolated home, and so begins a journey over the mountain on foot.

683. Roberts, Elizabeth Madox. *The Time of Man.* New York: Viking, 1926.

The Time of Man won the author a secure place in contemporary letters. It is a story of the inner life of Ellen Chesser, daughter and wife of Kentucky tobacco-farm tenants.

684. _____. *My Heart and My Flesh.* New York: Viking, 1927.

Theodosa Bell, a misfit in a small rural town in Kentucky, fails in love and also fails as a musician. Eventually she finds peace and settles down to a less complex life, teaching school in the country and planning to marry a sturdy farmer.

685. ———. *The Great Meadow.* New York: Viking, 1930.

A novel of pioneer Kentucky, the story of Diony Hall and Berk Jervis and their life at Harrod's Fort during the American Revolution, including captivity by Indians and struggles with the British. Diony thinks Berk is dead and marries another man. Berk returns in 1781 and Diony has to make a traumatic decision.

686. ———. *He Sent Forth a Raven.* New York: Viking, 1935.

Stoner Drake's wife dies and he vows never to set foot on his Kentucky farm at Wolflick again. He makes life miserable for his daughter, Martha, and later his granddaughter, Jocelle. Jocelle is strong and courageous and does not let Stoner dominate her as he dominated Martha.

687. ———. *Black Is My True Love's Hair.* New York: Viking, 1938.

Dena Jones elopes but her marriage proves to be disastrous. She struggles to readjust and find new romance, and does, with the miller's son. A poetic story about human aspirations.

688. Roberts, Mary Carter. "Mountain Ariel." *Amer. Forests* 40 (Oct. 1934): 451–54.

A short story about gathering wild honey in the mountains.

689. Robinson, Eliot Harlow. *Smiles, A Rose of the Cumberlands.* Boston: Page, 1919.

An idyllic novel of life, love, and medicine. It begins in the mountains of Virginia when Dr. MacDonald stumbles into the cabin where Smiles lives with her stepfather.

690. ———. *Smiling Pass: Being a Further Account of the Career of Smiles, A Rose of the Cumberlands.* New York: Burt, 1921.

A Cumberland mountain woman, Nurse Rose, comes home from the war and finds things have changed.

691. Rogers, Elizabeth Embree. *Biny's Choice.* Berea, Ky.: Berea Coll. Printing Department, n.d.

A lovely, ladylike Kentucky mountain girl, Sabina, chooses Tom, a serious-minded, steady young man, for her mate. He goes outside the area to educate himself. They marry and become the kind of family that makes "the salt of the mountain earth."

692. ———. "Sarepta's Schoolin'." *Berea Quarterly,* Aug. 1903, pp. 7–32.

A short story about a mountain girl's struggle to get an education. Her parents are violently opposed at first when it is evident that their child is not going to conform to the usual pattern of mountain girls. Gradually Sarepta wins her battle.

693. Rogers, Lettie Hamlett. *Birthright*. New York: Simon & Schuster, 1957.

A young schoolteacher is the main character in this novel about segregation in a North Carolina town.

694. Rollins, Kathleen. *Impassioned Foothills*. New York: Arcadia, 1937.

A story of Glorida Crosby, a talented girl of the Blue Ridge Mountains, in love with Tevis Malone, whose family and the Crosbys are archenemies. To escape, Gloria jumps at the chance to work and study art in New York.

695. Sandburg, Helga. *The Wheel of Earth*. New York: McDowell, Obolersky, 1958.

Ellen is a Kentucky mountain girl, born and reared in a Catholic family. Dominated by men—her father, her lover, her priest—she rebels. Taking her child, she finds employment in another state. Cyclic events reunite her with her lover, and they marry and return to settle on her family's farm.

696. _____. *The Wizard's Child*. New York: Dial, 1967.

Set in the Appalachian hills, this story is about a young girl who is said to talk and act in very strange ways at times. She is a source of concern to those who know her.

697. Saylor, Lettie Hoskins. *Brick without Straw: A Story of Kentucky Mountain Life*. Cincinnati: Hobson, 1943.

Druella Hartford, a mountain girl from a family so large it is running out of names, struggles to acquire an education. Wooed and won by a Bluegrass aristocrat, she continues to read and improve her mind, and eventually becomes an author.

698. _____. *Cradle Valley*. New York: Hobson, 1946.

The story centers around David Murray, who lives in the Kentucky mountains. The plot includes a feud, a homeless boy, and several strong female characters.

699. Scott, Evelyn D. *Witch Perkins*. New York: Holt, 1929.

A strange woman moves in next door to a young girl in the Kentucky mountains. The girl is soon convinced the woman is a witch.

700. Seckar, Alveva. *Zuska of the Burning Hills*. New York: Oxford Univ. Press, 1952.

Zuska, a girl from an impoverished family in a West Virginia coal town, stumbles on a secret which enables her to help her family.

701. Settle, Mary Lee. *O Beulah Land*. New York: Viking, 1956.

Hannah Bridewell, a street-wise Londoner, is caught in the act of stealing and sent to Virginia with a gang of convicts to work in the tobacco fields. Captured by Indians and kept for a time, she escapes and heads for the mountains. Hannah is a strong mountain woman; many others are portrayed in the book. Episodic in nature, this is a must for the serious scholar doing research on the mountain woman and her roots.

702. ———. *Know Nothing*. New York: Viking, 1960.
This book begins 63 years after the end of *O Beulah Land*. It gives a prominent role to the women, both strong and weak, who were pioneers in the mountains.

703. ———. *Fight Night on a Sweet Saturday*. New York: Viking, 1964.
A girl returns to West Virginia for her brother's funeral. This is the point at which she begins searching for meaning to his seemingly wasted life and useless death. All the sordidness of the mined-out area becomes symbolic of his destruction.

704. Sheppard, Muriel Earley. *Cabins in the Laurel*. Chapel Hill: Univ. of North Carolina Press, 1935.
Stories about mountain women: Frankie, who murders her husband and burns his body in the fireplace; and old Aunt Polly Boone, in some ways both a blessing and a curse to those who know her.

705. Short, Carroll Dale. "The First Year's Sowing." *Sou. Expos.* 5, no. 1 (1978): 19–21.
A short story about a mountain woman in the North Georgia hills. Her husband is not very strong and she eventually has to care for him when he hurts his back, and do all the farm chores, as well. She is a strong woman.

706. Sibley, Susan. *Woodsmoke*. Winston-Salem, N.C.: Blair, 1977.
Viyella is born and raised in the Carolina hills. Later she moves to the swampland of South Carolina, but she never forgets the smoky blue of the mountains she loved. Her children grow up and go their inevitable ways, some to tragedy, some to rich, fulfilling adventures. Finally, Viyella has a chance to move back to the old farm in the hills.

707. Siler, James H. "Getting in the D.A.R." *Appal. Heritage* 7 (Spring 1979): 42–47.
Mae Dorton wants to join the Daughters of the American Revolution. But she is descended from Louvinia Dorton, a woman who never married but had six children. She was resourceful, had a lot of pluck, and ran a mill and ferry to raise her children.

708. Simms, W. Gilmore. *Charlemont*. New York: Redfield, 1856.
In a settlement in a secluded valley in the Kentucky hills, Margaret Cooper meets Alfred Stevens, an outlander, falls in love,

and gives "her all" into his keeping. He soon tires of her and the hills, and rides away as he came, leaving her with a dead child and with shame attached to her name.

709. Sims, Marion McCamy. *Memo to Timothy Sheldon*. Philadelphia: Lippincott, 1938.

Lynn Sheldon, on vacation in the North Carolina mountains, meets a man she would like to marry. The only problem is that she already has a husband.

710. Sinclair, Bennie Lee. "The Lesson." *Appal. Heritage* 7 (Winter 1979): 22–23.

A short story set in the Georgia mountains, told from the point of view of a 12-year-old boy whose father deserted the family. The central characters are the boy, his mother, and her younger sister.

711. Skidmore, Hobart Douglas. *O Careless Love*. New York: Doubleday, 1949.

A wisely innocent mountain girl decides upon a meretricious career. When she arrives in the West Virginia town of Felicity, she has already been ejected from a town on the other side of Sour Mountain. Her arrival coincides with the annual drying up of the Golly River.

712. Skidmore, Hubert. *Becky Landers, Frontier Warrior*. New York: Macmillan, 1926.

A young Kentucky girl in pioneer days becomes the provider for her family. She associates with famous scouts and warriors.

713. ———. *I Will Lift Up Mine Eyes*. New York: Book League of America, 1936.

Set in the Blue Ridge, this book tells the story of Nat and Maw Cutlip and their four children. They bravely but futilely resist the encroachment of industrial civilization. Maw especially is well characterized.

714. ———. *Heaven Came So Near*. New York: Book League of America, 1938.

Maw Cutlip, the main character, first appeared in the author's *I Will Lift Up Mine Eyes*. In this sequel her husband dies and she must continue raising their four children.

715. Smith, Barbara. "Cattleman." *Appal. Heritage* 7 (Spring 1979): 59–61.

A story about Elmer and his wife, Moll, who live on a farm in Mingo County, Virginia. They lose their seven-year-old daughter after a horse runs away with her. Then the newborn calves begin dying, and Elmer is maddened by his inability to prevent their deaths. Then in shock and horror he discovers Moll is the culprit.

716. Smith, Irene D. *The Right to Live.* New York: House of Field, 1941.

Marth Ann, born in a backwoods settlement in Kentucky, marries early and unhappily and soon moves to a grubby West Virginia mine patch. After the death of her child at the end of a long, relentless strike, she returns home.

717. Smith, John F. "Little Deely, the Woodhauler's Daughter." *Amer. Child* 2 (Aug. 1920): 155–81.

A long, sad account of Little Deely and her family: beloved brother; sick, worn-out mother; hard-drinking, hard-fisted, mean father. The father had contracted syphilis and passed it on to his wife and daughter, and both die slow, painful deaths.

718. _____. "Pinkie, the Little Cotton Picker." *Amer. Child* 2 (Feb. 1921): 330–44; 3, (Nov. 1921): 247–66.

A tenant farmer and his wife and daughters are the subjects of this story. The author does not specify geographic location, but it could well be Georgia or parts of Alabama. The story presents both black and white women and white girls.

719. Smith, Lee. "Paralyzed." *Sou. Expos.* 4 (Winter 1977): 37–42.

A short story told in first-person narrative. The author, a Virginia woman, reveals the characters of women in both the physical and the psychological sense.

720. Smith, Lilly. *Call of the Big Eastatoe.* Columbia, S.C.: State Printing Co., 1970.

An autobiographical novel of rural and family life in the South Carolina mountains.

721. Smith, Patrick. *Angel City.* St. Petersburg, Fla.: Valkyril, 1978.

Jaret and Cloma Teeter sell their meager possessions and their wornout farm in the hills of West Virginia. Loading what they can take and their two children into a van, they "hit the migrant trail" to Florida. In the harsh environment of the migrant life, the beautiful daughter becomes virtually a white slave and Cloma, pregnant with her third child, loses touch with reality.

722. Smith, William Dale. *A Multitude of Men.* New York: Simon & Schuster, 1959.

Vera Mae and her brother Dudley are powerfully drawn characters in this novel of love and death and work in a West Virginia steel mill, set against the backdrop of a labor strike.

723. Southworth, Mrs. Emma D. E. N. *The Prince of Darkness.* Philadelphia: Peterson, 1869.

A story set in the Blue Ridge Mountains. It deals with a mystery and an investigation, a lost patrimony, a victim bride, an heiress, and so forth.

724. Stallworth, Anne Nall. *This Time Next Year*. New York: Vanguard, 1971.

This book has several female characters: Florrie, the narrator; her mother, Julia Birdsong; and mean, tight-fisted Aunt Mira. The story deals with Florrie's growing-up years and with Julia's dream of leaving the tenant farm and living in town.

725. Steele, Wilbur Daniel. "How Beautiful with Shoes." *Harper's* 165 (Aug. 1932): 314–54.

A mountain girl is pursued by mad Humble Jewett, who gently woos her with beautiful poetry. When at last he falls asleep, a mountain man comes and kills him. After the gentle madness of Jewett, the crude advances of the mountain man repulse her.

726. Stephens, Mary Jo. *Witch of the Cumberlands*. Boston: Houghton, Mifflin, 1974.

A mystery concerning a mine disaster unfolds when three children come to Devil's Mountain, as an old mountain woman prophesied they would.

727. Still, James. *River of Earth*. New York: Viking Press, 1940; Lexington: Univ. Press of Kentucky, 1978.

A classic, this book has been acclaimed for more than 30 years for its strong characterizations and realistic language. The woman, young girl, and grandmother are particularly well characterized. Anyone doing research on mountain women will find this a must.

728. _____. *On Troublesome Creek*. New York: Viking, 1941.

A novelette composed of nine episodes, each one basically a short story, which tell of the life and times of a miner's family living on Troublesome Creek in Eastern Kentucky. Women of all ages and young girls are strongly characterized.

729. _____. "Maybird Upshaw." *Amer. Mercury* 63 (Aug. 1946): 161–66.

The story of Maybird, a woman weighing 507 pounds whose *joie de vivre* matches her weight. She goes to visit her sister Trulla and gains so much weight she cannot get out of the door. The brother-in-law, the narrator, is mighty worried. Chuckling, laughing, smiling, are leitmotifs for Maybird; crossness, moaning, complaining are leitmotifs for Trulla. Great structural contrasts between the two mountain women.

730. _____. "Mrs. Razor." *Mt. Life & Work* 30 (Summer 1954): 34–37.

The author considers this story the best he has ever done. A classic, it has been used in various anthologies, psychoanalytic works, etc. A little girl imagines she is Mrs. Razor. She goes

through all the "troubles and tribulations" of a married woman
with a no-account husband and three little children.

731. ———. "The Nest." *Mt. Life & Work* 44 (Nov. 1968): 13–16.
A powerful short story about a mountain girl who is not wanted by
her stepmother and ignored by her father. Her trial begins when
they send her across a mountain in winter to spend the night with
her aunt.

732. ———. "Encounter on Keg Branch." *Mt. Life & Work* 45 (Feb.
1969): 14.
A short, short story—mountain man's description of women,
especially those in his family. He says of his common-law wife:
"people like her ought to have their heads pinched off when
they're born."

733. ———. "The Burning of the Waters." *Atlantic Monthly* 198, no.
4 (Oct. 1956): 55–60.
A delightful short story about a mountain woman and her family.
After several devious schemes to get her husband to move the
family, he says: "Women aim to have their own way . . . one
fashion or another they'll get it. They'll burn the waters of the
creek if that's what it takes."

734. ———. *Pattern of a Man.* Lexington, Ky.: Gnomon, 1976.
This book includes three stories from *On Troublesome Creek* and
others written later. Women and girls are well portrayed.

735. ———. *Sporty Creek.* New York: Putnam, 1977.
A narrative of a mountain family. There are some good charac-
terizations of mountain women in the chapters "Low Glory,"
"The Moving," "Locust Summer," and "Tight Hollow."

736. ———. *The Run for the Elbertas.* Lexington: Univ. Press of Ken-
tucky, 1980.
Another collection of Still's short stories, including seven from
On Troublesome Creek and six published separately elsewhere.
Several involve women, especially "The Burning of the Waters"
and "The Quare Day."

737. Stribling, Thomas Sigismund. *Bright Metal.* New York: Doubleday, Doran, 1928.
A Greenwich Village actress marries a Tennessee man and goes
home to the hills with her husband. She tries to understand the
men and women and what is expected of her in the role of a
mountain man's wife. Finally she gets involved in backwoods
politics.

738. Strong, Jason Rolfe. *The Starlight of the Hills: A Romance of the
Kentucky Mountains.* New York: Frederick Pustet, 1923.

Marjorie Byron, daughter of a mine operator, is a devout Catholic. Her lover drifts away from the church and becomes involved in labor troubles in the Kentucky mountains, causing distress to Marjorie. But all ends well.

739. Stuart, Jane. *Yellowhawk*. New York: McGraw-Hill, 1973.

Rhoda Miller, a schoolteacher, narrates the story of Yellowhawk, a town in Eastern Kentucky.

740. _____. *Passerman's Hollow*. New York: McGraw-Hill, 1974.

Hilda Lawson and her husband work their farm in a remote, lonely valley. She discovers that her husband is a weakling and on her shoulders falls the task of keeping the family together. She has four children, one of whom is mentally retarded.

741. Stuart, Jesse. *Head O' W-Hollow*. New York: Dutton, 1936; Lexington: Univ. Press of Kentucky, 1979.

A collection of 19 of Stuart's earliest short stories about men and women, boys and girls, in Eastern Kentucky. The characterizations of women and girls show various aspects of their life.

742. _____. "Braska Comes Through." *Amer. Mercury* 51 (Sept. 1940): 47–53.

A curious story about a mountain girl. Nebraska has a hard time seeing the light of repentance the way the fundamentalist preachers teach it. The local people decide she must have a baby before she can get right with God.

743. _____. *Trees of Heaven*. New York: Dutton, 1940; Lexington: Univ. Press of Kentucky, 1980.

A novel about two clans: Anse Bushman and his family—powerful, hard-working mountain farmers—and Boliver Tussie and his family—poor white squatters who love to hunt, fish, play the guitar, and sing. The story centers around Tarvin Bushman and Subrinea Tussie, who are in love and want to get married. The wives of Bushman and Tussie are also portrayed.

744. _____. *Men of the Mountains*. New York: Dutton, 1941. Lexington: Univ. Press of Kentucky, 1979.

A collection of Stuart's short stories which appeared in magazines between 1935 and 1940. The stories are robust and the women are pictured with various characteristics.

745. _____. *Taps for Private Tussie*. New York: Dutton, 1943.

A hilarious book about the large Tussie clan and a $10,000 insurance check from the government (because Kim Tussie has supposedly been killed in action). Portrayed are Aunt Vittie, Kim's widow, Grandma Tussie, and assorted kith and kin who come flocking around to share in Aunt Vittie's "wealth."

746. _____. *Tales from the Plum Grove Hills.* New York: Dutton, 1946.

> The third collection of Stuart's short stories. Almost all have women and girls, though not as main characters. Grandma in "The Sanctuary Desolated," Mom in "The Storm," Ma in "Spring Victory," Portia in "Bury Your Dead," and other women are portrayed.

747. _____. *Foretaste of Glory.* New York: Dutton, 1946.

> One night the "Northern Lights" stab the southern sky and the people in the small town think the end of the world has come. They run about seeking to confess their sins before they die. Among the women who take part in the events of this wild night are Sister Spence, Pastor of the Holiness Church, Sallie Bain, and Big Malinda Sprouse.

748. _____. *Clearing in the Sky and Other Stories.* New York: McGraw-Hill, 1950.

> A collection of stories, most of which have men and boys as main characters. But a few stories deal with women: "The Slipcover Sweater," "When Mountain Men Make Peace," and "Coming Down the Mountain."

749. _____. *Plowshare in Heaven.* New York: McGraw-Hill, 1958.

> A book of short stories, many of them having the viewpoint of a woman or in some way showing characteristics of women.

750. _____. "Spring Offensive." *Mt. Life & Work* 39 (Spring 1963): 11–15.

> A charming short story about a young girl who is not allowed by a neighbor boy to play war games.

751. _____. *Daughter of the Legend.* New York: McGraw-Hill, 1965.

> A lumberjack falls in love with a beautiful mountain girl, a Melungeon.

752. _____. *Come to My Tomorrowland.* Nashville: Aurora, 1971.

> A story about a young girl who is crippled by polio and who forms a special attachment to a deer with a broken hip.

753. Stutler, Boyd Blynn. *The Kinnan Massacre.* Parsons, W.V.: McClain, 1969.

> Mary Kinnan is taken captive by Indians but the rest of her family is massacred. This is a story of her sufferings and her courage and daring.

754. Sutton, Margaret. *Jemima, Daughter of Daniel Boone.* New York: Scribner, 1942.

> The story of Jemima Boone from six to sixteen. Most of the text is the well-known Boone story as seen through the eyes of a young girl. Though not Appalachian *per se*, this book is about a young

pioneer girl in the frontier days of Kentucky, and some of the pioneer girls and women of that era settled in the hills.

755. Sylvester, Letitia Vertrees. *My Kentucky Cousins*. Boston: Christopher, 1933.

A girl from the mountains discovers that she has some Bluegrass connections. Through this discovery her life is changed.

756. Tarleton, Fiswoode. *Bloody Ground: A Cycle of the Hills*. New York: Dial, 1929.

Twelve short stories about life and characters in Breathitt County, Kentucky. Women are portrayed in most of the stories.

757. Thomas, Jean. *Devil's Ditties*. Chicago: Hatfield, 1931.

Stories of people in the Kentucky mountains and how music plays a role in their lives. The author writes of special occasions such as weddings, births, deaths, and court days. Some of these stories depict the mountain women.

758. Thompson, Adele Eugenia. *Brave Heart Elizabeth: A Story of the Ohio Frontier*. Boston: Lee & Shepard, 1902.

A novel based on historical facts. Betty Zane lives in Wheeling, West Virginia, and along the Ohio River frontier country. She has much courage and goodness.

759. Thompson, Maurice. *At Love's Extremes*. New York: Cassell, 1885.

Milly White, born and raised in the Alabama hills, falls in love with world-traveler and artist John Reynolds, who has come to the hills to escape reminders of a lost love and a murdered man. He does not love Milly, but is not immune to her beauty.

760. Thorndyke, George Howard. *The Witch's Castle*. Knoxville: Life & Letters, 1903.

Though told from the male narrator's point of view, there are several women involved in the plot. Belinda Jenkins is a typical mountain mother, busy with her family and home. She regales the narrator (Thorndyke) with all the lore of the East Tennessee mountains, with stories about a witch, ghosts, and so forth. There is a mystery and a treasure hunt for buried gold, and all ends well.

761. Thornton, Marcellus Eugene. *My "Budie" and I*. New York: Neely, 1899.

A mountain girl, Louise Stewart, meets the owner-manager of a coal mine at Pigeon Roost, North Carolina. The two, from widely differing backgrounds, fall in love, and the story ends happily. Much of the book deals with coal mining during the decade 1880–1890.

762. Tidball, Mary Langdon. *Barbara's Vagaries*. New York: Harper, 1886.

Barbara Dexter, an unsophisticated North Carolina mountain girl, is in Washington, where she is the brunt of the malicious wit of a popular Washington hostess. After Barbara has triumphed socially over everyone, she disappears in a boating accident. Her suitor searches for her; eventually he finds her back in her hometown, and marries her.

763. Tiernan, Frances Christine Fisher. *Bonny Kate: A Novel*. Library of American Fiction, no. 1. New York: Appleton, 1881.

A stylized story about Kate, her family, and her friends in a beautiful mountain setting.

764. _____. *A Little Maid of Arcady*. Philadelphia: Kilner, 1893.

The story of a girl in the mountains of Western North Carolina and her relationships with family and friends.

765. Townsend, Meta Folger. *In the Nantahalas*. New York: Broadway, 1910.

A North Carolina mountain girl attempts to educate herself and escape the mountain milieu, to bridge the gap between her world and the outside world. She succeeds and comes home to teach the mountain children music, art, and nature studies.

766. Trosper, Betty. "The Dado Dream." *Mt. Life & Work* 37 (Fall 1961): 28–32.

A mountain woman has a dream which does not materialize for many years because she has an alcoholic for a husband.

767. Troubetzkoy, Amelie Rives Chanler. *Tanis, the Sang-Digger*. New York: Town Topics, 1893.

Tanis, a mountain woman, is a ginseng-digger. She and her neighbors are depicted as near savages, but she helps an outlander find his missing wife and wins a certain amount of respect and approval.

768. Troxel, Thomas H. "Why Little Rowena Never Grew Up." *Mt. Life & Work* 19 (Spring 1943): 6–10.

An amusing story of a young girl and her superstitious mother, which takes place in about 1925. Rowena describes herself as always having a hard time in life, and relates some of the superstitions which have affected her.

769. Twitchell, Charles P. "The End of the Feud." *Berea Quarterly* 18 (Apr. 1914): 21–28.

A good portrayal of a mountain woman who was "tall and large—a woman who had been strong as a man" before her troubles came upon her.

770. Van Every, Dale. *The Captive Witch*. New York: Messner, 1951.

A convincing account of life in the wilderness and early settlements. In 1780, Adam Frane has his personal troubles with a bossy young widow and a white girl he has rescued from the Cherokee.

771. Wallin, Clarence Monroe. *Gena of the Appalachians*. New York: Cochrane, 1910.

Gena, an orphan girl, lives with Jose Dillinburger, who abuses her until he is arrested for moonshining. Gena gets his land and moves in with a neighbor, who arranges to send her to college. She meets and marries Paul Waffington, a church worker.

772. Ward, Charlie. *Silk Stocking Row*. Parsons, W.V.: McClain, 1975.

Men and women living in a West Virginia coal camp are the characters in this novel. Several mountain women play major roles.

773. Weaver, Jack. "A Woman Can Ruin A Good Man." *Mt. Life & Work* 31 (Winter 1955): 8–9.

Bessie Jones and Jim Faircloth illustrate the title. Jim is a hard-drinking, hard-living man and Bessie is a church goer. A humorous story about just who gets the upper hand in their "partnership."

774. Weaver, John Downing. "Parting Words." *Fighting Words: Stories and Cartoons by Members of the Armed Forces of America*. Warfield Lewis, ed. Philadelphia: Lippincott, 1944.

A young man gets himself shot in the back by worthless Bush Henry. As he lies dying a mountain girl named Honey promises that she will avenge his death. She drowns Bush Henry in a well.

775. _____. "Meeting Time." *Harper's* 197 (Oct. 1945): 54–61.

A short story about a red-headed mountain woman who is a preacher. She meets and marries Rev. Poplum. Shortly thereafter she holds a revival and induces most of the men to give up liquor, tobacco, crude talk, and general sin.

776. Weverka, Robert. *Trouble on the Mountain*. New York: Bantam, 1975.

This story, based on "The Waltons" television series by Earl Hamner, Jr., is about the whole family. There are some excellent characterizations of young girls, a wife and mother, and a grandmother.

777. _____. *The Easter Story*. New York: Bantam, 1976.

Olivia Walton is an idealized mountain woman. In this story, based on "The Waltons" television series, Olivia lies stricken with a desperate illness that cripples her legs and sends the whole family into a crisis. It is a season of renewal and hope, however, and Olivia rises to meet the challenge.

778. Whittaker, Frederick. *Ruby Roland, The Girl Spy*. Beadle's Dime

Novels, no. 282. New York: Beadle & Adams, 1873.

Ruby Roland, an adopted daughter of Indians, watches over the frontier settlements and aids them against hostile savages and the English. She falls madly in love with George Rogers Clark and accompanies him to Vincennes disguised as a young adjutant. Later they are married.

779. Wilburn, W. R. "The Porch." *Appal. Heritage* 7 (Summer, 1979): 21–26.

The two central characters are Lewis Lafon and his wife, Minnie. She nags at him until he builds her a front porch. He finishes the porch and she is pleased and proud—until he walks out of her life.

780. Wilkinson, Sylvia. *Shadow of the Mountain*. Boston: Houghton, Mifflin, 1976.

A novel set in the North Carolina and Tennessee mountains, with several women characters. This author has much to say about mountain women which is not being said by other women writers.

781. Willett, Edward. *The Five Champions: Or, The Backwoods Belle*. Beadle's New Dime Novels, no. 462. New York: Beadle & Adams, 1867.

Lucy Simms is abducted by Indians. Her father promises her hand to the champion who rescues her. She is finally rescued by a veteran scout and her long-lost brother, Mart. Since neither is eligible, she marries Harry Denton, another champion who had done his best but failed to come to her aid.

782. ———. *The Scioto Scouts: Or, The Shawnees' Decoy*. Beadle's Dime Novels, no. 219. New York: Beadle, 1870.

Susan Archer, her brother Bartholomew, her mother and father, and her fiance, Stephen Alleyne, go floating down the Ohio River in 1790 to find a new home in Kentucky. Susan and her mother are abducted by Indians but are rescued by Buck Hardnett and his Delaware comrade, Wapawah. Later Stephen and Susan are married in frontier Kentucky.

783. Williams, Vinnie. *Walk Egypt*. New York: Viking, 1960.

A story of a strange and lonely woman in the North Georgia hills. She finds love and laughter for a time, only to lose them again.

784. Wilson, Clyde. *Our Bed Is Green*. New York: Ballou, 1934.

At the end of a horror-filled day, a North Carolina mountain girl is left an orphan, responsible for a younger brother. They spend several years at the Valle Crucis Mission School in North Carolina, then return to the hills.

785. Wilson, Neill Compton. *The Nine Brides of Granny Hite*. New York: Morrow, 1952.

Fourteen stories about the people in Cat-Track Hollow, probably set in Tennessee. Granny Hite, with a finger in most of the pies in the hollow, extracts many of the stories from the nine girls who are quilting their wedding quilts at her cabin.

786. Wolfe, Thomas. *Look Homeward, Angel*. New York: Grosset & Dunlap, 1929.

The story is primarily about Eugene Gant, his father and brothers, but his mother, iron-willed Eliza Gant, is also portrayed throughout this very powerful, semi-autobiographical book.

787. _____. "The Battle of Hogwart Heights." *Stories by Thomas Wolfe*. New York: Avon, 1944.

The story of the Joyner family in the Catawba region. Mrs. Joyner is a proper, refined woman who finds it difficult to accept many people of the region who are not from the best families.

788. _____. *The Short Novels of Thomas Wolfe*. C. Hugh Holman, ed. New York: Scribner, 1961.

Of the five novels in this collection, the most interesting is *Web of Earth*. It is primarily about Eliza Gant, modeled along the lines of Wolfe's mother.

789. Womble, Walter L. *Love in the Mists*. Raleigh, N.C.: Edwards & Broughton, 1892.

A mountain girl whose father has been killed by moonshiners joins forces with the revenuer to help him capture the gang.

790. Woolson, Constance Fenimore. "Up in the Blue Ridge." *Rodman the Keeper: Southern Sketches*. New York: Appleton, 1880.

The library was built following the Civil War, but is for the most part ignored by the hill folk. Honor, the librarian, spends half her time helping drum up subscriptions for the library. She is also involved with a New York literary man whom the mountain people believe to be a revenuer.

791. Woolwine, Thomas Lee. *In the Valley of the Shadows*. New York: Doubleday, 1909.

In the Tennessee hills there is a feud between the Taylor and Gentry families. The Taylor girl falls in love with the Gentry boy.

792. Wright, Mary Wolcott. "Joffy." *Mt. Life & Work* 28 (Spring 1952): 31–36.

A story of how a little girl is deeply touched by the old man next door. One day they take him to the hospital and the little girl walks twenty miles just to see him smile.

793. _____. "Miss Lily and the Bee." *Mt. Life & Work* 36 (Summer 1960): 15–19.

A short story about Miss Lily Deel, an old maid, who daydreams about the minister, a widower. There is a slightly sinister twist at the end of the story.

794. ———. "The Tunnel." *Mt. Life & Work* 36 (Fall 1960): 35–40, 60–61.

A story about Darrie, whose sister, Sherry Ann, was killed in a tunnel as the two girls walked to school. Now Darrie must show a new neighbor girl the way to school. Although there is a different route now, Darrie deliberately leads her through the tunnel. The new girl is almost killed by a train, and in saving her life Darrie comes to terms with her sister's death.

795. Yancey, William H. *The Gate Is Down*. New York: Exposition, 1956.

A story of love, duty, and the call of the land, set in the Alabama hills. The main character is Scott Calderwood, but several women figure in the story and are strongly and realistically characterized.

796. Yerby, Frank. *A Woman Called Fancy*. New York: Dial, 1951.

Fancy is 19 years old the night she runs away from her home in the South Carolina hills to prevent her parents from forcing her into marriage with a man old enough to be her grandfather. Most of the book deals with her life in a mill town and a city in Georgia, but Fancy never forgets the hills and her family there.

797. Young, Garnett. "Ribbons for Their Hair." *Mt. Rev.* 1 (Spring 1975): 4–6.

A short story about two young mountain girls that shows the imagination and resourcefulness of young females in Appalachia.

798. ———. "The Shy Hillbilly Singer." *Mt. Rev.* 5 (1976): 37–39.

A shy, young woman (somewhat resembling the country singer Loretta Lynn) tells how she didn't make it in the country music world.

Health Conditions & Health Care

799. "Amanda's Salve." *Foxfire* 10 (Fall 1976): 218–20.

From beef tallow, salve is made for use on any kind of infection or sore. The making and use of this salve are described by a mountain woman who, at the same time, reveals much about herself.

800. Anderson, Elsie. "Our Life with Grandmother, Rebecca Caudill Tackett." *Appal. Heritage* 6 (Summer 1978): 11–12.

A woman remembers when her grandmother was ill and the family moved in to help to take care of her. A good glimpse of an old woman, a young wife and mother, and a young girl.

801. Ballangee, Judith. "Lend-a-Hand Lives Up to Its Name." *Appalachia* 4 (Aug./Sept. 1971): 15–19.

The Lend-a-Hand health center, established in 1958 by a nurse and a schoolteacher in Knox County, Kentucky, is described and reviewed. Young girls and women have been served since its inception.

802. Barret, Liz. "Nature's Way." *Mt. Life & Work* 50 (July/Aug. 1974): 8–9.

Barret made the film "Nature's Way" for Appalshop in 1973. Here she explains how this was done and tells of a midwife, Lena Stephens, who has delivered over 5,000 babies.

803. Bass, Jack. "Hunger? Let Them Eat Magnolias." *You Can't Eat Magnolias*. H. Brandt Ayers and Thomas H. Naylor, eds. New York: McGraw-Hill, 1972.

A brief review of the South's attempt to combat disease and hunger. It includes short descriptions of difficulties Appalachian women encounter in feeding their young children because of inadequate welfare programs.

804. Belanger, Ruth. "Midwives Tales." *Goldenseal* 5 (Oct./Nov. 1979): 42–46.

Relates various interviews the author had with mountain midwives in West Virginia.

805. Bernard, Jacqueline. "Dark as a Dungeon Way Down in the Mines." *Ms.* 3 (Apr. 1975): 21.

Claims for black-lung benefits have been filed by two women in Tazewell County, Virginia.

806. _____. "Pikeville's Methodist Hospital: One More Rejection." *Sou. Expos.* 3 (Winter 1976): 27–28.

Nurses, aides, and other workers at the Appalachian Regional Hospital strike for better pay, better treatment. The three-year-long strike has been strangled by red tape and lack of support from the United Mine Workers and the Methodist Church.

807. Bland, Marion F. "Superstitions about Food and Health among Negro Girls in Elementary and Secondary Schools in Marion County, West Virginia." Master's thesis, West Virginia University, 1950.

Not available for annotation.

808. Bradley, Frances Sage, M.D. "Who Pays the Price?" *Mt. Life & Work* 6 (Oct. 1930): 8–10, 30.

A doctor writes about a mountain woman expecting her fourth or fifth child, and how a public health nurse persuaded her to have this baby in the hospital. Reveals some prejudices of mountain women.

809. _____. "The Redemption of Appalachia." *Hygeia* 9 (Jan. 1931): 26–30.

Lack of health education in the mountains is illustrated by the woman who sent for her children and would not let them go back to the boarding school because there was an outbreak of measles.

810. Breckinridge, Mary. "An Adventure in Midwifery." *Survey* 57 (Oct. 1, 1926): 25–27, 47.

The story of service to mountaineer women "from Hurricane Creek to Hell-fer-Sartin," as the nurse-midwives ride out from the Frontier Nursing Service Center in Leslie County, Kentucky.

811. _____. "Where the Frontier Lingers." *Rotarian* 47 (Sept. 1935): 9–12, 50.

The author tells about conditions among mountain women and the work of the Frontier Nursing Service.

812. _____. *Wide Neighborhoods*. New Yok: Harper, 1952; Lexington: Univ. Press of Kentucky, 1981.

The autobiography of the remarkable woman who founded the Frontier Nursing Service in Leslie County, Kentucky, and the story of the nurse-midwives who ride over the hills and up the hollows delivering babies and caring for mothers. Beginning in Chapter 17 are varied accounts of mountain life and mountain people, especially women.

813. "Carrie Stewart." *Foxfire 5*. Eliot Wigginton, ed. Garden City, N.Y.: Anchor Press/Doubleday, 1979.

Carrie Stewart, over 100 years old, lives in Franklin, North Carolina. She tells about her father, who was a slave, and her active life of rearing ten children and being a midwife.

814. Church, Ruth, and Stanley, Cathy. "Women Miners—in the 40s: Today." *Mt. Life & Work* 50 (Nov. 1974): 14–15.

Two women working in the Virginia mines describe their work; and two women who worked in the mines in the 1940s talk about filing for black-lung benefits.

815. Coogan, Mercy Hardie. "Wilkes-Barre's Nurse-Midwives." *Appalachia* 10 (June/July 1977): 1–7.

Reduction of the neonatal death rate in Wilkes-Barre, Pennsylvania, since 1973 has been the result of introducing a group of nurse-midwives.

816. _____. "Infants and Mothers 3, Mortality 0." *Appalachia* 12 (July/Aug. 1979): 1–13.

This article talks about mothers and infants in Appalachia and programs to reduce the mortality rate. Good photographs of women of various ages.

817. Darcy, Jean. "Women in Rebellion." *MAW* 1 (Nov./Dec. 1977): 7–11.

"Americans are finally discovering... that trained midwives are not just for women in inaccessible mountain hollows or for the poor... that they are the best caretakers for all healthy, normal pregnancies."

818. Dilley, Patty. "Forum." *Youth Mag.* 27 (Sept. 1976): 77.

A native of Conover, North Carolina, Dilley wants to do work in occupational health, especially with victims of brown lung, a disease found among cotton and textile mill workers. "Since none of the mills are unionized, it's difficult to get the companies to do anything about it."

819. Dixon, Ada. "Brown Lung in Southwestern Virginia." *Mt. Life & Work* 53 (Apr. 1977): 8–11.

Dixon worked for seven years in the Clintwood, Virginia, Garment Company factory. She got brown lung in the process and talks about the industry and her disability.

820. Edgar, Betsy Jordan. *We Live with the Wheel Chair.* Parsons, W.V.: McClain, 1970.

A warm, sympathetic account of family life in an historic home in West Virginia. The husband is confined to a wheel chair and the wife must make many adjustments in order to keep the family together.

821. Fell, Frances. "A Christmas 'Least One' on Hell-fer-Sartin." *Public Health Nurse* 22 (Dec. 1930): 605–07.

The experiences of the nurse-midwives at the Frontier Nursing Service as they work with mountain women.

822. Gardner, Caroline. *Clever Country: Kentucky Mountain Trails.* New York: Revell, 1931.

The story of the Frontier Nursing Service and the nurses who ride horseback to reach their patients—mountain women in Eastern Kentucky.

823. Gardner, Linda. "Showdown at Stinking Creek." *Youth Mag.* 27 (Sept. 1976): 36–43.

The author spent two years in the Appalachian mountains working on her master's thesis. She was horrified at the unsanitary living conditions maintained by some women, but developed close relationships with a few of them.

824. Hartz, Lynn Richardson. "Women of Appalachia." *Appalachia* 11 (Feb./Mar. 1978): 21–24.

Hartz, born and raised in West Virginia, does counseling and therapy work with Appalachian women. She says that women in some ways are stronger than men, and more resourceful, particularly the elderly women." They are accustomed to looking to their own resources."

825. Heney, Eva. "Bits from the Day's Work." *Mt. Life & Work* 2 (Oct. 1926): 27–29.

A mountain nurse tells of three incidents in a day's work.

826. Higginbotham, Phyllis. "From Our Mountain Nurses." *Mt. Life & Work* 2 (Oct. 1926): 26–27.

A few brief pages from a mountain nurse's diary, in which she talks about mountain women, childbirth, and children.

827. Hunter, Sally. "A Widow Speaks." *Mt. Life & Work* 50 (Dec. 1974): 18.

Hunter interviews the widow of a miner who was trapped inside Consolidation Coal Corporation's mine near Mannington, West Virginia. The company has not recovered the bodies of 23 of the men, even after six years. The widows have formed a group to fight for passage of the federal Health and Safety Act.

828. Hutchins, Louise. "Better Health for Mountain Mothers." *Mt. Life & Work* 34 (Autumn 1958): 16–20.

The Mountain Maternal Health League was formed (by Dr. Hutchins and others) to teach planned parenthood to mountain people.

829. "In the Mines . . . Two Women Remember." *Mt. Life & Work* 51 (Feb. 1975): 35.

Two of the first women miners on record are interviewed. They describe many aspects of their lives: duties, safety, and health.

830. Lansing, Elizabeth Carleton Hubbard. *Rider on the Mountains.* New York: Crowell, 1949.

A Boston society girl volunteers for a tour of duty with the Frontier Nursing Service. As she becomes acquainted with and sympathetic toward the mountain people, we see mountain women through her eyes.

831. Lester, Betty. "The Clinic the Neighbors Built." *Survey* 64 (Apr. 15, 1930): 73–74.

The women in Leslie County, Kentucky, wanted a two-room building constructed where the Frontier Nursing Service could hold weekly clinics. The article relates how the women got their building.

832. _____. "The Experiences of a Midwifery Supervisor in the Kentucky Hills." *Amer. Journal of Nursing* 31 (May 1931): 573–77.

The author is a nurse-midwife who came from overseas to work with the "nurses on horseback" in the remote hills of Kentucky. Interesting details of mothers and babies.

833. Looff, David H. *Appalachia's Children: The Challenge of Mental Health.* Lexington: Univ. Press of Kentucky, 1971.

Psychiatric clinics for disturbed children were run by the author in Eastern Kentucky. He describes child-rearing practices in the area and gives good characterizations of Appalachian mothers and girls.

834. Mannarino, Julie. "Rural Response to Rape." *Social Welfare in Appalachia* 8 (1976): 8–9.

Suggestions for rape report and referral systems are based on the system used at Fairmont Clinic in Fairmont, West Virginia.

835. Myers, Pauline. "Mountain Mothers of Kentucky." *Hygeia* 7 (Apr. 1929): 353–56.

An article describing problems mountain mothers face, with suggestions for the women and for health and social workers who come to the mountains.

836. Norton, Beatrice. "Coughing Up Support in the Carolinas." *Mt. Life & Work* 53 (Dec. 1977): 13–14.

Norton testified at a hearing on the need for federal legislation to aid victims of brown-lung disease. Her testimony is reproduced here.

837. Orth, Helen. "The Half-and-Half Nurse." *Mt. Life & Work* 5 (Oct. 1929): 20–21, 24.

An article about a mountain nurse and some of the people she encounters. There is a strong characterization of a young woman, the mother of three children, living in incredible poverty.

838. Pease, Nola. "Another Successful Clinic at Community Center, Wooton, Kentucky." *Mt. Life & Work* 2 (Oct. 1926): 27.

The story of a successful medical clinic serving Leslie County. Nola Pease was a mountain nurse.

839. Poole, Ernest. "The Nurse on Horseback." *Good Housekeeping* 94 (June 1932): 38–39, 203, 210.

Relates the work of the Frontier Nursing Service at Hyden, Kentucky.

840. _____. *Nurses on Horseback.* New York: MacMillan, 1932.

The story of the Frontier Nursing Service at Hyden, Kentucky, which has had a great impact on Eastern Kentucky, and has been of great service to the mountain women.

841. Prewitt, Martha. "Mothers and Babies in Leslie County." *Mt. Life & Work* 2 (Oct. 1926): 8.

The Kentucky Committee for Mothers and Babies, Inc., was founded by Mary Breckinridge to improve the facilities and methods of native midwives. Breckinridge also founded the Frontier Nursing Service in Leslie County, Kentucky.

842. Prichard, Arthur C. "Phoebia G. Moore, M.D.: The First Woman to Study Medicine at West Virginia University." *Goldenseal* 5 (Oct./Dec. 1979): 36–41.

The story of how Phoebia Moore broke down the wall of sex prejudice thrown around the medical courses at West Virginia University and received her M.D. in 1903.

843. Rash, Maxine Vanover. "Aunt Spicie." *Mt. Rev.* 5 (1976): 15–17.

Aunt Spicie was a mountain midwife—tough, resourceful, and superstitious.

844. Rasnick, Elmer. "Women File for Black Lung—Expecting Trouble." *Mt. Life & Work* 50 (Sept. 1974): 11.

Five women worked in the Laurel Creek Mines in Tazewell County, Virginia, from 1940 to 1952. Two plan to file for black-lung benefits but fear they will not be believed.

845. Silveri, Louis D. "Nursing on Troublesome." *Appal. Heritage* 7 (Summer 1979): 11–17.

An article about Erna Kuhn and her work as a public health nurse in Knott County, Kentucky, many years ago. She traveled by horseback all over the county, and talks about the people she nursed, especially the women.

846. *Southern Exposure* 6, no. 1 (1978).

A special issue on health care in Appalachia and some parts of the South. This issue should prove valuable for anyone doing research on mountain women and health.

847. Stahl, Ellen J. "Legal abortion in Cincinnati and Appalachian Women." *MAW* 1 (July/Aug. 1978): 7–14.

The author is doing research on Appalachian women who migrate to Cincinnati. She tells about the abortion clinics, groups opposing legalized abortion, and where the Appalachian woman fits in between the two. A good look at how Appalachian women feel about children, abortions, and unwanted pregnancies.

848. Stuart, Jesse. "Remedies That Stand Out in Memory." *Ky. Folklore Rec.* 22 (July/Oct. 1976): 59–63.

The author knew a woman who excelled in using home remedies. Her son, in an accident, had one finger severed and others almost cut through, and "she stopped the blood. Not one of her son's fingers bled."

849. Swerczynski, M. J. "A Home Birth." *MAW* 1 (Mar./Apr. 1978): 11–12.

A woman assists a midwife in a home delivery. She says home births are a joyous way for people to celebrate the cycle of life.

850. Taylor, Lucy. "Brown Lung." *Mt. Life & Work* 53 (Apr. 1977): 5.
Taylor talks about the 35 years she worked in a cotton mill.

851. Thomas, Mei. *Grannies' Remedies.* New York: Heineman, 1967 [1965].
Granny knew that the old home remedies had positive curative effects. Now the scientists are agreeing with her.

852. Tuttle, Emeth. "Mountain Mothers." *Mt. Life & Work* 3 (Jan. 1928): 11–12, 20.
When the Mothers' Aid Bill passed in 1923, the counties of North Carolina were able to divide $50,000 per year. Too often, however, many mothers could not be reached because of bad roads and the lack of money for a new county officer, a superintendent of public welfare.

853. Tyler-McGraw, Marie. "But After All Was She Not a Masterpiece as a Mother and a Gentlewoman . . . ." *Goldenseal* 3 (Oct./Nov./Dec. 1977): 28–34.
Anna Maria Reeves Jarvis, a nineteenth-century West Virginia woman who worked for health and peace, was the inspiration for Mother's Day.

855. Wharton, May Cravath. *Doctor Woman of the Cumberlands: The Autobiography of May Cravath Wharton, M.D.* Pleasant Hill, Tenn.: Uplands, 1953.
A deeply moving account of a woman doctor's life and practice in the Cumberland Mountains.

856. White, Debra. "Children and Violence." *MAW* 1 (July/Aug. 1978): 21–22.
The author tells of some agencies where Appalachian women and children can find help and counseling. "Child abuse doesn't happen only in poor, illiterate families."

857. Wicker, Allie. "Women." *Mt. Life & Work* 48 (Nov. 1972): 3.
The author was a member of the Eastern Kentucky Welfare Rights Organization. She talks about the clinic at Mud Creek and women's health problems.

858. Willis, Irene. "Women of Appalachia." *Appalachia* 11 (Feb./Mar. 1978): 18–21.
The author is a nurse-midwife and mountain woman who has spent years working with other mountain women. They are, she says, strong, tough, not inclined to whine, mean sometimes, but basically good, decent, hard-working, shrewd, and self-reliant.

859. Wilson-Clay, Barbara. "Cultural Myths and Abused Children." MAW 1 (July/Aug. 1978): 16–18.

Abused children present a real problem for society in Appalachia, as in other parts of the country. This article reveals some of the problems and asks some of the questions.

860. Withington, Alfreda Bosworth. "The Mountain Doctor." *Atlantic Monthly* 150 (Dec. 1932): 763–74.

Dr. Withington, after years of working in France with the Red Cross and the Rockefeller Foundation, returned to Kentucky to practice medicine in the mountains.

861. _____. *Mine Eyes Have Seen: A Woman Doctor's Saga.* New York: Dutton, 1941.

The author practiced medicine in the Kentucky mountains. An account of her experiences.

862. "Women and Health." *Mt. Life & Work*, Special Issue, 50 (June 1974): 1–25.

This issue contains articles covering many aspects of health conditions: "Assistance for Women," "Diagnosis: Work-Related Disease," "Facts for Women," "Please Mr. Computer," "Prepared Childbirth," "Our History: Mt. Midwives and Mothers," "To Be Happy," and "Women's Self-Help Group."

863. "Women's Alcoholism Center." *Mt. Life & Work* 50 (July/Aug. 1974): 7.

Nearly 1,000 women in a residential section of Cincinnati, including a number of migrants from the Appalachian mountains, have drinking problems. A drop-in center is being organized to help them.

864. Wood, Violet. *So Sure of Life.* New York: Friendship Press, 1950.

The story of doctor Robert F. Thomas and his wife Eva. She is a teacher and he the only doctor in the area. The author tells of their life in the Smoky Mountains and the people they meet there.

865. Young, Barbara. "Appalachian Women and Mental Health: A Discussion." MAW 1 (Nov./Dec. 1977): 13–15.

The author interviews two women who are professional mental health workers.

Industry

866. Ansley, Fran and Bell, Brenda. "Diagnosis: Work-Related Disease." *Mt. Life and Work* 50 (June 1974): 13–16.

Certain health and safety hazards face women in Appalachia who work in garment factories and cotton mills.

867. "Appalachian Women's Rights Organization Forms." *Mt. Life & Work* 51 (Mar. 1975): 28–30.

On February 16, 1975, a meeting took place in Floyd County, Kentucky, in which women spoke out about various aspects of their lives and labor. The conclusion many seemed to arrive at was that women are strong fighters but need the support of other women.

868. Arnow, Harriette S. "Progress Reached Our Valley." *Nation* 211 (Aug. 3, 1970): 71–77.

Arnow and her husband bought a 160-acre farm on Little Indian Creek on the South Fork at Cumberland, Kentucky. After a few years "progress" reached the lovely valley—Lake Cumberland was built and stripminers ravaged the hillsides. Most of the people had to move away; those who stayed live in constant fear of landslides and other destruction from a disturbed landscape.

869. Axelrod, Jennifer. "Appalachia, Women and Work." *MAW* 3 (Jan./Feb. 1978): 7–11.

A historical overview encompassing Appalachian women in unions, the labor force, coal mining, textile manufacturing, and hospital work.

870. Bernard, Jacqueline. "Moving Mountains: Appalachian Women Organize." *Ms.* 4 (Sept. 1975): 21.

The activities of the Appalachian Women's Rights Organization are briefly reviewed.

871. Dixon, Ada. "Brown Lung in Southwestern Virginia." *Mt. Life & Work* 53 (Apr. 1977): 8–11.

Dixon worked for seven years in the Clintwood, Virginia, Garment Company factory. She got brown lung in the process and talks about the industry and her disability.

872. Frederickson, Mary. "The Southern Summer School for Women Workers." *Sou. Expos.* 4 (Winter 1977): 70–75.

A definitive article about the workers education program, begun in 1927 and run until World War II. The school began at Sweet Briar College but later moved to Asheville, North Carolina. The staff sought to provide young workers from textile, garment, and tobacco factories with the analytic tools for understanding the social context of their lives.

873. Hedgepeth, Maurine. "J. P. Stevens—the Workers." *Mt. Life & Work* 53 (Apr. 1977): 29.

J. P. Stevens Company refused to rehire Hedgepeth after her pregnancy leave because she testified about management practices to the National Labor Relations Board.

874. Jackson, Addie. "J. P. Stevens—the Workers." *Mt. Life & Work* 53 (Apr. 1977): 30.

Jackson talks about her work at J. P. Stevens's Statesboro, Georgia, plant, which is now shut down.

875. Jackson, Clayton. "Johnson City." *Mt. Life & Work* 49 (Jan. 1973): 11–12.

Evelyn Reece fought to organize a union at Tennessee Plastics in Johnson City. Although the union was certified, the company refused to recognize it and Reece was fired. The author writes of the struggles of the workers and the company.

876. Janison, Elsie S. "A School for Women Workers in Industry in the South." *School and Society* 36 (Oct. 8, 1932): 473–75.

This educational experiment was undertaken for the women employees in North Carolina mills, and was housed at Fruitland Institute near Hendersonville. A worthy project and successful for the most part.

877. Kahn, Kathy. "A Sweatshop Don't Ever Pay Enough." *Mt. Life & Work* 49 (April. 1973): 14–21.

An interview with a woman who helped lead the Levi-Strauss strike in Fannin County, Georgia, and organize the McCaysville Industries.

878. Merzer, Meridee. "Kathy Kahn: Voice of Poor White Women." *Viva* 1 (Apr. 1974): 74–78.

The story of Kathy Kahn (author of *Hillbilly Women*), who came to Appalachia ten years ago and has been active as spokeswoman and organizer of women's groups.

879. Norton, Beatrice, "Coughing Up Support in the Carolinas." *Mt. Life & Work* 53 (Dec. 1977): 13–14.

Norton testified at a hearing on the need for federal legislation to aid victims of brown-lung disease. Her testimony is reproduced here.

880. Quinney, Valerie. "Three Generations in the Mill." *Sou. Expos.* 3 (Winter 1976): 66–72.

The story of three women, representing three generations, who have worked in the cotton mills and changed their idea of themselves and their work.

881. Sharp, Molly. "There's Always a Judas." *Such As Us: Southern Voices of the Thirties*. Chapel Hill: Univ. of North Carolina Press, 1978.

Sharp, living with her daughter and son-in-law (a Baptist preacher) in North Carolina, talks about her life, her daughter's work in the cotton mills, and the preacher's work in the mill villages.

882. Taylor, Lucy. "Brown Lung." *Mt. Life & Work* 53 (Apr. 1977): 5.

A short article about the 35 years Taylor worked in a cotton mill.

883. Williams, Clara. "No Union for Me." *Such As Us: Southern Voices of the Thirties*. Chapel Hill: Univ. of North Carolina Press, 1978.

A short narrative setting forth Williams's strong feelings about the unions in Virginia and North Carolina.

Life Styles

884. Alther, Lisa. "They Shall Take Up Serpents." *New York Times Mag.* June 6, 1976, pp. 18–20, 28, 35.

The author of *Kinflicks* interviews the pastor and members of the Holiness Church of God in Jesus Name of Carson Springs, Tennessee. Photographs of snake handling and descriptions of experiences show the involvement of mountain women in this religious rite.

885. Angier, Suzanne. "Florence and Lawton." *Foxfire* 7 (Fall 1973): 192–208, 225–27.

A mountain couple remember their youth, adventures, and way of life.

886. "Annie Perry." *Foxfire* 9 (Summer–Fall 1975): 143–62.

Through interviews conducted over a four-year period, the personality of an 83-year-old mountain woman shines.

887. Arnow, Harriette S. "Gray Women of Appalachia." *Nation* 211 (Dec. 28, 1970): 684–87.

Arnow talks about the devastation brought to the land by stripmining and poor conservation practices, and what this has done to the people. "It is here that one sees the gray woman—gray like everything about her . . . Driving on you see the woman again and again . . . waiting. For what? The next welfare check? A job?"

888. Baker, Madge. "I Know It's Me They're Calling When I Hear 'Ms. Tumbleweed.'" *Appal. Women* 1 (Fall 1979): 15, 28.

Baker, a native of Tennessee, is known to her fellow truck drivers as "Tumbleweed." She writes about her experiences driving a tractor-trailer.

889. Ballou, Nellie. "Feminism Invades Mountain Election." *New York Times*, Nov. 1, 1925, sect. 4, p. 13.

A report about the furor in one section of the mountains when a woman became a candidate for political office.

890. Behymer, F. A. "The Queen of the Barge Still Reigns Along Troublesome Creek." *St. Louis Post-Dispatch* Sunday magazine, Oct. 23, 1932, pp. 1–4. (Excerpts from this article also appear as "The Queen of Troublesome Creek, Kentucky," in *Literary Digest* 114[Nov. 19, 1932]: 26, 28.)

When all the men in her family were killed in a feud, Stella Combs came into power. She announced that she hoped for peace but would not hesitate to extend her realm if the opportunity came.

891. Bell, Priscilla. "I'm Angry Again! I'm a Hillbilly." *Mt. Life & Work* 52 (Aug. 1976): 11–12.

A young woman who was raised in the hills writes with deep emotion about what it is like to be a hillbilly woman living in a modern city.

892. Brandstetter, Anne. "Mountain Teens Learn at East End School." *Youth Mag.* 27 (Sept. 1976): 44–47.

Sue Schaeffer's parents were born and raised in Appalachia; the family now lives in Cincinnati's East End. The article is about her and others like her, migrants from the hills, attending the East End Alternative School.

893. Butler, Marguerite. "A Dream Come True." *Mt. Life & Work* 7 (Oct. 1931): 1–4.

The author tells about how the Southern Mountain Handicraft Guild came into being. Women are not described specifically, but they certainly made an important contribution to the work.

894. Campbell, John C. *The Southern Highlander and His Homeland.* New York: Russell Sage Foundation, 1921; Lexington: Univ. Press of Kentucky, 1969.

Chapters about women, young girls, and grandmothers contain

excellent descriptions of the life style of mountain women in the early part of the twentieth century.

895. Carter, Mary Nelson. *North Carolina Sketches*. Chicago: McClurg, 1900.

The author writes of people she met in North Carolina, many of whom are women. Each section is in the form of an interview.

896. Chaffin, Lillie D. "Regionalism." *Appal. Heritage* 7 (Fall 1979): 47–51.

The author, a mountain woman, talks about her writings, how she views the region and her place in it, education, and so forth.

897. Darden, Norma Jean, and Darden, Carole. *Spoonbread and Strawberry Wine*. Garden City, N.Y.: Anchor Press/Doubleday, 1978.

The authors researched their family backgrounds and wrote this collection of traditional recipes, photographs, health and beauty secrets, and stories about celebrations and rituals. Along with this are ten short biographies of women in the Appalachian region and the surrounding area.

898. Daugherty, Mary L. "Serpent-Handling as Sacrament." *Theology Today* 33 (Oct. 1976): 232–43.

The ritual of serpent handling is the way members of independent Holiness churches in West Virginia celebrate life, death, and resurrection.

899. Davis, Tom. *White Caps and Blue Bills*. [Revised edition of *The Sevier County White Caps*.] Knoxville: Sevier, 1937.

Davis writes of the formation and activities of the Ku Klux Klan in Tennessee. Included are accounts of numerous women who were either beaten or murdered by the Klan.

900. Doran, Lisa. "Quilting: A Nice Way to Keep People Warm." *Mt. Memories* 9 (Winter 1977): 17–22. Pippa Passes, Ky: Students of the Appalachian Oral History Project, Alice Lloyd College.

An article about mountain women and quilting.

901. Dowda, Rus. *Appalachian Women in the 19th Century and Their Image in the Murder Ballads of the Times*. Berea, Ky.: Council of the Southern Mountains, 1978.

The author was a Berea College senior who had done considerable research into the status of women.

902. Dykeman, Wilma. *Tennessee Women, Past and Present*. Selected additional material edited by Carol Lynn Yellin. Memphis: Tennessee Committee for the Humanities and Tennessee International Women's Decade Coordinating Committee, 1977.

A comprehensive book about women in Tennessee's history. The author knows her subject and writes with convincing clarity.

903. Edgar, Betsy Jordan. *We Live with the Wheel Chair.* Parsons, W.V.: McClain, 1970.

A warm, sympathetic account of family life in a historic home in West Virginia. The husband is confined to a wheel chair and the wife must make many adjustments in order to keep the family together.

904. Edwards, Beth Rader. "Appalachian Women? Survival Is the Game." *Mt. Life & Work* 52 (Aug. 1976): 22–23.

The Appalachian woman who comes to the city finds more problems than just those of housing, employment, and education. She must contend with blatant stereotypes which confine her to an almost subhuman status.

905. Elkinton, Linda Cooper. "Women." *Mt. Life & Work* 48 (Dec. 1972): 17–19.

Elkinton comments on the "Weekend for Women" at Camp Caesar, West Virginia, held in October 1973, and some of the events which took place as the women worked together and talked about their lives.

906. Fallow, George. "A Woman's Like a Dumb Animal." *Such As Us: Southern Voices of the Thirties.* Chapel Hill: Univ. of North Carolina Press, 1978.

Fallow, who worked in sawmills in Alabama, talks expansively about his life. In speaking of women he says: "A woman's like a dumb animal—like a cow or a bitch dog. You got to frail 'em with a stick now and then to make 'em look up to you."

907. Farr, Grover V. "The Appalachian Woman through the Eyes of Fiction." Prize-winning paper in the Weatherford-Hammond Essay Contest at Berea Coll., Berea, Kentucky, 1973.

The author examines fiction by Harriette Arnow, Wilma Dykeman, James Still, Harry Caudill, Gurney Norman, Catherine Marshall, and Jack Weller to show how they portray mountain women.

908. Farr, Sidney. "The Appalachian Woman as Portrayed by James Still in *River of Earth*." *Appal. Heritage* 4 (Spring 1976): 55–61.

"Still seems to have an unusually deep understanding of the little facets, the secret yearnings of the mountain woman, and he has presented her as she really is."

909. _____. "Dark Hollow and Other Memories." *Appal. Journal* 4 (Winter 1977): 164–168.

Conversations with the author's relatives concerning mountain life. Good characterization of the great-grandmother, a remarkable pioneer woman during the frontier days in Eastern Kentucky.

910. _____. "Beautiful Baskets from Wild Honeysuckle." *Organic Gardening* 25 (June 1978): 108.

Betty Mills, a Kentucky mountain woman, found a way to use what she had and came up with a handcrafted product which helps her support her family. When asked why she didn't go to a city to work, she replies: "We've lived in the mountains all our lives . . . we like being able to walk on land that is ours."

911. Farris, Nana. "Head Cheese: A Country Delicacy." *Ky. Folklore Rec.* 23 (Jan./Mar. 1977): 14–16.

Augusta (Gish) Reed tells how women made head cheese (souse) in her community to feed their families.

912. Fetterman, John. *Stinking Creek.* New York: Dutton, 1967.

The customs and social life of Knox County, Kentucky, are studied. Good photographs of mountain girls and women.

913. Fey, Mary. "Learning from Our Differences." *Mt. Life & Work* 48 (Nov. 1972): 5.

Fey was a participant at the Women's Conference at Camp Caesar in West Virginia. She tells about her reactions to the weekend.

914. Foster, Vickie. "Mountain Women." *Mt. Rev.* 2 (Mar. 1976): 11–14.

Mountain women are captured in this collection of photographs.

915. Frost, Mrs. William G. "The Women of the Mountains." *Berea Quarterly* 18 (Jan. 1915): 5–16.

A paper read before the Women's Missionary Society in Berea. The author traveled extensively in the Appalachian Mountains and met and talked with hundreds of women. "We cannot attempt character sketches," she says, "but will try to give a few 'snap shots' of women who won our hearts because of ability, self-possession, poise, unselfishness."

916. Gaines, Judith. "Images of Appalachian Women." *Appalachia* 12 (July/Aug. 1979): 26–36.

From September 1968 through May 1969, the Council on Appalachian Women sponsored "Images of Appalachian Women," a series of public forums. This article covers some of the meetings and contains short interviews with mountain women.

917. Garner, Mary E. "The Road Builders." *Mt. Life & Work* 7 (Apr. 1931): 26–27.

Lost Creek, Tennessee, was an isolated community reached by a rough, rocky road. This article deals with the ingenious methods two women employed to get the county and the men of the community to build a five-mile highway.

918. Gazeway, Rena. *The Longest Mile.* New York: Doubleday, 1969.
The author lived in the remote hollows of Kentucky for a short
time before she wrote the book. She pictures the life style especially of the women and young girls, as well as the men and boys.

919. Gitlin, Todd, and Hollander, Nanci. *Uptown: Poor Whites in
Chicago.* New York: Harper & Row, 1970.
Migrants from Appalachia have moved into ghettolike neighborhoods in large northern and midwestern cities such as Detroit,
Indianapolis, Chicago, and Columbus. This book about migrants
to Chicago transcribes recorded conversations which give us a
picture of the family, but especially of how the mountain woman
copes in urban situations.

920. Goldman, Pam. "Family Violence." *Mt. Rev.* 11 (Oct. 1976):
18–20.
A woman lawyer in Prestonsburg, Kentucky, talks about wife
abuse and child abuse in the mountains, and some steps to meet a
need in this area.

921. Green, Lewis. "Mary." *Mt. Rev.* 1 (Spring 1975): 37–38.
A description of a 74-year-old mountain woman and of her courage and fortitude.

922. Green, Rayna. "Magnolias Grow in Dirt: "The Bawdy Lore of
Southern Women." *Sou. Expos.* 4 (Winter 1977): 29–33.
While the author writes of southern women in general, what she
says is also typical of Appalachian women. This is the first article
known to deal with this subject.

923. Groce, Lois. "Sharecropping in the Fields." *Growin' Up Country.*
Clintwood, Va.: Resource and Information Center, Council of the
Southern Mountains, 1973.
Determination to have a better way of life is the thread linking
Lois and her parents in their daily labor.

924. "Gunmaking: Making the New Era Possible. Bud and Dottie Siler:
Lockmakers." *Foxfire* 5. Eliot Wigginton, ed. Garden City, N.Y.:
Anchor Press/Doubleday, 1979.
Dottie and Bud Siler of Asheville, North Carolina, have built a
business of producing locks for muzzle-loading guns, using an
investment casting process.

925. Ham, Tom. "Close-up of a Hillbilly Family." *Amer. Mercury* 52
(1941): 659–65.
An account of the way of life of the Long family in the North
Georgia hills.

926. Hamburger, Robert. "A Stranger in the House." *Sou. Expos.* 5,
no. 1 (1978): 22–31.
This article, part of a book in progress, looks at how black women

from the South have fared as domestic workers in the North. Two women speak: one from Fayetteville, North Carolina, the other from Virginia.

927. Hickey, Margaret, ed. "Forgotten Children: Miracle of Pilot Knob." *Ladies' Home Journal* 65 (Jan. 1948): 23–24, 110, 112.

An article about a remote community in the Tennessee mountains, about the Save-the-Children Federation and their work of community development, and about mountain women and girls. The women in the community helped build a school and community center.

928. Hill, Jennie Lester. "Home Life in the Kentucky Mountains." *Berea Quarterly* 7 (Nov. 1902): 11–18.

The author, a teacher at Berea College, traveled extensively in the mountains visiting the homes of former Berea College students.

929. Hurst, Taylor. "Marryin' Doesn't Excuse Her." *Mt. Life & Work* 3 (Oct. 1927): 21–24.

An article by a mountain doctor who was also truant officer for Perry County, Kentucky. It reveals the very young age at which mountain girls married then and the attitude of some of the mothers.

930. Hutchinson, Ruth. "Women." *Mt. Life & Work* 48 (Nov. 1972): 3.

The author was the first woman deputy in the history of Buchanan County, Virginia.

931. "Ida Belle Marcum: Little Laurel Lady." *Mt. Call* 1 (Mar. 1974): 4–6, 18.

An 89-year-old woman is interviewed. She describes many aspects of her life.

932. Johnston, Annie Fellows. "A Mountain Mailbag." Unfinished manuscript, n.d. Berea Coll. Archives, Berea, Ky.

This manuscript deals with men and women from Virginia who pioneered in the mountains of Eastern Kentucky.

933. Jordan, Sue. "Forum." *Youth Mag.* 27 (Sept. 1976): 82.

Jordan works as a chambermaid in the Pocono Mountains of Pennsylvania. "It's like slave labor—you work hard for little pay, and the tourists treat you like dirt."

934. Kahn, Kathy. *Hillbilly Women.* New York: Doubleday, 1972.

A series of taped, edited interviews with mountain women in Southern Appalachia and in some of the migrant ghettoes in northern cities. Nineteen women tell what it means to be a woman when you are poor, proud, and struggling to resist exploitation of your land and people.

935. Kinder, Alice J. *Mama's Kitchen Window.* Kansas City, Mo.: Beacon Hill, 1977.

Vignettes from life in the Kentucky hills. Chapters include: "Mama's Rose China Platter," "Mama's Sunday Bonnet," "Mama's Wedding Ring," "Mama and the Missionary Barrel," etc.

936. Kirkland, Winifred. "Mountain Mothers." *Ladies' Home Journal* 37 (Dec. 1920): 26–27.

This article about mountain women includes some illustrations. It is worth reading to see how popular magazines portrayed mountain women in 1920.

937. Lewis, Claudia. *Children of the Cumberlands.* New York: Columbia Univ. Press, 1946.

The author taught in a nursery school for two and a half years at the Highlander Folk School in Tennessee. A portrayal of mountain children and their mothers as perceived by a woman from outside the region.

938. "Lottie Thompson." *Mt. Trace* 1 (Spring 1975): 76–79.

A 92-year-old woman describes her life on a farm.

939. McKinney, Aunt Tobe. "Talking Is My Life." *Such As Us: Southern Voices of the Thirties.* Chapel Hill: Univ. of North Carolina Press, 1978.

Aunt Tobe is a Tennessee woman. "Now, I know some folks back through here in Big Ivy will say Aunt Tobe McKinney is a gossip. Law ha' mercy, a gossip is a sharp-tongued woman and I'm not that."

940. Maggard, Sally. "Eastern Kentucky Women—International Woman's Day." *Mt. Life & Work* 51 (Apr. 1975): 19–23.

A report of a meeting at Wheelwright in Floyd County, Kentucky, on International Woman's Day. Women born and raised in Appalachia speak about themselves.

941. Miller, Jennifer. "Quilting Women." *Sou. Expos.* 4 (Winter 1977): 25–28.

A good article about women in several Appalachian states who quilt, some for economic reasons and others for creative satisfaction.

942. Moffat, Adelene. "The Mountaineers of Middle Tennessee." *Journal of Amer. Folk-Lore* 4 (Oct./Dec., 1891): 314–20.

An article about mountaineers in general—men, women and children. It is worth reading for the general characteristics of women portrayed in the late 1800s.

943. Myers, Pauline. "Mountain Mothers of Kentucky." *Hygeia* 7 (Apr. 1929): 353–56.

An article describing problems mountain mothers face, with suggestions for the women and for health and social workers who come to the mountains.

944. Nelson, Linda. "Women." *Mt. Life & Work* 48 (Nov. 1972): 8.
"A Weekend for Women" brought together a variety of women in West Virginia. Among them were the daughters, wives, and sisters of coal miners, who discussed what it means to be related to a miner.

945. Pearl, Minnie. *Christmas at Grinder's Switch.* New York: Abingdon Press, 1963.
This witty television, radio, and public performance star gives a hilarious account of Christmas as celebrated by men and women in the Tennessee mountains.

946. Pelton, Robert W., and Carden, Karen W. *Snake Handlers: God-Fearers? or Fanatics?* Nashville: T. Nelson, 1974.
A documentary report liberally illustrated with photographs of people in different places of worship handling snakes as part of their rituals. Many of the participants are young girls and women.

947. Reeves, Florence. "A Kentucky Ballad Singer." *Mt. Life & Work* 12 (Jan. 1937): 18–19.
A short article about Aunt Phronnie, a mountain woman who sang ballads and songs "from the old country" of Scotland. It reveals her life style and the many ways she used her skills in raising sheep and children and gathering medicinal herbs, singing her ballads all the while.

948. ———. "A Mountain Coverlet." *Mt. Life & Work* 11 (Oct. 1935): 16–19.
A mountain woman tells about her weaving and her grandmother's handiwork, and some of the old drafts such as "Ladies Delight" and "Lee's Surrender."

949. Relham, Richard. "Doing Good." *Appal. Heritage* 7 (Spring 1979): 27–31.
The author, a retired minister, was told in the mining community a pathetic story about Carrie Suggs and her children being evicted from their home. He went to help, thinking Carrie was a widow. To his dismay, he found she was the "scarlet woman" of the hills, and he had been tricked into what could have been a compromising situation.

950. Ritchie, Jean. "Now Is the Cool of the Day." *Mt. Life & Work* 46 (May 1970): 3–11.
Ritchie talks about her childhood in Eastern Kentucky, stripmining and the destruction of the regions, and the joys of living as expressed in one song, "Now Is the Cool of the Day."

951. ———. *Singing Family of the Cumberlands.* New York: Oxford Univ. Press, 1955; Oak Publications, 1963.
A charming, tender, delightfully humorous account of Jean's

growing-up years in Appalachia, and of her family, friends, and people in the community.

952. Rosten, June. "Forum." *Youth Mag.* 27 (Sept. 1976): 79.

"One of the major problems of women in Appalachia today is employment," says Rosten, a staff member of the Southern Appalachian Ministry. "Jobs for women are few and the ones they do get are menial and very low-paying."

953. Shackelford, Laurel. "Home." *Mt. Rev.* 1 (Sept. 1974): 5–6.

A Louisville woman compares city life to her prior life style in Floyd County, Kentucky.

954. Shelton, Ferne, ed. *Pioneer Beauty Secrets: Old and New Cosmetics from the Kitchen and Garden.* High Point, N.C.: Hutcraft, 1966.

Mountain women, like women the world over, are interested in beauty.

955. Simmons, Lola. "From the Mountains Faring." *Such As Us: Southern Voices of the Thirties.* Chapel Hill: Univ. of North Carolina Press, 1978.

Lola says she and her common-law husband came "faring down from the mountains to Knoxville, and ain't never going back again. I miss them mountains sometimes. Yes, I miss that steep old land."

956. Speed, Judy, and Taylor, Becky. "Effie Lord's Cafe." *Foxfire* 11, no. 2 (Summer 1977): 135–41.

The owner of an old-fashioned restaurant (where customers help themselves in the kitchen) describes an average day and expresses her values in respect to her environment.

957. Sullivan, Ken. "Out in the Weeds and Briers: The Recollection of Rosie Lee Shanklin." *Goldenseal* 4 (Apr./Sept. 1978): 26–30.

The author talks with a 91-year-old woman, a native of Summers County, West Virginia, who speaks of her early (arranged) marriage, changes in the community, and differences in people.

958. Taney, Mary Florence. *Kentucky Pioneer Women.* Cincinnati: Clarke, 1893.

Rebecca Bryan Boone and Susanna Hart Shelby, natives of North Carolina, Keturah Leitch Taylor and Mary Hopkins Cable Breckenridge from Virginia, and Henriette Hunt Morgan and Susan Lucy Barry Taylor of Kentucky are the pioneer women depicted. They lived during a period when those who survived possessed courage and great strength.

959. Terrill, Tom E., and Hirsch, Jerrold, eds. *Such As Us: Southern Voices of the Thirties.* Chapel Hill: Univ. of North Carolina Press, 1978.

As the title says, these are southern voices speaking about their personal lives. A goodly number of the speakers are women and several are from the mountain areas. The material in this book was gathered and edited by the Federal Writers' Project—part of the WPA project of the 1930s.

960. Terry, Peggy. "Our America: A Self-Portrait at 200: The Hillbilly." *Newsweek* 88 (July 4, 1976): 54, 61.

An interview with a woman, originally from Kentucky and Oklahoma, facing poverty and prejudice in Chicago.

961. Thomas, Mei. *Grannies' Remedies.* New York: Heineman, 1967 [1965].

Granny knew that the old home remedies had positive curative effects. Now the scientists are agreeing with her.

962. Thornborough, Laura. "Americans the Twentieth Century Forgot." *Travel* 50 (Apr. 1928): 25–28, 42.

The author describes mountain people living in the Great Smoky Mountains in Tennessee. Several women are interviewed.

963. Toone, Betty L. *Appalachia: The Mountains, the Place, and the People.* New York: Franklin Watts, 1972.

This book covers several aspects of community life in the mountains. One section, "The Children of Appalachia," has a particularly good characterization of a mountain girl.

964. Turner, Debbie. "That's One Night I'll Never Forget." *Mt. Life & Work* 52 (June 1976): 22–26.

A young mountain girl tells about losing her husband during the explosion at the Scotia Mines in March 1976 and what it is like to be a young widow with a child in Eastern Kentucky.

965. Tyler-McGraw, Marie. "But After All Was She Not a Masterpiece as a Mother and a Gentlewoman . . . ." *Goldenseal* 3 (Oct./Nov./Dec. 1977): 28–34.

Anna Maria Reeves Jarvis, a nineteenth-century West Virginia woman who worked for health and peace, was the inspiration for Mother's Day.

966. Ulmann, Doris. *The Appalachian Photographs of Doris Ulmann.* Penland, N.C.: Jargon Society, 1971.

These rare photographs of mountain people, especially women, taken in the early twentieth century, should be studied by every serious researcher preparing material on Appalachian women.

967. Vogel, John. *This happened in the Hills of Kentucky.* Grand Rapids, Mich.: Zondervan, 1952.

The author, founder and director of the Galilean Children's Home in Corbin, Kentucky, offers revealing glimpses of young girls and mountain women.

968. White, Linda C. "Unemphatic Love." *Western Folklore* 34 (Apr. 1975): 154.

An article about the connotations of the word love as it is used in Cumberland County, Kentucky.

969. "Will and Magaline Zoellner." *Foxfire 5*. Eliot Wigginton, ed. Garden City, N.Y.: Anchor Press/Doubleday, 1979.

In the second half of the article (pp. 67–76) Magaline Zoellner, born in the North Carolina mountains, describes her childhood and growing up in the mountains. She talks of marrying at a young age and her life since then.

970. Willis, Bonnie T. "The Living Tradition." *Mt. Life & Work* 5 (Oct. 1929): 13–15.

Once each week there was a "Weavin' Day" at Penland, North Carolina, during which about 50 mountain women came to learn new designs and take home materials to weave during the week. There was much visiting and exchanging of personal news on "Weavin' Day."

971. Winter, Oakley, "Vesta, A 'Modern' Woman." *Mt. Life & Work* 40 (Winter 1965): 31–32.

Winter writes of her Tennessee grandmother, a strong woman who raised a large family. She had a keen mind and made it her business to keep track of the yield of the land as well as every detail of her household.

972. "With Looms in Their Homes." *Mt. Life & Work* 45 (Nov. 1969): 14–17.

Art teacher Naoma Powell created a craft center that enables mountain women to earn money from their woven products.

973. Witt, Matt. *In Our Blood*. New Market, Tenn.: Highlander Research Center, 1979.

A book of photographs and text about four coal mining families. In each case, the woman's point of view is given along with that of her husband.

974. "Women." *Mt. Life & Work* 48 (Nov. 1972): 3–8.

Letters from women who attended "A Weekend for Women" in West Virginia, and interviews with four women who have been active workers in the mountains.

975. "Women Stop School Busses." *Mt. Life & Work* 54 (Oct. 1978): 9–10.

An account of the women in Harlan County, Kentucky, who blocked school bus routes in an effort to stop Jericol Mines' armored trucks traveling the roads after a school bus was caught in the line of fire. This action shows the women changing to a more aggressive, militant stance, instead of staying home and letting the men do most of the fighting.

976. Wyker, Mossie Allman. "Yes! There Is Hope for Rural Appalachia." *World Call* 49 (Nov. 1967): 21–22.

Anna Hobbs, wife and mother of four, is the motivating force in developing her community, Kerby Knob, Kentucky.

Migrants

977. Alexander, Patricia. "I Am Home." *Appal. Women* 1 (Fall 1979): 17.

The poet, a Tennessee woman, writes this poem about living in Chicago and traveling home to the hills and her mother.

978. Ansley, Fran, and Thrasher, Sue. "The Ballad of Barney Graham." *Sou. Expos.* 4, no. 1 & 2 (1976): 137–42.

An interview with the woman who wrote the ballad about her father gives us an insight into her own character. She talks about the United Mine Workers, her father's death at the hands of company thugs, the hardships she and her family endured, and their migration to Ohio.

979. "Appalachian Women?" *Mt. Life & Work* 52 (Aug. 1976): 22–23.

In addition to problems of housing, employment, and education, mountain women in the city must deal with stereotypes about Appalachian people which are often reinforced by the media.

980. Arnow, Harriette S. *The Dollmaker.* New York: Macmillan, 1954.

This modern fiction classic reveals the characteristics of mountain women in a clear, forceful, and honest manner. Gertie Nevels is forced to move to industrial Detroit during World War II, and finds living conditions much worse than in the mountains. Arnow shows the mountain woman's inability to speak up for herself against her husband's wishes.

981. Bell, Priscilla. "I'm Angry Again! I'm a Hillbilly." *Mt. Life & Work* 52 (Aug. 1976): 11–12.

A young woman who was raised in the hills writes with deep emotion about what it is like to be a hillbilly woman living in a modern city.

982. Brandstetter, Anne. "Mountain Teens Learn at East End School."
Youth Mag. 27 (Sept. 1976): 44–47.

Sue Schaeffer's parents were born and raised in Appalachia; the
family now lives in Cincinnati's East End. The article is about her
and others like her, migrants from the hills, attending the East
End Alternative School.

983. Brown, James S. "The Family behind the Migrant." *Mt. Life &
Work* 44 (Sept. 1968): 4–7.

A short article discussing the mountain family's strong ties. Men
and women move to urban centers to live and work, but they
never forget those left in the mountains.

984. Coles, Robert. "Mountain Dreams." *Women of Crisis: Lives of
Struggle and Hope*, by Robert Coles and Jane Hallowell Coles. New
York: Delacorte, 1978.

A native of Harlan County, Kentucky, Hannah Morgan now lives
in Dayton, Ohio. The chapter shows her sense of injustice and
also her relationship with her family, especially her teenage
daughter.

985. Darcy, Jean. "Paradox of Patricia Rodionoff-Peck." MAW 1
(Sept./Oct. 1977): 5–10.

An interview with a sculptor who returned to her small hometown
after years in a large city.

986. Dayton Human Relations Commission. *Southern Appalachian
Migration*. Dayton, O.: Dayton Human Relations Commission, 1966.

The alienation experienced by Appalachians who migrate to cities
in the North is the focus of this study.

987. Dillard, Colonel John H. "The Story of Rowena Roberts." *Mt.
Life & Work* 4 (Apr. 1928): 19–20, 31.

A true story of a North Carolina mountain girl who makes good.
Against many odds the lovely Rowena gets an education because,
through long years of hardship, she never gives up her dream.
After her schooling is completed she leaves her native hills, gets
work in a big city, and is very successful.

988. Edwards, Beth Rader. "Appalachian Women? Survival Is the
Game." *Mt. Life & Work* 52 (Aug. 1976): 22–23.

The Appalachian woman who comes to the city finds more problems than just those of housing, employment, and education. She
must contend with blatant stereotypes which confine her to an
almost subhuman status.

989. Gitlin, Todd, and Hollander, Nanci. *Uptown: Poor Whites in
Chicago*. New York: Harper & Row, 1970.

Migrants from Appalachia move into ghettolike neighborhoods in
large northern and midwestern cities such as Detroit, Indi-

anapolis, Chicago, and Columbus. This book about migrants to Chicago transcribes recorded conversations which give us a picture of the family, but especially of how the mountain woman copes in urban situations.

990. Hamburger, Robert, "A Stranger in the House." *Sou. Expos.* 5, no. 1 (1978): 22–31.

This article, part of a book in progress, looks at how black women from the South have fared as domestic workers in the North. Two women speak: one from Fayetteville, North Carolina, the other from Virginia.

991. Hudson, Elsie. "Their First Home, the Haunted House." *Appal. Heritage* 6 (Summer 1978): 14–16.

Hudson writes about her mother, Annie Anderson, age 82. Both women are revealed—the old woman and the younger one, who has migrated to Michigan.

992. Kahn, Kathy. *Hillbilly Women.* New York: Doubleday, 1972.

A series of taped, edited interviews with mountain women in Southern Appalachia and in some of the migrant ghettoes in northern cities. Nineteen women tell what it means to be a woman when you are poor, proud, and struggling to resist exploitation of your land and people.

993. Miller, Tommie. "Life of the Urban Appalachian Woman." *MAW* 1 (Sept./Oct. 1977): 12–14.

An impressionistic essay on the problems of Appalachian women who have migrated to northern cities.

994. Montgomery, Bill. "The Uptown Story." *Mt. Life & Work* 44 (Sept. 1968): 8–19.

The author writes about Chicago Southern Center in the Uptown area of the city. As many as 1,400 Appalachian migrants pass through the doors of the center during any month. Glimpses of women, their thoughts, and how they deal with reality, as well as details of the whole family as migrants.

995. Rasnic, Steve. "Cincinnati and It's Raining." *Mt. Rev.* 4 (Sept. 1978): 7.

The author says he wrote this prose-poem after seeing an old lady in "Hillbilly Ghetto," a hunting knife strapped on her belly. The old woman says in the poem: "In the country your hands could do something: rebuild a church . . . move the creek over your land."

996. Schwarzweller, Harry K.; Brown, James S.; and Mangalam, Joseph J. *Mountain Families in Transition: A Case Study of Migration.* University Park: Pennsylvania State Univ. Press, 1971.

A study of what happened when families migrated from Beech Creek, an isolated, subsistence-farming mountain area of Eastern

Kentucky, to northern cities. While the whole family is studied, the student of Appalachian women may find some useful things here.

997. Shackelford, Laurel. "Home." *Mt. Rev.* 1 (Sept. 1974): 5–6.
A Louisville woman compares city life to her prior life style in Floyd County, Kentucky.

998. Smith, Patrick. *Angel City.* St. Petersburg, Fl.: Valkyril, 1978.
In this novel, Jaret and Cloma Teeter sell their meager possessions and their wornout farm in the hills of West Virginia. Loading what they can take and their two children into a van they "hit the migrant trail" to Florida. In the harsh environment of the migrant life, the beautiful daughter becomes virtually a white slave and Cloma, pregnant with her third child, loses touch with reality.

999. Stahl, Ellen J. "Legal Abortion in Cincinnati and Appalachian Women." *MAW* 1 (July/Aug. 1978): 7–14.
The author is doing research on Appalachian women who migrate to Cincinnati. She tells about the abortion clinics, groups opposing legalized abortion, and where the Appalachian woman fits in between the two. A good look at how Appalachian women feel about children, abortions, and unwanted pregnancies.

1000. Terry, Peggy. "Our America: A Self-Portrait at 200: The Hillbilly." *Newsweek* 88 (July 4, 1976): 54, 61.
An interview with a woman originally from Kentucky and Oklahoma facing poverty and prejudice in Chicago.

1001. "Women's Alcoholism Center." *Mt. Life & Work* 50 (July/Aug. 1974): 7.
Nearly 1,000 women in a residential section of Cincinnati, including a number of migrants from the Appalachian mountains, have drinking problems. A drop-in center is being organized to help them.

Music

1002. Ansley, Fran and Thrasher, Sue. "The Ballad of Barney Graham." *Sou. Expos.* 4, no. 1 & 2 (1976): 137–42.
An interview with the woman who wrote the ballad about her father gives us an insight into her own character. She talks about

the United Mine Workers, her father's death at the hands of company thugs, the hardships she and her family endured, and their migration to Ohio.

1003. "Aunt Sal's Song." *Appal. Heritage* 1 (Spring 1973): 8–10.
The verses of this song are given, along with photographs of Uncle William Creech, Aunt Sally Creech, and handmade relics.

1004. Baker, Edna Ritchie. "Memories of Musical Moments." *Appal. Heritage* 5 (Summer 1977): 59–64.
The importance of music for the Ritchie family is discussed. Lyrics from several songs are included.

1005. Berman, Connie. "Dolly Parton Scrapbook." *Good Housekeeping* 188 (Feb. 1979): 140–43, 203–09.
Dolly Parton tells of her childhood in the Smokey Mountains of Tennessee, and how she was able to realize her dreams of being a superstar and having a great deal of money.

1006. Brown, Rick, and Thrasher, Sue. "Loretta Lynn." *Sou. Expos.* 2 (Spring/Summer 1974): 20, 22.
An interview with the singer, daughter of an Eastern Kentucky coal miner. She talks about her life as a mountain girl and woman, and her music and career. Her music is interwoven so closely into her life that when she speaks of one she is also telling of the other.

1007. Cooper, Wilma Lee. "You Can't Talk about Women in Country Music. . ." An interview by Alice Gerrard. *Sing Out!* 26, no. 2 (1977): 2–7.
Cooper says of her background: "Grandmother married a Ware and had four children, and the littlest one was six months old . . . when Grandfather died. My grandmother worked like a man." Cooper reveals her own character and those of her grandmother and mother.

1008. "Cora Whitaker of Whitaker's Music Store: Roots." *Mt. Life & Work* 51 (May 1975): 26–27.
Cora has operated a music store since 1948 in Jenkins, Kentucky.

1009. Dickens, Hazel. "Songs: Mannington Mine Disaster and Black Lung." *Mt. Life & Work* 47 (Apr. 1971): 10–13.
Dickens provides words and music to her protest songs.

1010. _____. "As Country as I Could Sing." *Growin' Up Country*. Jim Axelrod, ed. Clintwood, Va.: Resource and Information Center, Council of the Southern Mountains, 1973.
Dickens talks with Alice Gerrard about life, being a woman, and singing country music.

1011. Dowda, Rus. *Appalachian Women in the 19th Century and*

Their Image in the Murder Ballads of the Times. Berea, Ky.: Council of the Southern Mountains, 1978.

The author was a Berea College senior who had done considerable research into the status of women.

1012. French, Katherine Jackson. Ballad Collection. Acc. no. 4, box 1, Southern Appalachian Archives. Berea Coll., Berea, Kentucky.

French spent years collecting ballads in the mountains. She came in contact with many women and stayed in their homes in her collecting trips. The ballad collection itself is a good source of the way women in Elizabethan England and Southern Appalachia were considered by society. The collection contains some correspondence and miscellaneous notes as well as a manuscript and the ballads themselves.

1013. Green, Archie, ed. "Aunt Molly Jackson Memorial Issue." *Ky. Folklore Rec.* 7 (Oct./Dec. 1961): 129–75.

A discographic compilation of works about this remarkable singer and songwriter from the mountains. Alan Lomax, Zonweise Stein, John Greenway, and D. K. Wilgus pay warm tribute to her. "I have brought to light the first in print vignette . . . by the late Ben Robertson . . . the folklorist who knew her best. [Mary Elizabeth Barnicle] has much to offer about her friend."

1014. Gunning, Sarah. "My Name is Sarah Ogan Gunning. . . ." *Sing Out!* 25, no. 2 (1976): 15–16.

A songwriter and singer of traditional songs writes about her life in the coal-mining counties of southeastern Kentucky.

1015. Horacek, Jeannie. "Women's Music." *Mt. Life & Work* 48 (Nov. 1972): 7.

In October 1972, the Women's Band traveled to Webster Springs, West Virginia, for the "Weekend for Women." The author discusses the importance of music for those in the women's movement.

1016. Lawrence, Randy. " 'Make a Way Out of Nothing.' One Black Woman's Trip from North Carolina to the McDowell County Coalfields." *Goldenseal* 5, no. 4 (Oct./Dec. 1979): 27–30.

An interview with a black woman who worked in a tobacco factory in North Carolina before her family migrated to the coal fields of West Virginia. She worked in various jobs, sang in church choirs, and had a firm belief that God takes care of His children.

1017. Ledford, Lily May. "The Role of Women in Country Music." *Sing Out!* 25, no. 2 (1976): 4–5.

Ledford, a member of the original Coon Creek Girls Band, speaks about the role of women in country music. Hers was the first women's singing group to break into commercial country music.

1018. Lynn, Loretta, with Vecsey, George. *Loretta Lynn: Coal Miner's Daughter.* Chicago: Regnery, 1976.

The singer's life from its beginning in Eastern Kentucky to stardom in Nashville. The book was made into a motion picture which was released in 1980.

1019. Reece, Florence. "Which Side Are You On?" *Sou. Expos.* 4, no. 1 & 2 (1976): 90.

A brief account of the author's background as daughter and wife of a miner, and how her famous song of that title came to be written.

1020. Reeves, Florence. "A Kentucky Ballad Singer." *Mt. Life & Work* 12 (Jan. 1937): 18–19.

A short article about Aunt Phronnie, a mountain woman who sang ballads and songs "from the old country" of Scotland. It reveals her life style and the many ways she used her skills in raising sheep and children and gathering medicinal herbs, singing her ballads all the while.

1021. Riddle, Almeda. *A Singer and Her Song.* Baton Rouge: Louisiana State Univ. Press, 1970.

The author is a noted singer of traditional ballads. A good glimpse into her background and life.

1022. Ritchie, Edna. "The Singing Ritchies." *Mt. Life & Work* 29 (Summer 1953): 6, 8–10.

The Ritchies are among the most famous singing families of the Southern Highlands. Edna, one of the daughters, tells what it was like growing up as one of the Ritchies.

1023. Ritchie, Jean. *Singing Family of the Cumberlands.* New York: Oxford Univ. Press, 1955; Oak Publications, 1963.

A charming, tender, delightfully humorous account of the well-known folksinger's growing-up years in Appalachia, her family, her friends, and people in the community.

1024. _____. "Now Is the Cool of the Day." *Mt. Life & Work* 46 (May 1970): 3–11.

Ritchie talks about her childhood in Eastern Kentucky, stripmining and the destruction of the region, and the joys of living as expressed in one song, "Now Is the Cool of the Day."

1025. _____. *Jean Ritchie Celebration of Life: Her Songs... Her Poems.* New York: Geordie, 1971.

A collection of music, poems, and songs, and photographs of Ritchie and her family in Eastern Kentucky.

1026. _____. "Black Waters." *Appal. Heritage* 1 (Summer 1973): 53–54.

Ritchie, noted folksinger and author, shares her feelings about the strip-mining in Perry County—her homeplace—in the words and music of this protest song.

1027. Ross-Robertson, Lola. "Ida L. Reed: 1864–1951; Barbour County Hymn Writer, Poet." *Goldenseal* 2 (Oct./Dec. 1976): 25–32.
   A brief biography of a remarkable woman and some selections from her writings.

1028. Stanley, Len. "Custom Made Woman Blues." *Sou. Expos.* 4 (Winter 1977): 92–93.
   Interviews with Hazel and Alice, a folksinging duo especially liked by women. Hazel was born and raised in West Virginia and worked in a textile mill before she got into folksinging. Her partner is a college-educated folksinger from Los Angeles.

1029. "The Two Sisters." James Watt Raine, collector. *Mt. Life & Work* 1 (Apr. 1925): 28.
   Mountain women heard their mothers and grandmothers sing this song, and they in turn sing it to their own children. Ballads such as this one formed the basis of many a romantic dream by mountain maidens.

1030. Thomas, Jean. *Devil's Ditties.* Chicago: Hatfield, 1931.
   Stories of people in the Kentucky mountains and how music plays a role in their lives. The author writes of special occasions such as weddings, births, deaths, and court days. Some of these stories depict the mountain women.

1031. ———. *The Sun Shines Bright.* New York: Prentice-Hall, 1940.
   The autobiography of Jean Thomas, the "Traipsin' Woman," who collected mountain ballads and songs.

1032. Tribe, Ivan M. *Molly O'Day, Lynn Davis, and the Cumberland Mountain Folks: A Bio-Discography.* Los Angeles: John Edwards Memorial Foundation, Univ. of California, 1975.
   Molly O'Day, a mountain woman, was a very successful country singer who studied the religions of the world and decided to become a preacher.

1033. Trivette, Janese. "Sing Me Back Home before I Die." *Plow*, Aug. 1976, 5–6, 14.
   An interview with Ruth and Lehman Stamper at their home in Poor Valley, Virginia. They talk about their hillside farm, the handcrafted items they make to sell, and their music. They also sing a number of songs for the author.

1034. West, Hedy. "No Fiddle in My Home." *Sing Out!* 26, no. 5 (1978): 2–6.
   This internationally known performer of songs from her native folk and other traditions writes about her grandmother, Lillie West, a folk singer from a singing family.

1035. "Which Side Are You On?" *Mt. Life & Work* 48 (Mar. 1972): 22–24.
   An interview with Florence Reece, who tells about her early years

and the coal-mining conditions behind her labor song "Which Side Are You On?" which tells of the conflict between union men and company thugs.

1036. Williams, Cratis. "Hedy West: Songbird of the Appalachians." *Appal. South* 1 (Summer 1965): 8–11.

Williams, a folk singer in his own right, writes with perception and clarity about folksinger Hedy West and her people, mountaineers since the American Revolution.

1037. Williams, Richard. "Omie Wise." *Ky. Folklore Rec.* 23 (Jan./ Mar. 1977): 7–11.

The ballad of Omie Wise is about a pregnant young woman who is murdered by her lover—a typical ballad showing the notorious double standard at work.

1038. "Women's Voices: Thoughts on Women's Music in America." *Sing Out!* 25, no. 2 (1976): 3–6.

A good article profiling some noted women, especially Lily May Ledford, one of the original Coon Creek Girls at Renfro Valley, Kentucky.

Oral History

Note: All items in this section consist of tapes and transcripts. The place listed in the heading indicates where the tape is deposited. Tapes and transcripts can be obtained by writing to the campus director of the Appalachian Oral History Project at the school that conducted the interview.

1039. Adams, Malinda. Emory, Va.: Emory and Henry Coll. Aug. 1973. 60 min.; 12 pp. Cynthia Legard, interviewer.

Adams was born in 1920 and lives in Saltville, Virginia. She discusses her role as a housewife, her crocheting and quilting, railroads, and box socials.

1040. Adkins, Susie. Pippa Passes, Ky.: Alice Lloyd Coll. Aug. 9, 1972. 20 min.; 14 pp. Don Sparkman, interviewer.

Adkins has lived on a farm all her life and remembers the community as it was years ago—early transportation, courting, soap making, and home remedies. She talks about the Depression and tells some Indian tales.

1041. Aldridge, Byrd. Boone, N.C.: Appalachian State Univ. June 11, 1974. 45 min.; 27 pp. Barbara Greenberg, interviewer.

Aldridge talks about her Foscoe, North Carolina, home. She speaks of tourists, the selling of mountain land, and land prices. She describes a typical summer day in her childhood.

1042. Allen, Alice. Jackson, Ky.: Lee's Junior Coll. June 15, 1972. 30 min.; 18 pp. Ron Allen, interviewer.

Allen talks at length about the Depression in the mountains and how people have changed since that time. "They have so much now; they've forgot all about their neighbors, the Lord, and everything else."

1043. Anderson, Ada. Jackson, Ky.: Lee's Junior Coll. Feb. 22, 1972. 60 min.; 33 pp. Sari Tudiver, interviewer.

Anderson was born in 1895 and died in 1974. She is a Breathitt County, Kentucky, housewife and gives detailed accounts of the Highland School and community, land tenure, and church activities.

1044. Arnette, Meda. Pippa Passes, Ky.: Alice Lloyd Coll. Jan. 16, 1971. 30 min.; 14 pp. Sue Richards and Kathy Hembry, interviewers.

This Magoffin County, Kentucky, woman talks about her education as a child, going to school, and politics. She also comments on early community gatherings and the Appalachian region.

1045. Ashley, Polly. Pippa Passes, Ky.: Alice Lloyd Coll. Dec. 31, 1971. 30 min.; 9 pp. Curtis Caudill, interviewer.

Ashley tells about her childhood, making molasses, and early health care; she also mentions politics and working in Detroit. She was 81 when interviewed.

1046. Ayers, Mrs. Floyd C. Boone, N.C.: Appalachian State Univ. July 17, 1973. 45 min.; 30 pp. Donna Clawson, interviewer.

Ayers, a retired schoolteacher, discusses education and her various teaching positions. She talks about the early days at Appalachian State University and the qualifications for teaching then.

1047. Baird, Bertha. Boone, N.C.: Appalachian State Univ. June 25, 1973. 30 min.; 12 pp. Tommy Pursley, interviewer.

Baird, a North Carolina housewife, was born in 1880. She discusses at some length childhood memories, education, politics, voting, the fight for the vote for women, and the time she migrated to Oklahoma.

1048. Barnett, Dora. Jackson, Ky.: Lee's Junior Coll. Mar. 9, 1972. 150 min.; 68 pp. Sari Tudiver, interviewer.

Barnett worked at the election polls until 1971. Included are details of her family history and how a family of eleven was supported off the land and their livestock. She talks about shuck-

and feather-beds, gin mills, county politics, and mountain people.

1049. Bays, Alice. Pippa Passes, Ky.: Alice Lloyd Coll. July 27, 1973. 45 min.; 17 pp. Luther Frazier, interviewer.

Bays talks about farming, farm methods, planting by the signs of the zodiac, camping, soap-making, and smoking meat.

1050. Bingham, Grace. Boone, N.C.: Appalachian State Univ. July 23, 1973. 50 min.; 24 pp. Carolyn Shelton, interviewer.

Bingham is a retired postmistress. She gives a history of her community and discusses her childhood and the Depression.

1051. Bingham, Virginia O. Emory, Va.: Emory and Henry Coll. July 1973. 40 min.; 9 pp. Ann Henderson, interviewer.

Bingham is a member of the board of directors of the Progressive Community Club of Washington County, Virginia. She talks about the club and the Office of Economic Opportunity.

1052. Booker, Elizabeth. Emory, Va.: Emory and Henry Coll. Sept. 1973. 60 min.; 19 pp. Jeanne Seay, interviewer.

Booker talks about the old convent in Abingdon, Swedenborgian Church, and the old Abingdon fairgrounds.

1053. Bradley, Margaret J. Emory, Va.: Emory and Henry Coll. July 1973. 60 min.; 8 pp. Dan Matthews and Kathy Shearer, interviewers.

Bradley talks about old businesses and families of Abingdon, Stonewall Jackson Institute, the Cave House, Stuart Cattle Ranch, and Sinking Springs Presbyterian Church.

1054. Brown, Amanda. Emory, Va.: Emory and Henry Coll. June 1973. 60 min.; 3 pp. Shelia Hill, interviewer.

Brown talks about her early life and her family, crafts, superstitions, the Depression, church hymns, and keeping money.

1055. Brown, Pearl. Jackson, Ky.: Lee's Junior Coll. n.d. Anna Pellat, Sandy Miller, Phyllis Williams, interviewers.

Brown talks about the first train into Hazard, coal camps, and how the scrip system worked.

1056. Bryant, Aunt Easter. Pippa Passes, Ky.: Alice Lloyd Coll. July 28, 1972. 60 min.; 38 pp. Kathy Fleming and Kathy Burke, interviewers.

Bryant, a native of Letcher County, Kentucky, and daughter of "Devil" John Wright, talks about her early childhood, religion, and transportation. She tells stories about the Ku Klux Klan and moonshining, and also discusses and defends her father's actions.

1057. Burke, Flotilla. Pippa Passes, Ky.: Alice Lloyd Coll. June 29, 1973. 75 min.; 23 pp. Luther Frazier, interviewer.

Burke discusses social activities such as dating, corn-shucking, and the Fourth of July celebrations, crafts, canning, and making soap and molasses.

1058. Burke, Hattie Mae. Pippa Passes, Ky.: Alice Lloyd Coll. June 22, 1972. 37 min.; 23 pp. Dennis Ray King, interviewer.

Burke is a Floyd County, Kentucky, merchant. She talks at length about her family, childhood, schooling, dating, and the simpler way of life in the past. She discusses politics and religion both of which mean a great deal to her. "I say there's two things I was, an Old Regular Baptist and a Democrat."

1059. Burke, Sophia. Pippa Passes, Ky.: Alice Lloyd Coll. June 27, 1972. 20 min.; 6 pp. Dennis King, interviewer.

Burke, born in 1895, is a housewife and farmer. She recalls her childhood memories, education, quilting, soap making, and the Depression.

1060. Burnham, Mary. Boone, N.C.: Appalachian State Univ. Mar. 19, 1973. 60 min.; 32 pp. Lester Harmon, interviewer.

Burnham is bookkeeper for the Valle Crucis Mission School. She talks about her childhood and schooling, and the history of the Mission School.

1061. Byers, Lottie. Boone, N.C.: Appalachian State Univ. Aug. 21, 1974. 120 min.; 68 pp. Barbara Greenberg, interviewer.

Byers, a housewife, lives in Zionville, North Carolina. She discusses doctors and midwives, natural cures for sicknesses, migrating to Knoxville, politics, farming, and planting by the signs of the zodiac.

1062. Byrd, Mrs. Ben. Boone, N.C.: Appalachian State Univ. July 9, 1974. 60 min.; 41 pp. Barbara Greenberg, interviewer.

Byrd, a farmer's wife, talks about the farm, machinery, planting by the moon, the 1940 flood, spinning, and weaving.

1063. Campbell, Sina. Pippa Passes, Ky.: Alice Lloyd Coll. June 1, 1972. 20 min.; 12 pp. Don Sparkman, interviewer.

Campbell speaks about early schooling in an "old, big log schoolhouse . . . chimney halfway up the house, cracks you could pitch a dog through" She discusses community events, social events, and the Depression.

1064. Carpenter, Mattie Childers. Jackson, Ky.: Lee's Junior Coll. June 6, 1973. 23 min.; 15 pp. Dwight Haddix, interviewer.

Carpenter, of Breathitt County, comes from a family of nine children who moved to Kentucky from Virginia. She talks about her family's history and describes the hotels, stores, the ice plant, watching the log boom, and fires in the early days of Jackson.

1065. Caudill, Angeline. Pippa Passes, Ky.: Alice Lloyd Coll. Mar. 20, 1972. 25 min.: 7 pp. Vicki McCarty, interviewer.

Caudill was born in 1907 and resides in Cable, Ohio. She talks about the boardinghouse her parents ran in Paintsville, Kentucky, her childhood, church, medicine, outlaws, and how to kill and cure hogs.

1066. Caudill, Mr. & Mrs. Emery. Pippa Passes, Ky.: Alice Lloyd Coll. June 29, 1972. 25 min.: 12 pp. Dennis King, interviewer.

The Caudills, natives of Knott County, Kentucky, talk of their life together. Mr. Caudill speaks of mountain remedies, the union, and the Depression. Mrs. Caudill tells of her childhood, schooling, church, soap-making, and quilting. "My grandma told me, a woman wasn't no good if she didn't make about eight quilts before she got married. So, I made eight quilts, four was finished and four wasn't."

1067. Caudill, Martha. Pippa Passes, Ky.: Alice Lloyd Coll. 1971. 15 min.; 9 pp. Curtis Caudill, interviewer.

Martha Caudill talks about the one-room school, what her teachers were like, social events, and medical care.

1068. Chandler, Gypsie. Pippa Passes, Ky.: Alice Lloyd Coll. Mar. 22, 1973. Time unknown; 14 pp. Vicki McCarty, interviewer.

A schoolteacher and native of Lawrence County, Kentucky, Chandler talks about her personal history, her family's first car, the Depression, early doctors, education, deaths, and funerals.

1069. Childress, Mary Ann. Pippa Passes, Ky.: Alice Lloyd Coll. Oct. 19, 1973. 50 min.; 10 pp. Cora Lee Hairston, interviewer.

Childress is a Letcher County, Kentucky, housewife. She talks of her childhood, her philosophy of life, the church, the Bible, and God.

1070. Clark, Martha. Pippa Passes, Ky.: Alice Lloyd Coll. Sept. 5, 1971. 30 min.; 14 pp. Clara Higgins and Arnell Oden, interviewers.

Clark, a pastor for the Church of God in Letcher County, Kentucky, talks about how she got her third-grade education, and the segregation in the schools. She says blacks were allowed only up to the third grade and attended school three months out of the year, separate from the whites. She talks about her religious beliefs and what it's like being a woman preacher.

1071. Clark, Reely. Pippa Passes, Ky.: Alice Lloyd Coll. May 30, 1972. 30 min.; 11 pp. Carolyn Hunter, interviewer.

Clark tells of her childhood: "Mother would put me on the bed with the baby beside the fireplace to keep it warm and the other children was tied in chairs.... I've tended that baby many a time."

1072. Coffey, Lillie. Boone, N.C.: Appalachian State Univ. July 10, 1974. 45 min.; 31 pp. Glenn Knowles, interviewer.

Coffey talks about the history of Linville, North Carolina, and about quilting parties, doctors in the area, medicine, marriage, and family life.

1073. Cole, John, and Cole, Nola. Pippa Passes, Ky.: Alice Lloyd Coll. May 11, 1971. 30 min.; 24 pp. Kathy Shepherd, interviewer.

A retired miner and his wife talk about their youth, education, home remedies, doctors, and religion. They also give their views on mines, camps, camp life, social life, and planting crops by the signs of the moon. Mrs. Cole sings an old ballad at the end of the interview.

1074. Cole, Mattie. Emory, Va.: Emory and Henry Coll. June 1973. 45 min.; 8 pp. Cynthia Legard, interviewer.

Cole is a retired teacher. She discusses the history of Chilhowie, Virginia, education, organization, Martha Washington College, and home remedies.

1075. Cole, Maude P. Emory, Va.: Emory and Henry Coll. July 1973. 45 min.; 7 pp. Cynthia Legard, interviewer.

Cole is a Chilhowie, Virginia, housewife and retired school-teacher. She talks about her early life and family history, the Mill Creek Community, home remedies, and crafts.

1076. Cole, Virginia Irene. Emory, Va.: Emory and Henry Coll. July 1973. 25 min.; 6 pp. James H. Groseclose, interviewer.

Cole, who operates a farm, discusses her early life, schooling, customs, the Civil War, churches, and crafts.

1077. Collins, Grace. Jackson, Ky.: Lee's Junior Coll. Feb. 26, 1972. 40 min.; 15 pp. Alpha Jane Bailey, interviewer.

Collins is a mountain woman who went back to school after raising her family. She finished high school and college and began teaching at the age of 45. She talks about her struggles and her experiences trying to get an education.

1078. Collins, Madeline. Pippa Passes, Ky.: Alice Lloyd Coll. Dec. 28, 1971. 30 min.; 15 pp. Amy Collins, interviewer.

Madeline Collins migrated from the region to try to find better work, and later returned. She speaks of her family, her husband, and the two businesses they had: a truck mine and a sawmill.

1079. Collins, Mary. Pippa Passes, Ky.: Alice Lloyd Coll. Dec. 29, 1971. 60 min.; 23 pp. Amy Collins, interviewer.

Collins recalls experiences she had as a child, hardships in a one-room school, mining, and going to Alice Lloyd College.

1080. Combs, Blanche. Boone, N.C.: Appalachian State Univ. July 3, 1973. 75 min.; 24 pp. Carolyn Shelton, interviewer.

Combs, a schoolteacher, relates experiences she has had in teaching, discusses changes which have taken place in the educational system, and speaks of the time she migrated to the West, where she lived for a number of years.

1081. Combs, Nettie. Pippa Passes, Ky.: Alice Lloyd Coll. July 10, 1975. 50 min.; 17 pp.

Combs talks about the self-sufficiency of the farm, how to make maple syrup, molasses, and soap. She talks about doctors, midwives, and old-time preachers.

1082. Combs, Ollie. Pippa Passes, Ky.: Alice Lloyd Coll. Aug. 21, 1975. 40 min.; 20 pp. Ron Daley, interviewer.

Better known as Widow Combs, Ollie Combs gained national recognition in 1965 when she stood in front of a bulldozer to prevent the stripmining of her land. She discusses the reasons why she made her stand, the events leading to her arrests, the chances for a shoot-out, and the various conversations with other participants. She told the stripmine operators: "God did not make bulldozers to destroy what people have got and you are not going to destroy what I've got to get what you want under the ground."

1083. Conley, Lurania. Pippa Passes, Ky.: Alice Lloyd Coll. Sept. 17, 1971. 15 min.; 11 pp. Avery Chaffins, interviewer.

Conley tells how the women in her early life raised sheep and describes the process of making cloth. She describes how the women raised and preserved foods, churned butter, and made soap and home remedies.

1084. Cook, Anna Mae. Pippa Passes, Ky.: Alice Lloyd Coll. Aug. 5, 1973. 50 min.; 10 pp. Cora Lee Hairston, interviewer.

Cook talks about the differences between the Methodist and Holiness churches and tells why she joined the Holiness Church. She talks about faith healing.

1085. Cook, Lula. Pippa Passes, Ky.: Alice Lloyd Coll. May 30, 1972. 25 min.; 9 pp. Michiyo Cook, interviewer.

Cook, a housewife from Pike County, Kentucky, tells of her childhood, domestic activities, family, and politics. She also recalls when television, cars, and electricity reached her community.

1086. Cook, Nellie. Boone, N.C.: Appalachian State Univ. July 27, 1973. 45 min.; 26 pp. Karen Ward, interviewer.

Living in the Bamboo Community at Boone, Cook discusses her home, community, schools, and churches. She tells ghost stories and talks about witches and haunted houses.

1087. Couch, Marie Turner. Jackson, Ky.: Lee's Junior Coll. June 6, 1973. 30 min.; 12 pp. Wanda T. Miller, interviewer.

Couch was a schoolteacher for 39 years, mainly in one-room schools in Breathitt County, Kentucky, though she also taught in

Perry and Harlan counties. She describes conditions in a one-room school in Breathitt County around 1967. She believes one-room schools are far superior to the consolidated schools replacing them.

1088. Cozart, Eliza B. Emory, Va.: Emory and Henry Coll. Feb. 1974. 60 min.; 12 pp. Kathy Shearer, interviewer.

Cozart, an Abingdon, Virginia, housewife, talks about the tobacco business in Washington County and the tobacco market begun by her husband.

1089. Creighton, Mildred. Pippa Passes, Ky.: Alice Lloyd Coll. Sept. 27, 1971. 15 min.; 6 pp. Dennis Cook and Kenny Slone, interviewers.

Creighton is a Knott County, Kentucky, librarian. She talks about the school system when she was a child, the games the children played, superstitions, and home remedies.

1090. Critcher, Josie. Boone, N.C.: Appalachian State Univ. Aug. 8, 1973. 20 min.; 18 pp. Karen Ward, interviewer.

Critcher talks about religion, the Depression, quilting, crocheting, politics, and schools.

1091. Daniels, Thelma. Pippa Passes, Ky.: Alice Lloyd Coll. July 7, 1972. 30 min.; 10 pp. Don Sparkman, interviewer.

Daniels discusses education, churches, and politics. Most of the interview is about welfare. "We're putting a second generation of people in that program," she says, "and that's a terrible way of life."

1092. Davidson, Mattie. Pippa Passes, Ky.: Alice Lloyd Coll. July 7, 1973. 15 min.; 4 pp. Connie Sargent, interviewer.

Davidson talks about her life and the life of the community during the Depression.

1093. Davis, Brenda. Pippa Passes, Ky.: Alice Lloyd Coll. June 26, 1974. 25 min.; 12 pp. Luther Frazier, interviewer.

Davis was raised in Floyd County, Kentucky, but migrated to Ann Arbor, Michigan. She talks about why she moved, problems encountered, meeting black people, and the jobs she held.

1094. Davis, Margaret R. Emory, Va.: Emory and Henry Coll. July 1973. 30 min.; 7 pp. Jeanne Seay, interviewer.

Davis tells about attending Stonewall Jackson Institute and talks about the Tennessee Lumber Company and the Andrew Russell house.

1095. Day, Panny Hogg. Pippa Passes, Ky.: Alice Lloyd Coll. 1971. 50 min.; 28 pp. Ricky Day, interviewer.

Day talks about her childhood and self-sufficiency, transportation, superstitions, and the 1927 flood. She also tells several amusing stories.

1096. Drake, Sarah. Jackson, Ky.: Lee's Junior Coll. Jan. 5, 1972. 60 min.; 25 pp. Kathy Carroll, interviewer.

Drake raised eight children by farming and selling pine roping and decorations for Christmas. She has exciting stories of life in a coal camp, going hunting with the men, election fights, the Depression, and tobacco crops.

1097. Dungan, Mildred W. Emory, Va.: Emory and Henry Coll. Jan. 1974. 105 min.; 15 pp. Bill Patterson and Peggy Cartwright, interviewers.

Dungan talks about Damascus, Virginia, during her childhood, education, transportation, and Martha Washington College.

1098. Dunn, Grace. Jackson, Ky.: Lee's Junior Coll. June 1972. 60 min.; 49 pp. Diane Schiffer, interviewer.

Dunn is an articulate mountain woman. She talks about midwifery, making lye soap, blacksmithing, and the Free Will Baptist Church.

1099. Edmisten, Loura. Boone, N.C.: Appalachian State Univ. June 9, 1973. 20 min.; 10 pp. Karen Ward, interviewer.

Edmisten talks about her family, schools, religion, politics, and transportation. She also discusses entertainment, crafts, and courting.

1100. Edmondson, Margaret Cole. Emory, Va.: Emory and Henry Coll. Aug. 1973. 40 min.; 8 pp. James H. Groseclose, interviewer.

Edmondson is a retired schoolteacher and merchant. She talks about education, running a hardware store, and her early life.

1101. Eggers, Lela. Boone, N.C.: Appalachian State Univ. July 22, 1974. 60 min.; 48 pp. Barbara Greenberg, interviewer.

Eggers, who lives at Beaver Dam Community in Vilas, North Carolina, talks about the 1940 flood, how to dry food to preserve it, home remedies, folktales, digging roots, and what winters are like in the mountains.

1102. Ehle, June. Pippa Passes, Ky.: Alice Lloyd Coll. July 12, 1972. 45 min.; 22 pp. Carolyn Hunter, interviewer.

Ehle talks about clothes being rationed, schools, coal mines, stamps, the WPA, using newspapers for wallpaper, and working at anything to get food for her family.

1103. Farthing, Maude. Boone, N.C.: Appalachian State Univ. Mar. 20, 1974. 60 min.; 38 pp. Laura Dawkins and Mike McNeely, interviewers.

Farthing talks about her community, schools, churches, prominent families, log rollings, threshers, and corn-shuckings.

1104. Feltner, Angeline. Pippa Passes, Ky.: Alice Lloyd Coll. June 4, 1972. 50 min.; 34 pp. Timothy Morris, interviewer.

Feltner remembers her childhood, her early life on the farm, the one-room school she attended, transportation, making molasses and soap, curing meat, courting, and home remedies.

1105. Fields, Lonnie. Pippa Passes, Ky.: Alice Lloyd Coll. Aug. 9, 1973. Time unknown; 13 pp. Hester Mullins, interviewer.
The interview covers life on the farm in the mountains and Fields's childhood.

1106. Fitch, Mae. Pippa Passes, Ky.: Alice Lloyd Coll. Nov. 27, 1971. 20 min.; 14 pp. Avery Chaffins, interviewer.
Fitch talks about her family, including her grandfather who lived to be 102 years old. She attended a one-room school as a child and mentions some of the games the children played.

1107. Foster, Emma. Pippa Passes, Ky.: Alice Lloyd Coll. June 16, 1971. 20 min.; 8 pp. Kenny Slone and Josia Ann Dye, interviewers.
Foster was 81 years old when interview took place. She talks about her family life, education, home remedies, religion, and the community of Drift.

1108. Foster, Lilly. Pippa Passes, Ky.: Alice Lloyd Coll. Feb. 20, 1972. 17 min.; 12 pp. Stephen Peake, interviewer.
Foster spent her childhood in Alabama and the last 52 years in Kentucky. She talks about her family life and her husband, a miner. She says of the Depression: "We had a certain day to get something to eat. We had to go line up like cows. I never did get in that line."

1109. Foutes, Leona. Pippa Passes, Ky.: Alice Lloyd Coll. July 25, 1975. 180 min.; pp unknown. Joey Elswick, interviewer.
A teacher for 30 years, Foutes talks about education, early campus life at Alice Lloyd College, the college's contribution to the mountains, and her philosophy.

1110. Frazier, Bertha. Pippa Passes, Ky.: Alice Lloyd Coll. June 5, 1973. 40 min.; 21 pp. Luther Frazier, interviewer.
Frazier talks about her childhood, her personal history, farming, her education, religion, making soap and molasses, curing meat, and weaving. She also speaks of her husband's work in the mines.

1111. Frazier, Cora. Pippa Passes, Ky.: Alice Lloyd Coll. Dec. 19, 1973. 75 min.; 37 pp. Don and Laurel Anderson, interviewers.
Frazier talks about education in Letcher County, Kentucky. She discusses the trustee system and her experiences during her 40-year career as a teacher, and how her grandparents sold valuable mineral rights to coal companies.

1112. Fullerton, Eula. Emory, Va.: Emory and Henry Coll. June 1973. 45 min.; 22 pp. Ann Henderson, interviewer.
Fullerton is a retired welfare worker. She discusses her early life

and family, farming, education, Emory and Henry College, welfare programs in Washington County and Southwest Virginia, the poor farm, and the United Mine Workers.

1113. Gayheart, Bessie. Pippa Passes, Ky.: Alice Lloyd Coll. Nov. 21, 1975. 60 min.; 25 pp. Ron Daley, interviewer.
Gayheart is a Knott County, Kentucky, housewife and community activist. She talks about the welfare system and the problems and abuses she faced as a recipient. She also discusses her anti-stripmining activities, her fight against overweight coal trucks, and her opinion about an unfair political and educational system.

1114. Gillenwater, Hattie. Emory, Va.: Emory and Henry Coll. Aug. 1973. 25 min.; 5 pp. Jeanne Seay, interviewer.
Gillenwater discusses her father, who was a miller, moving by covered wagon, crafts, and preserving foods.

1115. Greene, Hattie Greer. Boone, N.C.: Appalachian State Univ. July 31, 1973. 50 min.; 20 pp. Donna Clawson, interviewer.
Greene talks about mountain crafts, including weaving and candle-making. She also makes comments on mountain home remedies such as boneset and catnip teas.

1116. Greene, Mary Glenn. Emory, Va.: Emory and Henry Coll. June 1973. 30 min.; 7 pp. Shelia Hill, interviewer.
Greene was a domestic worker. She discusses the Plum Creek community, her family, church, crafts, and the Depression.

1117. Greer, Viola. Boone, N.C.: Appalachian State Univ. June 14, 1973. 45 min.; 22 pp. Karen Ward, interviewer.
Greer's interview includes information about her birthplace, her family, and her education. She also discusses religion in some detail, and preachers, music in the church, and church dinners.

1118. Gwyn, Louise L. Emory, Va.: Emory and Henry Coll. Aug. 1973. 45 min.; 12 pp. Cynthia Legard, interviewer.
A Marion, Virginia, housewife, Gwyn talks about her early life and family, education, churches, crafts, farming, and herb gathering.

1119. Hager, Frances (Granny). Pippa Passes, Ky.: Alice Lloyd Coll. Jan. 3, 1973. 105 min.; 44 pp. Mike Mullins, interviewer.
Granny Hager discusses many things: her family, childhood, education, and various jobs held. She talks in great detail about the Depression, politicians, and unionization in Harlan and Perry counties. Granny Hager died in 1975.

1120. Hall, Becky. Pippa Passes, Ky.: Alice Lloyd Coll. June 15, 1973. 60 min.; 40 pp. Diana Hall, interviewer.
Hall discusses her family life along with comments on the elections, home cooking, black lung, welfare, unions, farm life, early

transportation, and Hoover as President ("liked to starved to death that summer"). Hall also speaks of the lighter side of life and games the children used to play.

1121. Hall, Gladys. Pippa Passes, Ky.: Alice Lloyd Coll. June 15, 1971. 13 min.; 13 pp. Millie Hall and Carter Hall, interviewers.

Hall, a schoolteacher who lives in Knott County, Kentucky, talks about teaching in a one-room school. She also discusses her childhood and the community, and law enforcement.

1122. Hall, Julia. Jackson, Ky.: Lee's Junior Coll. May 1972. 45 min.; 16 pp. Ron Allen, interviewer.

Hall is a housewife, gardener, and cook at Lee's Junior College. She tells of the hardships her family survived during the Depression, gives the Hall family history, and talks about the change in churches, people, and communities.

1123. Hall, Nora. Pippa Passes, Ky.: Alice Lloyd Coll. June 10, 1971. 25 min.; 13 pp. Millie Hall and Carter Hall, interviewers.

Hall is a Knott County, Kentucky, housewife, though she was born and raised in Letcher County. She talks about her education in a two-room school, her childhood, and social events.

1124. Hamby, Maude. Boone, N.C.: Appalachian State Univ. Jan. 23, 1973. 50 min.; 18 pp. Alex Greene, interviewer.

This Deep Gap, North Carolina, woman talks about hunting, railroads, homemade medicines, and the Depression. She and her husband discuss cattle, work in the coal mines, land, family background, food, and their opinions of life today.

1125. Hampton, Edith. Boone, N.C.: Appalachian State Univ. Aug. 14, 1973. 25 min.; 20 pp. Karen Ward, interviewer.

Hampton discusses religion, the Depression years, politics, political leaders, and home remedies.

1126. Hampton, Winifred. Boone, N.C.: Appalachian State Univ. July 31, 1973. 40 min.; pp. unknown. Karen Ward, interviewer.

Winifred Hampton is a saleswoman. She discusses schools, religion, her family history, politics, and outlaws of early times.

1127. Harris, Mattie Virginia. Emory, Va.: Emory and Henry Coll. May 1973. 20 min.; 3 pp. Dennis A. Harris, interviewer.

Harris describes herself as a housewife. She discusses Broadford community, stores, doctors, the Harris family, churches, and revivals.

1128. Hartley, Hazel. Boone, N.C.: Appalachian State Univ. Aug. 9, 1973. 35 min.; 19 pp. Karen Ward, interviewer.

Hartley discusses the many and varied aspects of the lives of Appalachian women. She talks about various jobs she has held, craft work, making medicines, and early utensils used in cooking and cleaning.

1129. Hayes, Flora T. Emory, Va.: Emory and Henry Coll. July 1973. 25 min.; 9 pp. Jerry Hill, interviewer.

Hayes talks about her early life and family from the standpoint of a member of a black community.

1130. Hays, Martha. Jackson, Ky.: Lee's Junior Coll. June 20, 1973. 30 min.; 8 pp. Archie Bowling, interviewer.

Hays talks about her early life and how her older brothers and sisters had to raise the younger ones when their mother died. She describes the old way in which mountain women washed clothes.

1131. Helton, Mary. Emory, Va.: Emory and Henry Coll. July 1973. 60 min.; 13 pp. Cynthia Legard, interviewer.

Helton is a housewife and a basket weaver. She talks about gypsies in the area, basket weaving, the Depression, remedies, education, churches, crafts, and cooking.

1132. Henderson, Ella V. Emory, Va.: Emory and Henry Coll. Dec. 1973. 105 min.; 15 pp. Kathy Shearer, interviewer.

Henderson, a Saltville, Virginia, storekeeper, talks about the Regular Baptist Church, the old store used as a voting place, and old hymns.

1133. Hill, Amy Rouse. Emory, Va.: Emory and Henry Coll. July 1973. 30 min.; 7 pp. James H. Groseclose, interviewer.

Hill, who was born in 1896, discusses early life and family, churches, education, customs, crafts, economic conditions, superstitions, and electricity.

1134. Hill, Elizabeth. Emory, Va.: Emory and Henry Coll. June 1973. 30 min.; 5 pp. Shelia Hill, interviewer.

Hill was employed at Glade Spring Products at the time of her interview. She talks about what it is like to be a member of a black community, her early life, and education.

1135. Holliday, Ethel. Pippa Passes, Ky.: Alice Lloyd Coll. Oct. 30, 1971. 10 min.; 7 pp. Gary Ferguson, interviewer.

Holliday was born in 1896 in Perry County, Kentucky. She talks about going to school, the teachers, and her husband, who is a sheriff. She goes into depth about the mines and the union.

1136. Hounshell, Callie. Jackson, Ky.: Lee's Junior Coll. Dec. 13, 1973. 10 min. 3 pp. Paulette King, interviewer.

Although the tape is short, it contains some excellent information about mountain superstitions, witches, healers, and planting by the signs of the moon.

1137. Hounshell, Josie. Jackson, Ky.: Lee's Junior Coll. June 1973. 40 min.; 26 pp. Benny Chandler, interviewer.

Josie Hounshell talks about a variety of subjects—wool pickings, bean stringings, log rollings, and how the community joined together to get work like this done. She also relates the hardships she faced having to raise children alone while making only 50 cents a day.

1138. Howell, Buena Ramsey. Pippa Passes, Ky.: Alice Lloyd Coll. June 28, 1971. Medda Campbell and Harriet Connor, interviewers.

Howell is a librarian in Breathitt County. When she was 10 years old, she came to Alice Lloyd College to go to school. She talks about classes, rules, and duties, and tells an amusing incident about a cure for the itch.

1139. Huff, Melvina. Pippa Passes, Ky.: Alice Lloyd Coll. June 8, 1973. 60 min.; 22 pp. Hester Mullins, interviewer.

Huff talks about elections: "First time women got to vote, I was tickled to death." She discusses moonshine, social life, parties and tales, and outlaws.

1140. Hunter, Dixie. Pippa Passes, Ky.: Alice Lloyd Coll. July 14, 1972. 30 min.; 7 pp. Carolyn Hunter, interviewer.

Dixie Hunter is a coal miner's wife and a coal miner's daughter. She talks about living in the mining camp and the unions.

1141. Isenhour, Bernice. Emory, Va.: Emory and Henry Coll. June 1973. 45 min.; 20 pp. James R. Martin, interviewer.

Isenhour, an employee at Fieldcrest Mills, discusses her early life and background, education, working, politics, voting, unionization, and the flood of 1937.

1142. Johnson, Edna Hensley. Jackson, Ky.: Lee's Junior Coll. Feb. 16, 1972. 30 min.; 10 pp. Gary Sewell and Jim Blazier, interviewers.

Johnson was born in 1904. She gives a brief family history of the Hensleys and Vires, and talks about her occupations as court recorder, seamstress, and merchant. Included are a Civil War story and some scenes her grandfather recalled of early Jackson.

1143. Johnson, Fronie. Pippa Passes, Ky.: Alice Lloyd Coll. July 27, 1971. 50 min.; 40 pp. Luther Frazier, interviewer.

Johnson lives in Floyd County, Kentucky. She discusses the doctors in the area, religion, home remedies, funerals, sewing, education, her personal history, and her work as a midwife.

1144. Johnson, Mary. Pippa Passes, Ky.: Alice Lloyd Coll. June 8, 1972. 40 min.; 13 pp. Jeff Reynolds, interviewer.

This Pike County native tells about her parents' move to Doron by wagon, the ministers, and her education in a one-room school.

1145. Johnson, Mary. Pippa Passes, Ky.: Alice Lloyd Coll. June 6, 1974. 30 min.; 13 pp. Timmy Mullins, interviewer.

A store owner for many years, Johnson talks about running the store, the Depression, and her early home life.

1146. Johnson, Virgie. Pippa Passes, Ky.: Alice Lloyd Coll. June 7, 1974. 20 min.; 11 pp. Luther Frazier, interviewer.

Johnson talks about the simpler life in the mountains, how important the family is, and the changes mining has brought to the community. She speaks very strongly against stripmining.

1147. Jordan, Lottie. Pippa Passes, Ky.: Alice Lloyd Coll. Oct. 25, 1971. 20 min.; 10 pp. Steven Peake, interviewer.

Jordan, born in Alabama in 1885, picked cotton for a while before she moved to Kentucky. "When the Yankees come and freed the colored people that's when a heap of folks got killed and it made spirits [ghosts]." She talks about ghosts, superstitions, home remedies, and early transportation.

1148. Joseph, Odessa Noble. Jackson, Ky.: Lee's Junior Coll. June 1972. 60 min.; 28 pp. Mary Lou Moore, interviewer.

Joseph, a retired schoolteacher, describes logging activities and the building of the L & N Railroad through Haddix, Kentucky, in 1910. She tells of people stealing food and children begging during the Depression, and comments on government programs, progress in education over the years, the 1927 flood, and summer graveyard meetings.

1149. Kidd, Josephine. Pippa Passes, Ky.: Alice Lloyd Coll. 1972. 40 min.; 15 pp. Doug McIntosh, interviewer.

Kidd was born in 1900. She talks about logging and the log house she lived in, recreation, the railroad, drilling for oil, elections, life in the coal camps, the Depression, and herbs and their uses.

1150. Kidd, Phoebe. Pippa Passes, Ky.: Alice Lloyd Coll. June 1, 1972. 60 min.; 17 pp. Carolyn Hunter, interviewer.

This Floyd County, Kentucky, native tells about her childhood—family, land, food, clothing. She gives some examples of witches and strange happenings, and discusses soap and molasses making, doctoring, and the Depression.

1151. Kincaid, Mrs. J. S. Boone, N.C.: Appalachian State Univ. Nov. 4, 1974. 105 min.; 62 pp. Jim Pippin, interviewer.

Kincaid, a retired schoolteacher, talks about her life, teaching school, her husband's work in the lumber industry, and the hauling and processing of timber.

1152. King, Ethel. Pippa Passes, Ky.: Alice Lloyd Coll. June 15, 1972. 25 min.; 8 pp. Donald Hall and Dennis King, interviewers.

King, of Knott County, Kentucky, tells about her life on a farm and how to make butter.

1153. Kolling, Ruth D. Emory, Va.: Emory and Henry Coll. July 1973. 30 min.; 11 pp. Ann Henderson, interviewer.

Kolling was born in 1895. She talks very articulately about welfare work in Washington and Russell counties, her family, the Council of the Southern Mountains, and Berea College.

1154. Landrum, Hazel. Jackson, Ky.: Lee's Junior Coll. Sept. 1973. 30 min.; 13 pp. Dwight Haddix, interviewer.

Landrum is a retired nurse. She worked with the Breathitt County Health Department for several years and discusses in detail the enjoyment and fulfillment her work gave her and the role she had in the polio epidemic. She recalls her experiences in the 1957 flood, and various means of transportation in Breathitt's early days.

1155. Landrum, Sarena. Jackson, Ky.: Lee's Junior Coll. Sept. 1973. 60 min.; 32 pp. Sari Tudiver, interviewer.

A retired schoolteacher, Landrum speaks of churches and having services in her home, teaching in a one-room school, and free schools. She remembers visiting Lexington during the Spanish-American War, and soldiers marching from Salyersville to Jackson. She also talks about Hoover days and gives details of the bank closings and how they affected commodities and businesses. Landrum was born in 1877 and died in 1975.

1156. Lightfoot, Lena. Jackson, Ky.: Lee's Junior Coll. Sept. 15, 1975. 45 min.; 12 pp. Jack Williams and Janie Mills, interviewers.

Lightfoot tells what it is like to be a black schoolteacher in Kentucky. She talks about her family history and the role of the church in her life.

1157. Little, Lura. Emory, Va.: Emory and Henry Coll. June 1973. 15 min.; 6 pp. Cynthia Legard, interviewer.

Little discusses the Depression and its effect on Tazewell, Virginia. She also discusses superstitions and farming.

1158. Lowe, Margaret. Emory, Va.: Emory and Henry Coll. May 1974. 60 min.; 6 pp. Mary Harrison, interviewer.

Lowe, a retired domestic worker, talks about her early life, family, education, and job opportunities.

1159. Lowe, Margaret P. and Lowe, Booker. Emory, Va.: Emory and Henry Coll. July 1973. 30 min.; 7 pp. Mary Harrison, interviewer.

Mr. & Mrs. Lowe talk about the Depression, education, the WPA and the CCC, and race relations from the viewpoint of black members of a community.

1160. Lowrance, Aggie. Boone, N.C.: Appalachian State Univ. June 26, 1974. 60 min.; 33 pp. Barbara Greenberg, interviewer.

Lowrance, a craftswoman, discusses the Blue Ridge Hearthside Crafts Association and her involvement with it. She also relates much of the history of the Valle Crucis Mission School and talks about weaving, spinning, and the craft-designing process.

1161. McKee, Francis M. Emory, Va.: Emory and Henry Coll. Aug. 1973. 90 min.; 18 pp. Laura Stevenson, interviewer.

McKee is a retired schoolteacher. She talks about her family, teaching in the area, one-room schools, farm life, transportation, canning, preserving foods, and churches.

1162. Madden, Bertie. Pippa Passes, Ky.: Alice Lloyd Coll. June 3, 1975. 40 min.; pp. unknown. Darrell Madden, interviewer.
Madden primarily talks about food and gives recipes.

1163. Madden, Charlotte. Pippa Passes, Ky.: Alice Lloyd Coll. June 10, 1971. 60 min.; 14 pp. Harriet Connor and Medda Campbell, interviewers.
Madden talks about Alice Lloyd and the college, the area before Mrs. Lloyd came, how she was received, and her influence in the early days.

1164. Manley, Evelyn. Emory, Va.: Emory and Henry Coll. July 1973. 45 min.; 6 pp. Laura Stevenson, interviewer.
Evelyn Manley, now retired, talks about her early life and her family, teaching in a one-room school, and her nursing career.

1165. Martin, Marie. Pippa Passes, Ky.: Alice Lloyd Coll. June 18, 1971. 60 min.; 24 pp. Carter Hall, interviewer.
Martin talks about her education and self-sufficient living on the farm, her family, social events, the community, transportation, and elections.

1166. Mullins, Alva. Pippa Passes, Ky.: Alice Lloyd Coll. June 23, 1971. 20 min.; 13 pp. Millie Hall, interviewer.
Mullins is the wife of a coal miner. She talks about her youth, her brief school career, community occupations, recreation, and transportation.

1167. Mullins, Hester. Pippa Passes, Ky.: Alice Lloyd Coll. Nov. 15, 1975. 60 min.; 27 pp. Ron Daley, interviewer.
Mullins is a student and former Oral History worker. She discusses the differences between life in the mountains and in Lexington, where she goes to school. She describes Appalachian culture, biases against Appalachians, and the stereotypes of mountain people.

1168. Mullins, June. Pippa Passes, Ky.: Alice Lloyd Coll. June 9, 1973. 40 min.; 10 pp. Hester Mullins, interviewer.
The interview with Mullins covers such topics as planting seeds, food preservation, and peddling crops.

1169. Mullins, Sylvania. Jackson, Ky.: Lee's Junior Coll. June 16, 1973. 60 min.; 19 pp. Sari Tudiver and Norma Strong, interviewers.
Mullins, from Breathitt County, Kentucky, talks extensively of her experiences as a midwife, and gives an account of cooking in a coal-camp car and working in a canning factory.

1170. Napier, Rhoda. Pippa Passes, Ky.: Alice Lloyd Coll. Aug. 14, 1972. 50 min.; 51 pp. Sandra Richter, interviewer.

Born in 1901, Rhoda Napier lives in Floyd County, Kentucky. She talks about her early home life, school days, churches, courting, superstitions, and politics, about making soap and molasses, hunting for ginseng, snakeroot, and May apples, and the prices for these things.

1171. Neace, Leanna Napier. Jackson, Ky.: Lee's Junior Coll. June 1972. 30 min.: 26 pp. Debbie Davison and Philip Sheffel, interviewers.

An articulate mountain woman talks about the Noble family history (her mother's), tells a Civil War story, and talks about the Ku Klux Klan, hard farm work, hogs and geese being driven through the mountains, and the rivers black with log rafts.

1172. Noble, Julia. Pippa Passes, Ky.: Alice Lloyd Coll. Nov. 11, 1971. 15 min.; 11 pp. Clara Higgins, interviewer.

Noble was raised in Alabama and migrated to Kentucky when she was an adult. She discusses the Depression, superstitions, and race relations, and tells some ghost stories.

1173. Pettis, Georgette W. Emory, Va.: Emory and Henry Coll. June 1973. 30 min.; 6 pp. Shelia Hill, interviewer.

Pettis discusses her early life and her family, education in the mountains, domestic employment, and churches.

1174. Prater, Mae. Pippa Passes, Ky.: Alice Lloyd Coll. July 8, 1975. 90 min.; 33 pp. Ron Daley, interviewer.

This mountain woman talks about life in a Knott County coal camp. She discusses in detail cooking, early ways of doing things, the Depression, the first refrigerator and washing machine she ever had, and home remedies.

1175. Pratt, Bevie. Pippa Passes, Ky.: Alice Lloyd Coll. June 30, 1971. 40 min.; 12 pp. Josia Dye and Kenny Slone, interviewers.

Pratt is a sister to Congressman Carl Perkins. She tells of her childhood, Hindman Settlement School, and the George Clark Training School for Teachers.

1176. Price, Julie. Boone, N.C.: Appalachian State Univ., June 11, 1973. 30 min.; 16 pp. Carolyn Shelton, interviewer.

Price talks about a woman's place in life, husbands, raising children, the WPA and CCC, the Depression, superstitions, and ghosts.

1177. Raleigh, Ella. Jackson, Ky.: Lee's Junior Coll. Oct. 28, 1971. 40 min.; 14 pp. Ron Allen, interviewer.

Raleigh compares life in the past to the present—clothing, schools, food preservation, violence, recreation, and religion.

1178. Ramey, Delphia. Pippa Passes, Ky.: Alice Lloyd Coll. July 24,

1974. 60 min.; 27 pp. Luther Frazier and Laurel Anderson, interviewers.

Ramey talks about children's responsibilities on a farm during her childhood, about caring for her dad when he went blind, and making featherbeds.

1179. Rexroad, Shirley M. Emory, Va.: Emory and Henry Coll. June 1973. 45 min.; 17 pp. Laura Stevenson, interviewer.

Rexroad was employed at Virginia Glove Factory at the time of the interview. She discusses her family background, education, farming, entertainment, customs and stories, politics, and race relations.

1180. Rife, Flora. Pippa Passes, Ky.: Alice Lloyd Coll. 1973. 105 min.; 49 pp. Rex Wilson, interviewer.

Rife takes a broad look at life on the farm and discusses recreation, education, home remedies, bad men, food, and working. She tells some interesting anecdotes about moonshining and revenuers.

1181. Roberts, Sophia. Pippa Passes, Ky.: Alice Lloyd Coll. June 9, 1972. 30 min.; 8 pp. Carolyn Hunter, interviewer.

Roberts, who is married to a tenant farmer, gives a general view of life on a farm, and mentions washing clothes and making soap. She was born in 1894.

1182. Sale, Gladys. Jackson, Ky.: Lee's Junior Coll. March 13, 1973. 60 min.; pp. unknown. Sari Tudiver, interviewer.

Sale talks about the history of Lee County and the first school, the Missionary Episcopal Church that flourished there for 95 years, the flood of 1890, and the McGuires, the first people to come to Lee County.

1183. Scott, Annie. Pippa Passes, Ky.: Alice Lloyd Coll. Oct. 10, 1973. 50 min.; 10 pp. Cora Lee Hairston, interviewer.

Scott is a widow, originally from Alabama, who has lived in Kentucky 41 years. This interview covers her family, childhood, religious beliefs, and the Depression.

1184. Shelton, Mary. Boone, N.C.: Appalachian State Univ. June 14, 1973. 25 min.; 16 pp. Carolyn Shelton, interviewer.

Shelton talks about her family, education, religion, children, and jobs she has had. Part of the interview deals with spinning, weaving, and knitting.

1185. Sherwood, Anne. Boone, N.C.: Appalachian State Univ. July 23, 1973. 40 min.; 25 pp. Carolyn Shelton, interviewer.

Sherwood, a retired schoolteacher, discusses education and its role in her life, and the effects of the Depression on education in the mountains.

1186. Shores, Myrtle. Boone, N.C.: Appalachian State Univ. June 14, 1973. 50 min.; 12 pp. Carolyn Shelton, interviewer.

Shores lives in Todd, North Carolina. She discusses her family, farming, jobs, and children. Other topics include animals, religion, politics, the Depression, and the medicinal value of barks, roots, and herbs.

1187. Shull, Mamie Graybeal. Boone, N.C.: Appalachian State Univ. Apr. 3, 1973. 90 min.; 25 pp. Bill Brinkley, interviewer.

Shull talks about home remedies, child-rearing, crafts, canning and drying food, education, and religion. She also speaks about the Depression, legends and folktales, old-timey cooking, and sugar orchards.

1188. Skeens, Frances Weaver. Emory, Va.: Emory and Henry Coll. June 1973. 60 min.; 9 pp. Ann Henderson, interviewer.

Skeens, a retired schoolteacher, talks about growing up in Emory, farming, education, crafts, hog-killing, and the Depression.

1189. Slone, Alice. Pippa Passes, Ky.: Alice Lloyd Coll. June 14, 1972. 75 min.; 46 pp. Laurel Anderson, interviewer.

Slone was a schoolteacher until retirement. She speaks about her early home life, family relationships, and the values her parents taught her. She discusses the Civil War's impact on family life in the twentieth century and why she was called "hell-fire" Nance.

1190. Slone, Margaret. Pippa Passes, Ky.: Alice Lloyd Coll. Aug. 25, 1972. 40 min.; 14 pp. Don Sparkman, interviewer.

Slone talks about her family, schooling, childhood, religion, the first car she ever saw, making soap and molasses, chairmaking, and weaving, and what she heard her mother say about the Civil War.

1191. Slone, Susy. Pippa Passes, Ky.: Alice Lloyd Coll. July 7, 1971. 20 min.; 10 pp. Millie Hall and Douglas Hale, interviewers.

Slone talks about the many aspects of education in the mountains, tells some of the things they did at social gatherings, and talks about transportation.

1192. Slone, Verna Mae. Pippa Passes, Ky.: Alice Lloyd Coll. Jan. 25, 1974. 120 min.; 55 pp. James Still and his Folk Speech Class, interviewers.

Slone, author of *What My Heart Wants to Tell*, covers a variety of subjects, although emphasis is on Appalachian homelife. She talks about doctoring in the mountains, and describes her wedding and other important events in her life. She and James Still discuss the founding of the Hindman Settlement School and Alice Lloyd College.

1193. Smallwood, Margie. Pippa Passes, Ky.: Alice Lloyd Coll. June 1, 1972. 30 min.; 13 pp. Jeff Reynolds, interviewer.

Smallwood discusses her childhood, education, courting customs, and recreation. She describes the first car she ever saw, and the first railroad. She concludes with some stories.

1194. Smith, Geneva. Pippa Passes, Ky.: Alice Lloyd Coll. July 22, 1975. 47 min.; 10 pp. Ronnie Thacker, interviewer.

Smith, a schoolteacher, discusses her ancestors, early churches in Knott County, the forced relocation of her family from the Carr Creek Dam area, the impact of the Civil War on the mountains, and a Confederate, Captain Hiram Stamper.

1195. Smith, Shellie. Pippa Passes, Ky.: Alice Lloyd Coll. July 29, 1971. Josia Dye and Kenny Slone, interviewers.

Smith lives in Knott County, Kentucky. She talks about her childhood, school days, superstitions, home remedies, and her grandmother, who was a faith healer.

1196. Smythers, Mrs. Strader J. Emory, Va.: Emory and Henry Coll. July 1973. 60 min.; 12 pp. Strader Blankenship, interviewer.

Smythers says she is a housewife. She talks about her early life and family, farming, education, running a store at Poplar Camp, crafts, feuds, welfare, and moonshining.

1197. Sowards, Sallie. Pippa Passes, Ky.: Alice Lloyd Coll. June 1, 1972. 25 min.; 11 pp. Jeff Reynolds, interviewer.

Sowards, from Pike County, Kentucky, is a housewife who professes to be a witch doctor. She discusses her early life, her education, recreation, and courting. There is also information about witch doctors, superstitions, and "Bad" John Hall.

1198. Sparkman, Martha. Pippa Passes, Ky.: Alice Lloyd Coll. Sept. 21, 1972. 40 min.; 10 pp. Don Sparkman, interviewer.

Martha Sparkman was born in 1932 in Knott County, Kentucky. She tells interesting anecdotes about her childhood, education, politics, transportation, making molasses and soap, chairmaking, and mountain superstitions.

1199. Stewart, Annie. Pippa Passes, Ky.: Alice Lloyd Coll. June 16, 1972. 30 min.; 8 pp. Carolyn Hunter, interviewer.

Stewart talks about "the good old days" of going to school, courting, her husband, and home remedies.

1200. Strong, Pearlie. Jackson, Ky.: Lee's Junior Coll. July 7, 1975. 30 min.; 7 pp. Leslie Dunn and Greg Caudill, interviewers.

Strong is an extremely articulate mountain woman who provides an interview of the first quality. She discusses a variety of topics, such as family history, feuds, and working.

1201. Strother, Virginia Dare. Boone, N.C.: Appalachian State Univ. June 19, 1973. 60 min.; 24 pp. Karen Weaver, interviewer.

Strother is a weaver. The major topics of the interview include weaving, quilting, carding, and spinning. She talks about old patterns and explains the various weaving processes.

1202. Stuart, Oakie. Emory, Va.: Emory and Henry Coll. July 1973. 40 min.; 9 pp. Jerry Hill, interviewer.

Stuart, a domestic worker, talks about her early life and family, Clarksville community affairs, education, her father's employment on the railroad, churches, remedies, WPA, CCC, and welfare.

1203. Sturgill, Alpha. Pippa Passes, Ky.: Alice Lloyd Coll. Aug. 9, 1972. 60 min.; 21 pp. Judy Mullins, interviewer.

Alpha Sturgill and her mother-in-law tore down a moonshine still one time, she recalls. She talks also about her school days, religion, clothing, and transportation.

1204. Sturgill, Mayme M. Emory, Va.: Emory and Henry Coll. June 1973. 20 min.; 7 pp. Cynthia Legard, interviewer.

Sturgill is a retired storekeeper. She discusses her early life, family background, churches, crafts, the WPA, the Depression, and what it is like to run a store.

1205. Sweeney, Suzanne Ivans, and Sadler, Ethel. Emory, Va.: Emory and Henry Coll. June 1973. 120 min.; 24 pp. Ann Henderson, interviewer.

Sweeney and Sadler, who live in Santa Barbara, California, and Austell, Georgia, respectively, reminisce about school days at Martha Washington College.

1206. Tackett, Bertha. Pippa Passes, Ky.: Alice Lloyd Coll. Oct. 11, 1971. 20 min.; 9 pp. Carlos Combs, interviewer.

This Floyd County, Kentucky, housewife discusses her early childhood, education, religion, transportation, occupations, the two World Wars, and the way things have changed. She feels the old days were better because everybody had to work and do their part.

1207. Tackett, Josie. Pippa Passes, Ky.: Alice Lloyd Coll. June 13, 1972. 35 min.; 14 pp. Jeff Reynolds, interviewer.

Tackett, of Pike County, Kentucky, tells some stories about hangings and murders. She talks about witch doctors and other superstitions, and tells of an experience that happened to her when she was bewitched.

1208. Thacker, Mary. Pippa Passes, Ky.: Alice Lloyd Coll. June 21, 1975. 45 min.; 15 pp. Terri Singleton, interviewer.

Thacker recalls her school years, early transportation, a hanging at Whitesburg, Kentucky, and the Depression.

1209. Townsend, Dorothy. Boone, N.C.: Appalachian State Univ. June 27, 1974. 60 min.; 38 pp. Barbara Greenburg, interviewer.

Townsend is a craftswoman and well-digger. She discusses various aspects of living and working on a farm, doing crafts, digging roots, and gathering herbs.

1210. Turley, Ada Kitts. Emory, Va.: Emory and Henry Coll. June 1973. 30 min.; 8 pp. Strader E. Blankenship, interviewer.

Turley, from Wytheville, Virginia, discusses her family, cooking, education, and religion, and how to preserve food. She talks about migrating to Nebraska and speaks of the Ceres community, music, dances, and feuds.

1211. Turner, Elizabeth. Jackson, Ky.: Lee's Junior Coll. July 4, 1974. 45 min.; 11 pp. Mary Lou Jackson, interviewer.

Turner, who presently lives in Tucson, Arizona, talks about the one-room school in the Appalachian mountains and how it operated. She also says children have changed a great deal through the years.

1212. Turner, Lorena. Pippa Passes, Ky.: Alice Lloyd Coll. n.d. 95 min.; 24 pp. Ron Daley, interviewer.

Turner is from Highland County, Ohio. She talks about the Depression, its effect on her family and other people, and how she lived on eleven cents one month. She recalls that her dad had the first windmill, engine, and car in Brown County, Ohio.

1213. Turner, Norma Ward. Pippa Passes, Ky.: Alice Lloyd Coll. May 4, 1971. 50 min.; 13 pp. Sissy Ackman, Terry Hensley, and Danny Turner, interviewers.

Turner talks about doctors and home remedies for hives, thrush, whooping cough, colds, warts, and nail wounds. She talks about Sam Adams, a lawman at Wheelwright who was murdered, and sings a ballad about him. She discusses schools and tells about "Bad" John Hall and "Machine Gun" Kelly.

1214. Umbarger, Catherine. Emory, Va.: Emory and Henry Coll. Aug. 1973. 90 min.; pp. unknown. Cynthia Legard, interviewer.

Umbarger is a retired schoolteacher. She discusses Konnarock Training School at Konnarock, Virginia.

1215. Umberger, Katrina. Emory, Va.: Emory and Henry Coll. Aug. 1973. 35 min.; 9 pp. Cynthia Legard, interviewer.

Umberger, a retired librarian, discusses White Top Mountain, Konnarock Training School, and the White Top Mountain Music Festival.

1216. Van Dyke, Dorothy. Boone, N.C.: Appalachian State Univ. July 31, 1973. 30 min.; 20 pp. Karen Ward, interviewer.

Van Dyke talks about her home, schools, religion, gardening, quilting, medicines, and types of soap.

1217. Waddell, Crady. Pippa Passes, Ky.: Alice Lloyd Coll. Aug. 4, 1971. Ken Slone, interviewer.

Waddell talks about her childhood, work at the Hindman Settlement School, and her family. She recalls some superstitions and home remedies.

1218. Waters, Hattie Owens. Emory, Va.: Emory and Henry Coll. June 1973. 60 min.; 12 pp. Cynthia Legard, interviewer.

Waters was born in 1901 and makes her home in Konnarock, Virginia. She discusses being a housewife, her early life and her family, the railroad, and digging ginseng.

1219. Watson, Lelia. Boone, N.C.: Appalachian State Univ. June 9, 1973. 25 min.; 12 pp. Mike NcNeely, interviewer.

Watson talks about the Civil War, early schools, and the educational systems in the mountains.

1220. Watson, Rilda. Pippa Passes, Ky.: Alice Lloyd Coll. Apr. 29, 1971. 6 min.; 5 pp. Roger Stalker, interviewer.

Watson talks about people connected with Alice Lloyd and her mother. She tells folktales and gives remedies for the thrush and the sneezes.

1221. _____. Pippa Passes, Ky.: Alice Lloyd Coll. Sept. 14, 1972. 60 min.; 30 pp. Don Sparkman, interviewer.

Most of the interview is taken up with the Depression and Watson's life during that time.

1222. Webb, Sallie. Pippa Passes, Ky.: Alice Lloyd Coll. Sept. 17, 1972. 25 min.; 8 pp. Genia Maciag, interviewer.

Sallie Webb was born in 1885. A retired mountain schoolteacher, she gives a general interview about life as she grew up.

1223. Whitaker, Mamie. Pippa Passes, Ky.: Alice Lloyd Coll. July 26, 1972. 15 min.; 12 pp. Carolyn Hunter, interviewer.

Born in 1884, this Perry County, Kentucky, native recalls childhood events, her education, clothing, courting, churches, medicine, the Depression, and mining.

1224. Williams, Flora. Emory, Va.: Emory and Henry Coll. June 1973. 30 min.: 6 pp. Cynthia Legard, interviewer.

Williams, a Chilhowie, Virginia, housewife, discusses her early life and family, the Bethel community, churches, and schools in the area.

1225. Wright, Draxie. Pippa Passes, Ky.: Alice Lloyd Coll. June 24, 1975. 55 min.; 22 pp. Laurel Anderson, interviewer.

Wright discusses her move from a Pike County farm to a coal camp and how much she enjoyed living in the camp. She compares camp life to life on the farm.

1226. Yates, Zeola. Pippa Passes, Ky.: Alice Lloyd Coll. June 8, 1972. 30 min.; 11 pp. Carolyn Hunter, interviewer.

Yates discusses her family, her childhood, chores, church, courting, going to school, food, recreation, marriage, superstitions, and the Depression.

Poetry

1227. Alexander, Patricia. "I Am Home." *Appal. Women* 1 (Fall 1979): 17.

The poet, a Tennessee woman, writes about living in Chicago and traveling home to the hills and her mother.

1228. Amburgey, Gail; Coleman, Mary Joan; and Hansel, Paulette. *We're Alright But We Ain't Special*. Beckley, W.V.: Soupbean Productions, Mountain Union Books, 1976.

This book of poems is a collaboration of three mountain poets. Amburgey and Coleman are West Virginia natives, and Hansel was born and raised in Eastern Kentucky.

1229. Bernard, Jacqueline. "Mountain Voices: Appalachian Poets." *Ms.* 5 (Aug. 1976): 34, 36–38.

Four women who participated in the First Conference of Native Southern Appalachian Writers at New Market, Tennessee, are interviewed.

1230. Bowman, Joan. "Rachel Dobson." *Appal. Heritage* 7 (Summer 1979): 18–19.

A poem about an aged mountain woman who remembers trying to cut an angel off little Tommy Sizemore's tombstone because she wanted to play with the "toy angel."

1231. Brewer, Amanda. *I Sing of Appalachia*. Appalachia, Va.: Young, 1967.

Brewer is a mountain poet, proud of her native hills. Her poems reflect a woman's perceptions of the world around her.

1232. Chaffin, Lillie D. *8th Day 13th Moon*. Pikeville, Ky.: Pikeville Coll. Press, 1975.

A book of poetry in which Chaffin tells of the world for the Appalachian woman as she sees it.

1233. Cheek, Pauline B. "Of a Mind To." *Appal. Heritage* 7 (Spring 1979): 18.

The story of Granny and the organ she bought. Asked years later how she got it and paid for it, she would reply: "I reckon I was of a mind to have one, and I never did get out of heart."

1234. Cushman, Rebecca. *Swing Your Mountain Gal: Sketches of Life in the Southern Highlands.* Boston: Houghton Mifflin, 1934.

Sketches written in verse form. The author says in the foreword that they are based on real life.

1235. Day, Edith Eleanor. *The Girl of Luna's Creek.* Petersburg, W.V.: Great Court Press, 1949.

Young mountain girls dream of leprechauns and fairies and the knight in shining armor, just like girls the world over. This is a narrative poem about a young girl's encounter with a fairy who represents, to her, the spirit of the mountains.

1236. Dickens, Hazel. "Songs: Mannington Mine Disaster and Black Lung." *Mt. Life & Work* 47 (Apr. 1971): 10–13.

Hazel Dickens provides words and music to her protest songs.

1237. Frazier, Kitty. "Louise McNeill and the Women in Her Poetry." *MAW* 1 (Sept./Oct. 1977): 25–26.

Some of the characters from this West Virginia poet's writings are presented.

1238. Goodale, Dora Reed. *Mountain Dooryards.* Illustrated by Mary Rogers. 2nd ed. Berea, Ky.: Council of the Southern Mountains, 1961.

Sensitive poems about the mountain way of life, narrated by mountain people. Especially good are poems from the viewpoint of young girls, wives, mothers, and grandmothers.

1239. Graves, Nell. "Pentecostal Woman." *Appal. Journal* 3 (Summer 1976): 398.

A poem describing a Pentecostal woman, both physically and spiritually.

1240. Hartz, Lynn. "Modern Woman." *Appal. Women* 1 (Fall 1979): 27.

A poem about a modern mountain woman whose work and responsibilities seem endless.

1241. Howard, Lee. "Mountain Women." *Sou. Expos.* 4 (Winter 1977): 34–35.

A collection of poems about Appalachian women. The author, who grew up in the Kentucky mountains, says, "Appalachian women have more faces than these few poems can mirror, but there are some wrinkles that always form around the eyes, some

same angle in every smile, some common sound in the telling of
every life."
1242. Lawson, Sidney. "Appalachia, 1965." *Mt. Life & Work* 40
(Winter 1965), cover.
A poem telling how one mountain woman views her native hills
and her people since stripmine operations began in Appalachia.
1243. McGee, Betsy Ann. "My Grandmother Believed in Signs." *Appal. Heritage* 7 (Spring 1979): 12.
A poem characterizing Grandmother and relating her belief in
portents and dreams.
1244. McNeill, Louise. *Mountain White.* Dallas: Kaleidoscope, 1931.
A book of poetry from this West Virginia native, who often speaks
for other mountain women.
1245. _____. *Gauley Mountains.* New York: Harcourt, Brace, 1939.
The whole history of McNeill's West Virginia home and people is
here in her poems, some of them speaking from the woman's
viewpoint.
1246. _____. *From a Dark Mountain.* Charleston, W.V.: Morris
Harvey, 1972.
More poetry from this mountain woman.
1247. Marano, Russell. "Flora." *Appal. Heritage* 7 (Summer 1979):
38–39.
After Flora's husband was killed in the mines, she moved her five
children to the ghetto in a big city. By doing laundry for people
she scraped together enough money to keep the children in
school.
1248. Marshburn, Sandra. "Differences." *Appal. Women* 1 (Fall
1979): 27.
A woman who was once young and admired her mother's "spots
and lines" now finds herself aging in a different way from her
mother.
1249. "A Mountain Woman's Poem." *Mt. Life & Work* 1 (July 1925):
Inside cover.
A mountain woman talks about her life and hopes to be remembered for her kind words and good deeds to mankind.
1250. Rasnic, Steve. "Cincinnati and It's Raining." *Mt. Rev.* 4 (Sept.
1978): 7.
The author says he wrote this prose-poem after seeing an old lady
in "Hillbilly Ghetto," a hunting knife strapped on her belly. The
old woman says in the poem: "In the country your hands could do
something: rebuild a church . . . . move the creek over your land."
1251. Ritchie, Jean. "Now Is the Cool of the Day." *Mt. Life & Work*
46 (May 1970): 3–11.

Ritchie talks about her childhood in Eastern Kentucky, stripmining and the destruction of the region, and the joys of living as expressed in one song, "Now Is the Cool of the Day."

1252. ———. *Jean Ritchie Celebration of Life: Her Songs... Her Poems*. New York: Geordie, 1971.

A collection of music, poems, and songs, and photographs of Ritchie and her family in Eastern Kentucky.

1253. ———. "Black Waters." *Appal. Heritage* 1 (Summer 1973): 53–54.

Ritchie, noted folksinger and author, shares her feelings about the stripmining in Perry County, Kentucky—her homeplace—in the words and music of this protest song.

1254. Tremble, Stella. *Thorns and Thistledown*. New York: Comet, 1954.

A collection of poems by a mountain poet, sensitively portraying a woman's perceptions of and reactions to the world of nature.

1255. Williams, Richard. "Omie Wise." *Ky. Folklore Rec.* 23 (Jan./ Mar. 1977): 7–11.

The ballad of Omie Wise is about a pregnant young woman who is murdered by her lover—a typical ballad showing the notorious double standard at work.

Religion & Folklore

1256. Agee, James. *A Death in the Family*. New York: Avon, 1938.

This novel deals with death and how different members of the family handle the loss of a loved one. Mary Follet, a Tennessee woman, is portrayed convincingly and with sensitivity.

1257. Alther, Lisa. "They Shall Take Up Serpents." *New York Times Mag.*, June 6, 1976, pp. 18–20, 28, 35.

The author of *Kinflicks* interviews the pastor and members of the Holiness Church of God in Jesus Name of Carson Springs, Tennessee. Photographs of snake-handling and descriptions of experiences show the involvement of mountain women in this religious rite.

1258. "Aunt Addie Norton." *Foxfire* 10 (Fall 1976): 192–210.

Born in 1890 in the Persimmon Community, Raban County, Georgia, Aunt Addie talks of her life and beliefs.

1259. Baxter, Tamara R. "The Curin." *Appal. Heritage* 7 (Spring 1979): 13–17.

A short story narrated by a young girl. She and a friend hide in the friend's house to watch Granny heal a sick child.

1260. Bell, Charles Bailey. *A Mysterious Spirit: The Bell Witch of Tennessee*. Nashville: Charles Elder, 1972.

A mysterious spirit came to live with a Tennessee family and formed a close attachment to the wife and mother. The spirit, later called the Bell Witch, was kind to the mother but tormented other family members, especially teenaged Betsy.

1261. Bland, Marion F. "Superstitions about Food and Health among Negro Girls in Elementary and Secondary Schools in Marion County, West Virginia." Master's thesis, West Virginia Univ., 1950.

Not available for annotation.

1262. Cadle, Dean. "Cry in the Wilderness." *Appal. Heritage* 7 (Summer 1979): 42–48.

A short story told from the viewpoint of Birdie Walker, who has his own reasons for wanting the new preacher run out of town. He gets Alice Rowe, "that woman on the hill," to play a trick on the preacher and the people at the revival. The trick backfires on Birdie when Alice is converted and becomes a changed woman.

1263. Campbell, Marie. *Tales from the Cloud-Walking Country*. Bloomington: Indiana Univ. Press, 1958.

When the author taught at the Mountain Settlement School on Caney Creek in Knott County, Kentucky, she met many mountain women who told her folktales. Seventy-eight of those tales are recorded here, old European folktales told in mountain dialect.

1264. Cole, Effie. "Granny's Diary." *Mt. Rev.* 5 (1975): 19–20.

Excerpts from a diary kept by a literate woman in Civil War days, a woman recently settled in the mountains. Characteristic of the hardihood of pioneer women and some of their superstitions.

1265. Daugherty, Mary L. "Serpent-Handling as Sacrament." *Theology Today* 33 (Oct. 1976): 232–43.

The ritual of serpent-handling is the way members of independent Holiness churches in West Virginia celebrate life, death, and resurrection.

1266. Day, Edith Eleanor. *The Girl of Luna's Creek*. Petersburg, W.V.: Great Court Press, 1949.

Young mountain girls dream of leprechauns and fairies and the knight in shining armor, just like girls the world over. A narrative poem about a young girl's encounter with a fairy who represents, to her, the spirit of the mountains.

1267. Depree, Gladis Lenore. *The Self-Anointed.* New York: Harper & Row, 1978.

Depree is the daughter of John Vogel, founder and director of a home for orphaned children in Corbin, Kentucky. She talks freely of her life there and the other girls in the establishment, and of her escape from physical bondage and from the bondage of an unhealthy love shown her (and the other girls) by her father.

1268. Dickinson, Eleanor, and Benzinger, Barbara. *Revival!* New York: Harper & Row, 1974.

A book about revival meetings in the Great Smoky Mountains. About two-thirds of each congregation are women.

1269. "Ethel Corn." *Foxfire* 7 (Winter 1973): 260–67.

A woman speaks of her life, her faith, her views of contemporary life, and the war in Vietnam.

1270. Gillespie, Paul. "Granny Reed: A Testimony." *Sou. Expos.* 4, no. 3 (1976): 33–37.

"A proud member of the church of God in Western North Carolina," a 90-year-old woman describes her life in the mountains and her religious experiences.

1271. Graves, Nell. "Pentecostal Woman." *Appal. Journal* 3 (Summer 1976): 398.

A poem describing a Pentecostal woman, both physically and spiritually.

1272. Hannum, Alberta Pierson. *Look Back with Love: A Recollection of the Blue Ridge.* New York: Vanguard, 1969.

A personal remembrance of a time that was, and perhaps will never be again. . . of mountain friends . . . a different look at the Appalachian people."

1273. Harrington, Etta. "Witch Stories." *Foxfire* 9 (Winter 1975): 364–72.

Excerpted from a book manuscript are "stories told at night by father and grandparents" of the narrator. We gain insight into the narrator's lifestyle as she relates the stories.

1274. Huff, Jane. *Whom the Lord Loveth: The Story of James A. Huff.* New York: McGraw-Hill, 1961.

A wife's account of her brief and happy marriage to a young, seriously ill minister from East Tennessee.

1275. Kroll, Harry Harrison. *Three Brothers and Seven Daddies.* New York: Long and Smith, 1932.

A book filled with witches, ogres, prophets, sinister villains, etc. A

number of women are portrayed: Tennsy Obids, young and beautiful; Granny Pigeon, the witch of the community; a stepmother
who keeps trying to crowd into her stepson's bed; and others.

1276. McBroyer, Emma Lee Van Arsdell. *Grandmother Bond*. Lawrenceburg, Ky.: Lawrenceburg Printing Co., 1976.

A short biography of the author's grandmother, who was born and
raised in Barbourville, Kentucky, and later moved to Anderson
County with her bridegroom, a minister.

1277. McGee, Betsy Ann. "My Grandmother Believed in Signs." *Appal. Heritage* 7 (Spring 1979): 12.

A poem characterizing Grandmother and relating her beliefs in
portents and dreams.

1278. Myers, Elizabeth P. *Rock of Decision*. Grand Rapids: Eerdmans,
1931.

In this novel, a Blue Ridge Mountain girl, Phoebe Bradford,
cannot understand at first why Christians have to suffer. She
almost hates God, but through experience learns God's place in
her life.

1279. Pelton, Robert W., and Carden, Karen W. *Snake Handlers:
God-Fearers? or Fanatics?* Nashville: Nelson, 1974.

A documentary report liberally illustrated with photographs of
people in different places of worship handling snakes as part of
their rituals. Many of the participants are young girls and women.

1280. Read, Opie. *The Wives of the Prophets*. Chicago: Laird & Lee,
1894.

Up the Cumberland River in Tennessee is an old settlement
called Bolga, said to have been settled in 1697 when a new religious order arrived from England. This novel is about five women
chosen to serve their three years each as wife of the prophet, and
the intruder from outside who brings heartaches and trouble to
the people.

1281. Relham, Richard. "Doing Good." *Appal. Heritage* 7 (Spring
1979): 27–31.

The author, a retired minister, was told in the mining community
a pathetic story about Carrie Suggs and her children being evicted
from their home. He went to help, thinking Carrie was a widow.
To his dismay, he found she was the "scarlet woman" of the hills,
and he had been tricked into what could have been a compromising situation.

1282. Ridgway, Florence Holmes. "A Charge to Keep: Narratives and
Episodes Devoted to the Women Who Helped Build a Place for Wor-
ship and for Learning on the Berea Ridge." Berea, Ky.: Berea Woman's
Club, 1954. Typescript in Berea Coll. Archives.

This drama articulates the special courage and devotion of the women who helped found Berea College. The personal stories of Matilda Fee and Elizabeth Rogers support the author's contention that "there were mothers of Berea as well as fathers." The church, the college, the town, all owe their existence to the labors and sacrifices of these women.

1283. _____. "Women's Industrial: A Story of Sharing." *Mt. Life & Work* 32 (Autumn 1956): 30–35.

How the Berea Women's Christian Temperance Union formed an association concerned with the welfare of those in need.

1284. Ritchie, Jean. *Apple Seeds and Soda Straws*. New York: Walck, 1965.

Some love charms and legends as related by Appalachian folksinger Jean Ritchie.

1285. Sharp, Molly. "There's Always a Judas." *Such As Us: Southern Voices of the Thirties*. Chapel Hill: Univ. of North Carolina Press, 1978.

Sharp, living with her daughter and son-in-law (a Baptist preacher) in North Carolina, talks about her life, her daughter's work in the cotton mills, and the preacher's work in the mill villages.

1286. Stewart, Judy. "Superstitions." *Appal. Heritage* 1 (Summer and Fall 1973): 8–19, 23–24: 2 (Winter 1974): 57–63.

A rather extensive look at superstitions, customs, signs, and portents, and practices associated with death and burial in the Southern Appalachian mountains. Women are included in every aspect.

1287. Stuart, Jesse. "Braska Comes Through." *Amer. Mercury* 51 (Sept. 1940): 47–53.

A curious story about a mountain girl. Nebraska has a hard time seeing the light of repentance the way the fundamentalist preachers teach it. The local people decide she must have a baby before she can get right with God.

1288. _____. "Remedies That Stand Out in Memory." *Ky. Folklore Rec.* 22 (July/Oct. 1976): 59–63.

The author knew a woman who excelled in using home remedies. Her son, in an accident, had one finger severed and others almost cut through, and "she stopped the blood. Not one of her son's fingers bled."

1289. Tribe, Ivan M. *Molly O'Day, Lynn Davis, and the Cumberland Mountain Folks: A Bio-Discography*. Los Angeles: John Edwards Memorial Foundation, Univ. of California, 1975.

O'Day, a mountain woman, was a very successful country singer who studied the religions of the world and decided to become a preacher.

1290. Troxel, Thomas H. "Why Little Rowena Never Grew Up." *Mt. Life & Work* 19 *(Spring 1943): 6–10.*

An amusing story of a young girl and her superstitious mother, which takes place about 1925. Rowena describes herself as always having a hard time in life, and relates some of the superstitions which have affected her.

1291. White, Alma. *The Story of My Life.* New Jersey: Pillar of Fire, 1919.

White, one of seven sisters, was born in 1862 at Kinnikinneck in Lewis County, Kentucky. Her mother and sisters were typical mountain women. She yearned for an education, was later converted, became a minister, and founded the Pillar of Fire Church.

Studies & Surveys

1292. Anderson, Frances Gaines. "Leisure Time Interests and Activities of Girls in High School." Master's thesis, West Virginia Univ., 1942.

A study in which West Virginia mountain girls are used as a sample group.

1293. *Appalachia in the Sixties: Decade of Reawakening.* David S. Walls and John D. Stephenson, eds. Lexington, Ky.: Univ. Press of Kentucky, 1972.

Articles written by people who have lived with, worked with, and watched the people of Appalachia. The book was compiled as a follow-up to Kennedy's program in the early 1960s. The following chapters deal with women: "In Hazard," "Life in Appalachia— The Case of Hugh McCaslin," and "Fair Elections in West Virginia."

1294. Beshears, Ralph L. "A Descriptive Study of Juvenile Delinquency in Selected Counties in the State of North Carolina." Master's thesis, Appalachian State Teacher's Coll. 1958.

A study of mountain girls as well as boys.

1295. Bliss, Russell L. "Teenage Dating Behavior in Two Eastern Kentucky High Schools." Master's thesis, Univ. of Kentucky, 1957.

Dating patterns in two Eastern Kentucky mining communities were found to be similar to those elsewhere, but the mountain young people tended to date earlier and to be more serious in seeking marriage partners than urban high school students. The attitudes and practices of boys and girls are analyzed separately, especially with regard to sexual involvement.

1296. Brown, James Stephen. "The Conjugal Family and the Extended Family Group." *Amer. Sociological Rev.* 17 (June 1952): 297–306.

Brown did his field work in the Beech Creek area of Eastern Kentucky. While the article deals with family structures as a whole, there are some references to mountain women.

1297. Bryant, Elizabeth Jean. "The Attitudes of Freshman Female Students towards Physical Education at Western Carolina University." Master's thesis, Western Carolina Univ., 1971.

Not available for annotation.

1298. Burger, Bettijane. "Social Bonds: A Study of Shelters Aiding Battered Wives." *MAW* 1 (July/Aug. 1978): 25–30.

Burger is with the Charleston, West Virginia, chapter of the National Organization for Women, working in a Task Force on Battered Wives. In Kanawha County (which includes Charleston) the task force found there were 250 reported cases of wife abuse each month.

1299. Campbell, John C. *The Southern Highlander and His Homeland.* New York: Russell Sage Foundation, 1921; Lexington: Univ. Press of Kentucky, 1969.

Chapters about women, young girls, and grandmothers contain excellent descriptions of the life style of mountain women in the early part of the twentieth century.

1300. Caudill, Harry M. *Night Comes to the Cumberlands.* Boston: Little, Brown, 1962.

For almost two decades this book has been used by researchers and students interested in the Appalachian area. Mountain women are described on pp. 40–45, specifically, but are mentioned throughout the book.

1301. Coleman, Mary E. *Five-Year Report of Pilot Project Involving Young Homemakers in Low-Income Rural Areas in Alabama.* Auburn, Ala: Auburn Univ. Cooperative Extension Service, 1969.

Homemaking skills such as cooking, sewing, and general home management are taught to young housewives by program assistants in five counties, three of which are in Appalachia.

1302. Dayton Human Relations Commission. *Southern Appalachian Migration.* Dayton, O.: Dayton Human Relations Commission, 1966.

The alienation experienced by Appalachians who migrate to cities in the North is the focus of this study.

1303. Dickinson, Eleanor, and Benziger, Barbara. *Revival!* New York: Harper & Row, 1974.

A book about revival meetings in the Great Smoky Mountains. About two-thirds of each congregation are women.

1304. Dykeman, Wilma. *Tennessee Women, Past and Present.* Selected additional material edited by Carol Lynn Yellin. Memphis: Tennessee Committee for the Humanities and Tennessee International Women's Decade Coordinating Committee, 1977.

A comprehensive book about women in Tennessee's history. The author knows her subject and writes with convincing clarity.

1305. Gazeway, Rena. *The Longest Mile.* New York: Doubleday, 1969.

The author lived in the remote hollows of Kentucky for a short time before she wrote the book. She pictures the life style especially of the women and young girls but she also includes men and boys.

1306. Gitlin, Todd, and Hollander, Nanci. *Uptown: Poor Whites in Chicago.* New York: Harper & Row, 1970.

Migrants from Appalachia have moved into ghettolike neighborhoods in large northern and midwestern cities such as Detroit, Indianapolis, Chicago, and Columbus. This book about migrants to Chicago transcribes recorded conversations which give us a picture of the family, but especially of how the mountain woman copes in urban situations.

1307. Hays, Diana L. "As Close As I Can Get: A Study of the Women of the Southern Mountains." Master's thesis, Goddard-Cambridge Graduate Program, 1978.

A series of essays make up this study, which covers a period of about 75 years and reveals Southern Appalachian women as they faced industrialization in the early years of this century, adjusted to the cash economy, and finally begin to talk about issues that face them at the national and local levels.

1308. Hochstrasser, Donald L.; Arthur, Gerry; and Lewis, Michael. "Fertility Decline in Southern Appalachia: An Anthropological Perspective." *Human Organization* 32 (1973): 331–36.

The authors review the demographic literature on fertility decline in Southern Appalachia and make a case for the anthropological community approach to explain it. This study could be of help to researchers dealing with the stereotypes of mountain women.

1309. Kolassa, Kathryn M. "Foodways of Selected Mothers and Their Adult Daughters in Upper East Tennessee." Doctoral dissertation, Univ. of Tennessee, 1974.

Because of the media and other environmental factors, the importance of the mother in the cultural transmission of foodways may not be as great as was originally thought.

1310. Looff, David H. *Appalachia's Children: The Challenge of Mental Health*. Lexington: Univ. Press of Kentucky, 1971.

Psychiatric clinics for disturbed children were run by the author in Eastern Kentucky. He describes child-rearing practices in the area and gives good characterizations of Appalachian mothers and girls.

1311. Martorella, Marjorie. *The Legal Status of Homemakers in West Virginia*. Washington, D.C.: Center for Women Policy Studies, 1977.

Not available for annotation.

1312. Matthews, Elmora M. *Neighbor and Kin: Life in a Tennessee Ridge Community*. Nashville: Vanderbilt Univ. Press, 1965.

A sociological study of what happens to people in a hill community who have intermarried and lived in a relatively closed community since 1786.

1313. Miller, Danny. "Mountain Women in Fact and Fiction of the Early Twentieth Century." *Appal. Heritage* 6 (Summer and Fall 1978, Winter 1979): 48–56, 66–72. 16–21.

Deals with stereotypes of mountain women as portrayed in literature of the early twentieth century. The author sums up: "There was some truth in the characterization of mountain women at the turn of the century. But there was also much that was exaggerated or romanticized."

1314. Miller, Nora. *The Girl in the Rural Family*. Chapel Hill: Univ. of North Carolina Press, 1935.

A good study of girls and women in Appalachia. Chapter headings include: "The Mountain Farm Family," "The Soft Coal Mine Family," "The Cotton Farm Family," "The Tobacco Farm Family."

1315. Moore, Martha Kiser. "The Appalachians of Wilma Dykeman's Fiction." Master's thesis, East Tennessee State Univ., 1975.

A close look at the way Dykeman portrays Appalachian people. Since Dykeman is noted for her characterizations of mountain women, this affords another viewpoint on them.

1316. Noble, Lucinda Ann. "Structural Analysis of Mothers' Attitudes towards Child Rearing in Four Communities in Appalachia." Doctoral dissertation, Univ. of North Carolina, 1969.

A look, both generally and specifically, at child-rearing customs and attitudes.

1317. Schultz, Leroy G., project administrator. *Wife Battering in the Small Community: A Social Policy Analysis—1976*. Morgantown: West Virginia Univ. School of Social Work, n.d.

Not available for annotation. It is a known fact that the reported cases of wife battering reach a shocking number in various Appalachian counties.

1318. _____. *The Control of Prostitution in West Virginia: A Social Policy Analysis—1977.* Morgantown: West Virginia Univ. School of Social Work. n.d.
> Not available for annotation.

1319. Schwarzweller, Harry K.; Brown, James S.; and Mangalam, Joseph J. *Mountain Families in Transition: A Case Study of Migration.* University Park: Pennsylvania State Univ. Press, 1971.
> A study of what happened when families migrated from Beech Creek, an isolated, subsistence-farming, mountain area of Eastern Kentucky, to northern cities. While the whole family is studied, the student of Appalachian women may find some useful things here.

1320. Shackelford, Laurel, and Weinberg, Bill, eds. *Our Appalachia: An Oral History.* New York: Hill & Wang, 1977.
> This book portrays the people, life, culture, and history of the region. The scholar interested in researching Appalachian women will find source material in the sections in which mountain women are interviewed.

1321. Stahl, Ellen J. "Legal Abortion in Cincinnati and Appalachian Women." *MAW* 1 (July/Aug. 1978): 7–14.
> The author is doing research on Appalachian women who migrate to Cincinnati. She tells about the abortion clinics, groups opposing legalized abortion and where the Appalachian woman fits in between the two. A good look at how Appalachian women feel about children, abortions, and unwanted pregnancies.

1322. Surface, Bill. *The Hollow.* New York: Coward-McCann, 1971.
> A study of several families in Eastern Kentucky, including a number of women.

1323. Swisher, Basil G. S. "A Survey of the Attitudes of Women in Monongalia County, West Virginia, Toward the Use of Contraceptives." Master's thesis, West Virginia Univ., 1970.
> Not available for annotation.

1324. Terry, Geraldine B. *The Labor Force: Characteristics of Women in Low-Income Rural Areas of the South.* n.p.: Southern Cooperative Series, 1966.
> Includes statistics and information from several mountain counties.

1325. Testerman, Violet M. "A Comparative Study of Certain Personality Traits between Female Physical Education Majors and Non-Majors at Appalachian State University." Master's thesis, Appalachian State Univ., 1972.
> Not available for annotation.

1326. Weller, Jack E. *Yesterday's People.* Lexington: Univ. Press of Kentucky, 1965.

While most of this book is about Appalachia and Appalachian people in general, one section (pp. 58–86) deals specifically with mountain women and their attitudes toward their husbands, children, other people, education, and religion.

1327. "Women in Appalachia." *Appalachian Issues & Resources.* Knoxville, Tenn.: Southern Appalachian Ministry in Higher Education, 1975.

"Women in Appalachia are as varied as the races and classes and ethnic groups and geography that make up our region," reads the opening statement in this short article published in an "informational catalog."

1328. *Women's Work in Tennessee.* Memphis, Tenn.: Jones-Briggs, 1916.

The Tennessee Federation of Women's Clubs sponsored this book, which covers mountain settlement work, health improvement projects, prison reform, biographical sketches, and other topics.

Index

This index includes the names of all authors and most titles listed in the bibliography. Subjects are also indexed, except for those dealt with in the fiction, oral history, and poetry sections. The names of persons interviewed on oral history tapes are indexed, with an asterisk (*) following the number. Although some items appear more than once in the subject listings above, only the first appearance is indexed. The numbers here refer to entries rather than pages.

DATE DUE

SEP 3 0 1982